107 Great Chess Battles 1939–1945

Alexander Alekhine

Edited and Translated by Edward Winter

Dover Publications, Inc., New York

Published in Canada by General Publishing Company, Ltd., 30 Lesmill Road, Don Mills, Toronto, Ontario.
Published in the United Kingdom by Constable and Company, Ltd., 3 The Lanchesters, 162–164 Fulham Palace Road, London W6 9ER.

This Dover edition, first published in 1992, is an unabridged and corrected republication of the work originally published by the Oxford University Press, Oxford, England, in 1980. The subtitle giving the years, 1939–1945, when all but one of the games in this collection were played, has been added to the Dover edition. The Dover edition is published by special arrangement with Oxford University Press, 200 Madison Avenue, New York, NY 10016.

Manufactured in the United States of America
Dover Publications, Inc., 31 East 2nd Street, Mineola, N.Y. 11501

Library of Congress Cataloging-in-Publication Data

Alekhine, Alexander, 1892–1946.
   107 great chess battles : 1939–1945 / Alexander Alekhine ; edited and translated by Edward Winter.
     p.   cm.
  Includes index.
  ISBN 0-486-27104-8
  1. Chess—Collections of games. I. Title.
GV1452.A38 1980
794.1′57—dc20
                                                92-13030
                                                    CIP

Preface

Alexander Alekhine, chess champion of the world for over sixteen years, was one of the greatest players of all time. He also wrote some of the finest chess books ever produced, of which the last published in English was *My Best Games of Chess 1924–1937* (London, 1939). He continued writing extensively throughout the war years, mostly for publication in Spanish, but virtually none of this material has ever been translated into English.

The present book is a compilation of 107 games annotated by Alekhine between 1939 and his death in 1946. The supreme genius of the complicated position guides us patiently and entertainingly through the most fascinating of chess battles. Often he delights us with his candid views on fellow masters and rivals for his world title.

I should like to thank Mr. Bernard Cafferty for kindly clearing up a number of obscure points, and also the editor of the *British Chess Magazine* for permission to reprint Game 68 and the remarkable tribute to Capablanca that precedes it.

Collecting together these games and translating the notes has been an immensely enjoyable and rewarding task and I sincerely hope that the reader will derive as much pleasure and benefit from them.

Edward Winter
London 1979

Contents

PART ONE: OPEN GAMES

Ruy López

Game	Players	Occasion	Page
1	Pleci-Friedemann	Buenos Aires 1939	1
2	Kashdan-Reshevsky	Sixth match game 1942	3
3	Keres-Rabar	Munich 1942	5
4	Kashdan-Reshevsky	Eighth match game 1942	7
5	Alekhine-Schmidt	Salzburg 1942	9
6	Alekhine-Rey Ardid	Second match game 1944	10
7	Alekhine-Zollner	Cracow 1942	13
8	Foltys-Keres	Salzburg 1943	15
9	Alekhine-Junge	Cracow 1942	17
10	Alekhine-Barcza	Munich 1942	18
11	Sämisch-Alekhine	Prague 1943	20
12	Alekhine-Pomar	Gijón 1944	21
13	Alekhine-Rohacek	Munich 1941	25
14	Pomar-Pérez	Madrid 1945	28
15	Röpstorff-Bogoljubov	Warsaw 1942	30
16	Kashdan-Reshevsky	Second match game 1942	32
17	Kashdan-Reshevsky	Fourth match game 1942	34
18	Cruz-Apscheneek	Buenos Aires 1939	37
19	Kieninger-Alekhine	Munich 1941	39

Four Knights Game

20	Lundin-Michel	Buenos Aires 1939	42

Three Knights Game

21	Pahl-Werkmeister	Berlin 1942	44

Philidor's Defence

22	Piazzini-Tartakower	Buenos Aires 1939	46
23	Von Bardeleben-Alekhine	Düsseldorf 1908	49

Scotch Gambit

24	Medina–Keres	Madrid 1943	52
25	Ribeiro–Pomar	Match 1945	54

PART TWO: SEMI-OPEN GAMES

French Defence

26	Bogoljubov–Alekhine	Cracow 1942	57
27	Yanofsky–Dulanto	Buenos Aires 1939	59
28	Lundin–Raud	Buenos Aires 1939	61
29	Pleci–Endzelins	Buenos Aires 1939	64
30	Keres-Ståhlberg	Buenos Aires 1939	65
31	Alekhine–Bartosek	Prague 1943	69
32	Keres–Flores	Buenos Aires 1939	71
33	Pomar–Alekhine	Madrid 1945	73
34	Apscheneek–Alekhine	Buenos Aires 1939	76

Caro-Kann Defence

35	Keres–Mikenas	Buenos Aires 1939	80
36	Pomar–Rico	Bilbao 1945	83
37	Richter–Kieninger	Cracow 1940	84
38	Pomar–Sanz	Madrid 1945	86
39	Alekhine–Eliskases	Buenos Aires 1939	87
40	Alekhine–Richter	Munich 1942	90
41	Brinckmann–Heinicke	Frankfurt 1942	94
42	Capablanca–Czerniak	Buenos Aires 1939	95
43	Alekhine–Naharro	Madrid 1941	98

Sicilian Defence

44	Milner-Barry–Foltys	Buenos Aires 1939	99
45	Rometti–De Ronde	Buenos Aires 1939	101
46	Hasenfuss–Teteris	Lithuania 1942	103
47	Keres–Foltys	Munich 1942	104
48	Foltys–Stoltz	Munich 1942	106
49	Alekhine–Tsvetkov	Buenos Aires 1939	107
50	Alekhine–Podgorny	Prague 1943	110

Alekhine's Defence

| 51 | Reed-Danielsson | Buenos Aires 1939 | 114 |

King's Pawn, Nimzowitsch Defence

| 52 | Rojahn-Czerniak | Buenos Aires 1939 | 116 |

PART THREE: CLOSED GAMES

Queen's Gambit Declined, Orthodox Defence

53	Grau-Eliskases	Buenos Aires 1939	119
54	Ståhlberg-Piazzini	Buenos Aires 1939	121
55	Alekhine-Kunerth	Cracow 1942	123
56	Menchik-Graf	Buenos Aires 1939	125
57	Alekhine and W. Cruz v Silva Rocha, Charlier, and O. Cruz	Rio de Janeiro 1939	129
58	Lundin-Silva Rocha	Buenos Aires 1939	132
59	Kahn-Schmidt	Buenos Aires 1939	134

Queen's Gambit Declined, Slav Defence

| 60 | Reshevsky-Kashdan | Eleventh match game 1942 | 136 |
| 61 | Ståhlberg-Van Scheltinga | Buenos Aires 1939 | 139 |

Queen's Gambit Accepted

| 62 | Opocensky-Lundin | Buenos Aires 1939 | 141 |

Queen's Pawn, Nimzowitsch Defence

63	Reshevsky-Kashdan	Seventh match game 1942	143
64	Enevoldsen-Alekhine	Buenos Aires 1939	146
65	Bolbochán-Poulsen	Buenos Aires 1939	150
66	Petrov-Mikenas	Buenos Aires 1939	152
67	Capablanca-Mikenas	Buenos Aires 1939	155
68	Enevoldsen-Capablanca	Buenos Aires 1939	158
69	Pomar-Ticoulat	Balearic Islands 1944	161
70	Reshevsky-Kashdan	Fifth match game 1942	162
71	Tartakower-Enevoldsen	Buenos Aires 1939	164
72	Pomar-Ribeiro	Match 1945	166
73	Junge-Bogoljubov	Munich 1942	168

King's Indian Defence

| 74 | Flores–Najdorf | Buenos Aires 1939 | 170 |

Grünfeld Defence

75	Flores–Czerniak	Buenos Aires 1939	172
76	Russher–Walcicer	Cracow/Warsaw 1942	174
77	Grau–Mikenas	Buenos Aires 1939	175
78	Reshevsky–Kashdan	First match game 1942	179
79	Reshevsky–Kashdan	Third match game 1942	182
80	Reshevsky–Kashdan	Ninth match game 1942	185
81	Kashdan–Reshevsky	Tenth match game 1942	188

Queen's Indian Defence

82	Opocensky–Capablanca	Buenos Aires 1939	190
83	Alekhine–Keres	Munich 1942	193
84	Opocensky–Keres	Buenos Aires 1939	194
85	Bogoljubov–Rellstab	Cracow 1940	199

Queen's Pawn, Benoni Defence

| 86 | Van Scheltinga–Opocensky | Buenos Aires 1939 | 200 |

Dutch Defence

| 87 | Petrov–Tartakower | Buenos Aires 1939 | 202 |

Budapest Gambit

| 88 | Van Scheltinga–Tartakower | Buenos Aires 1939 | 205 |

Albin Counter Gambit

| 89 | Sämisch–Medina | Madrid 1943 | 208 |

Queen's Pawn Game

90	Petrov–Grau	Buenos Aires 1939	209
91	Mikenas–Czerniak	Buenos Aires 1939	212
92	Mikenas–Alekhine	Buenos Aires 1939	214
93	Czerniak–Tartakower	Buenos Aires 1939	218
94	Trompowsky, Silva Rocha, and Charlier v Alekhine and O. Cruz	Rio de Janeiro 1939	222

| 95 | Trompowsky-Vaitonis | Buenos Aires 1939 | 223 |
| 96 | Bogoljubov-Alekhine | Salzburg 1943 | 225 |

English Opening

97	Czerniak-Alekhine	Buenos Aires 1939	230
98	Leepin-Alekhine	Munich 1941	233
99	Keres-Richter	Munich 1942	235
100	Sajtar-Alekhine	Prague 1943	237

Réti's Opening

101	Engels-Bergqvist	Buenos Aires 1939	240
102	Ståhlberg-Rojahn	Buenos Aires 1939	243
103	Ståhlberg-Castillo	Buenos Aires 1939	245

Catalan System

104	Foltys-Michel	Buenos Aires 1939	247
105	Barcza-Bogoljubov	Munich 1942	250
106	Alekhine-Rabar	Munich 1942	251
107	Alekhine-Bogoljubov	Warsaw 1943	253

107 Great Chess Battles
1939–1945

PART ONE : OPEN GAMES

Ruy López

GAME 1

Buenos Aires 1939
Ruy López

White: I. PLECI (Argentina)
Black: G. FRIEDEMANN (Estonia)

1	e4	e5
2	Nf3	Nc6
3	Bb5	a6
4	Ba4	Nf6
5	0-0	Be7
6	Re1	b5
7	Bb3	d6
8	c3	Na5

I venture to predict that within a space of three years this premature move (correct clearly would be 8 ... 0-0 9 h3 Na5) will be universally and definitively abandoned in favour of castling.

9	Bc2	c5
10	d4	Qc7
11	a4!	Rb8
12	axb5	axb5
13	dxe5	dxe5
14	Nxe5?	

This capture (which should have been replaced by 14 Nbd2, threatening 15 Nxe5 etc., with advantage) is rightly considered by theory to be too dangerous. But the reasons that have been given to support this opinion have been incomplete or unconvincing. The present game therefore offers a good opportunity to arrive at a solution of this little opening problem.

14	...	Qxe5
15	Rxa5	Ng4
16	g3	

The only alternative, 16 f4, would give Black a winning attack after 16 ... Qc7 17 Ra1 c4 etc.

16	...	Qh5
17	h4	

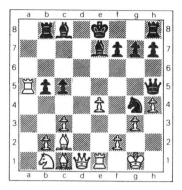

Position after 17 h4

17 ...   Bxh4!

Many spectators (some of them experts of proven international renown) were surprised that Friedemann did not here play the 'book' move 17 . . . g5 with the suggested continuation 18 Bxg5 Bxg5 19 Qd6 Bxh4 20 Qxb8 Bd8 etc. Probably the Estonian master saw over the board that his opponent would have at his disposition the much stronger move 19 Qd5 which, after 19 . . . h6 20 Qxc5 or 19 . . . f6, would bring Black grave problems. For this reason his decision to sacrifice the piece was not only justified by the circumstances but also, in a way, necessary. It should be noted too that the preparatory move 17 . . . 0-0 would be ineffective on account of 18 Qd5 Ne5 19 Bd1.

18   gxh4   Qxh4

19   Qf3

Clearly forced.

19 ...   Qh2+

20   Kf1   Ne5

The key to the combination, allowing the queen's bishop to participate.

21   Qg3

After 21 Bf4 Nxf3 22 Bxh2 Nxh2+, followed by 23 . . . Ng4, Black with his extra pawn would have won easily.

21 ...   Qh1+!

A difficult decision since it seems incredible that after 21 . . . Bh3+ 22 Ke2 Bg4+ 23 Ke3! (if 23 Kf1 it is mate in four with 23 . . . Qh1+ etc.), Black, despite the possibility of playing 23 . . . Nc4+, has no satisfactory continuation for his attack since after this knight check the White king, at f4, would be attacking the enemy bishop. After 23 . . . g5? it would be mate in three were White to capture the queen. But in this case White would protect his c4 square and have no further worries. Friedemann's move thus provides evidence of a profound examination of the position.

22   Ke2   Qh5+

23   f3   Nxf3!

A fresh and perfectly correct sacrifice. It is evident that the knight is untouchable because of 24 . . . Bg4 but nor can the rook be captured. If 24 Qxb8 then 24 . . . Ne5+ 25 Kf2 Qh2+ 26 Kf1 0-0 and wins.

24   Kf2!   Nxe1

25   Kxe1   Qh1+

26   Kf2

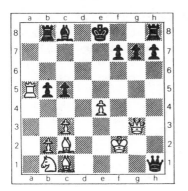

Position after 26 Kf2

26 ...   Qxc1?

An unbelievable error after such
inspired play. Black, probably under
time-pressure, completely overlooks
the check that follows. Otherwise
he would doubtless have played
26 . . . 0-0 27 Bf4 (27 Qxb8? Qxc1
loses rapidly) Rb6 28 e5 Rg6!
29 Bxg6 fxg6 30 Nd2 h6, after
which White would really have to

struggle to obtain a draw.

27 Qe5+

Now Black is lost.

27 ...	Kd8
28 Qd6+	**Ke8**
29 Ra7!	

Decisive.

29 ...	Qxc2+
30 Nd2	**Rb7**
31 Ra8	**Rc7**
32 Ke2!	

The finishing touch.

31 ...	Qa4
33 Rxa4	**bxa4**
34 Qxc7	**Bg4+**

A spite check.

35 Ke3   Black resigns

A game of theoretical value and unusual vitality.

GAME 2

Sixth match game, New York 1942
Ruy López

White: I. KASHDAN
Black: S. RESHEVSKY

1	e4	e5		7	Bb3	d6
2	Nf3	Nc6		8	c3	Na5
3	Bb5	a6		9	Bc2	c5
4	Ba4	Nf6		10	d4	Qc7
5	0-0	Be7		11	h3	
6	Re1	b5				

Perfectly playable would be the immediate move 11 Nbd2 since the firm pin 11 . . . Bg4 offered no danger.

| 11 | . . . | 0-0 |

12 a4

This demonstration on the queen's side is out of place here because Black can reply with a simple developing move. 12 Nbd2 and 12 Bg5 are good moves for White.

| 12 | . . . | Bd7 |

13 Nbd2?

Fine made the same tactical mistake against Reshevsky in the AVRO tournament. Necessary first was 13 axb5 which would keep the balance. Now Black will force a clearly superior ending.

13	. . .	cxd4
14	cxd4	Rfc8
15	axb5	

In his game Fine preferred to sacrifice a pawn by 15 Bd3 but finally he succumbed despite the obstinate tenacity of his resistance. The alternative sought by Kashdan is, in its turn, rather poor.

15	. . .	Qxc2
16	Qxc2	Rxc2
17	Rxa5	Bxb5
18	Ra1	

Neither now nor on the following move can he take the e-pawn because the entry of the bishop into the action at b4 would be fatal.

| 18 | . . . | Rac8 |
| 19 | b3 | Bf8 |

An unnatural move which in fact is not the best. 19 . . . Kf8 also parries the threat of freedom by 20 Ba3 exd4 21 e5 and if White continues as in the game Black gains a valuable tempo.

| 20 | dxe5 | dxe5 |
| 21 | Ba3! | |

The exchange of this bishop frees White's game but nonetheless he is still far from the safety of being able to obtain a draw since the Black bishop is in an assured position.

21	. . .	Bxa3
22	Rxa3	Rc1
23	Rxc1	Rxc1+
24	Kh2	Rc2
25	Ra1	Kf8

Equally safe would be 25 . . . Nd7 26 Nc4 (still the best chance) f6 27 Na3 Rxf2 28 Nxb5 axb5. White can win the b-pawn but he would lose his e-pawn and Black, with four pawns against two on the king's side, would have great chances of winning.

| 26 | Kg1 | Nd7 |

With the serious threat 27 . . . Nc5. White's following pawn sacrifice is practically forced.

| 27 | Nc4 | Bxc4 |

This certainly means the winning of a pawn but it leaves White hope in view of the absence of the Black a-pawn. I would have preferred to play 27 . . . f6 (strongly threatening 28 . . . Nc5) as 28 Na3 Rb2 29 Nxb5 axb5 30 Rd1 Ke7 31 Rd3 b4, followed by 32 . . . Nc5 would be clearly favourable to Black.

28	bxc4	Rxc4
29	Rxa6	Rxe4
30	Ra7	Ke7

Leaving aside the question of whether Black can force a win with the material available (in my view the win is possible, though technically very difficult), one thing is obvious: with the text move Reshevsky lets slip this last chance. Black should play 30 . . . Ke8! Then if 31 Ng5 Rd4 32 Nxh7? Black would win by 32 . . . f6 33 g4 (against the threat of 33 . . . Rh4) g5! and White would not have, as in the game, the saving move 34 h4.

31 Ng5!

This threatens the rook and both the h-pawn and the f-pawn.

31	. . .	Rd4
32	Nxh7!	

Now this paradoxical move which definitely saves the game is possible.

32	. . .	f6
33	g4	

Position after 33 g4

33	. . .	Kf7

If 33 . . . g5, White escapes by 34 h4!! Rxg4+ 35 Kf1 (threatening 36 Rxd7+) Rxh4 36 Nxf6, leading to a theoretically drawn endgame.

34	g5	f5
35	Kf1	Rd6

The king cannot approach the knight, either via g8, because of 36 g6 or via g6, because of 36 Rxd7. No resource remains.

36	g6+	Rxg6
37	Rxd7+	Kg8
38	Re7	Kxh7

Drawn

GAME 3

Munich 1942
Ruy López

White: P. KERES
Black: B. RABAR

1	e4	e5	3	Bb5	a6
2	Nf3	Nc6	4	Ba4	Nf6

5	0-0	Be7
6	Re1	b5
7	Bb3	d6
8	c3	0-0
9	a4	

Keres knows that the reply 9 . . . b4 considerably reduces White's initiative because in a game played in Moscow a few years ago he obtained a satisfactory position, not to say a superior one, after 10 d4 exd4 11 cxd4 Bg4 12 Be3 Na5 13 Bc2 c5. However, Keres assumes that his young adversary will be ignorant of this line, and he is certainly right.

9	. . .	Rb8?

This move is a strategic error since it helps White to obtain a dominant central position.

10	axb5	axb5
11	d4	

This threatens to win a piece and obliges his opponent to exchange, opening up a dangerous line of attack.

11	. . .	exd4
12	cxd4	Bg4
13	Nc3	Qd7
14	Be3	Bd8

So as to be able to answer 15 d5 with 15 . . . Ne7.

15	Qd3	

Allowing Black the move 15 . . . Bxf3, which gives certain defensive chances, in exchange for the pos-session of the two bishops.

15	. . .	Bxf3
16	gxf3	Ne7
17	Kh1	Ng6
18	Rg1	Nh5

These manoeuvres do not imply a desire to counter-attack but simply to defend against the growing pressure in the centre of the board of the White infantry. But this object could also have been achieved through 18 . . . Re8 19 f4 b4 etc.

19	Qf1	Kh8

Black believes he has the chance to manoeuvre his pieces with a view to a counter-offensive, but he succeeds in doing nothing except losing more tempi. The move 19 . . . c6 was necessary.

20	Ne2!	

Now the reply 20 . . . f5 would be refuted by 21 Qh3 and if 20 . . . Nh4 then 21 Ng3 etc.

20	. . .	c6
21	f4	

This advance reduces the already limited possibilities of Black, whose only hope will now consist of a desperate sacrifice.

21	. . .	d5
22	f5	Nh4

If 22 . . . Ne7 then naturally 23 Qh3.

23	f3	Qe8

If 23 . . . Re8, 24 Nf4 with a violent attack.

24	Nf4	Nf6
25	Qh3	

If now 25 . . . Ng8 there would

follow 26 e5, and if 26 . . . Qd7,
27 f6 Qxh3 28 fxg7 mate.

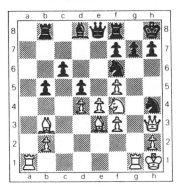

Position after 25 Qh3

25 . . .   **Nxe4**

At first sight this sacrifice seems to
be very strong but Keres has foreseen such an eventuality for some
time and has to hand the appropriate
recipe.

| **26** | **fxe4** | **Qxe4+** |
| **27** | **Ng2** | **Nxf5** |

After 27 . . . Qxf5 there follows
28 Qg3 Nxg2 29 Rxg2 Bf6 30 Bc2
Qd7 31 Rf1 Rg8 32 Bxh7 Kxh7
33 Rxf6 etc.

28 Bf4 !

Forcing the gain of material.

28	**. . .**	**Rb7**
29	**Rae1**	**Qxd4**
30	**Qxf5**	**Qxb2**
31	**Be5 !**	**Qxb3**
32	**Re3**	**Black resigns**

After 32 . . . Qc4 there would
follow 33 Bxg7+ Kxg7 34 Nf4+
Kh8 35 Qxh7+ Kxh7 36 Rh3+,
followed by mate.

GAME 4

Eighth match game, New York 1942
Ruy López

White: I. KASHDAN
Black: S. RESHEVSKY

1	**e4**	**e5**
2	**Nf3**	**Nc6**
3	**Bb5**	**a6**
4	**Ba4**	**Nf6**
5	**0-0**	**Be7**
6	**Qe2**	

This variation offers White at least
as many chances as 6 Re1. The
choice of line of play is a matter of
taste and style.

6	**. . .**	**b5**
7	**Bb3**	**d6**
8	**a4**	**Bg4**

Definitely not 8 . . . b4 because of
9 Qc4.

| **9** | **c3** | **0-0** |

10	h3	Bd7

If 10 . . . Bh5 White plays 11 d3 or the immediate 11 g4 and Black's queen's bishop has little future.

11	d4	Qc8
12	Rd1	b4
13	cxb4	

White does not judge at its proper value the defensive strength of the Black knight at b4. More chances are offered by maintaining the tension in the centre with 13 a5.

13	. . .	exd4
14	Nxd4	Nxb4
15	Nc3	c5!

Black does not leave his opponent the necessary time to develop his pieces and proceeds with a series of exchanges which frees him from all difficulties.

16	Nf3	Be6
17	Bc4	

Equally uninspiring would be 17 Nd5 Bxd5 18 exd5 Re8 etc.

17	. . .	Bxc4
18	Qxc4	Qe6
19	Qxe6	fxe6
20	e5	dxe5
21	Nxe5	Nfd5

The active position of his pieces compensates Black adequately for the isolation of his pawns.

22	Ne4	Rfd8
23	Bg5	Bxg5
24	Nxg5	Nf4
25	g3	Ne2+

26	Kg2	Nd4

As may be seen, Black's defence offers no difficulties.

27	Rac1	Rd5
28	Re1	

If 28 f4 Black would have the effective reply 28 . . . Nb3.

28	. . .	h6
29	Ngf3	Nxf3
30	Kxf3	Rf8+
31	Kg2	

Black to move

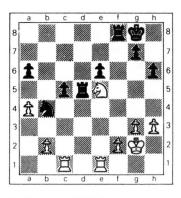

Position after 31 Kg2

31	. . .	Rxe5

This forces liquidation and a draw.

32	Rxe5	Nd3
33	Rexc5	Rxf2+

The point of the combination.

34	Kg1	Nxc5
35	Rxc5	Rxb2
36	Rc6	a5
37	Rc5	Ra2
38	Rxa5	e5

39	Rxe5	Rxa4

Drawn

This easily comprehensible game shows the dynamic force of Reshevsky's defence.

GAME 5

Salzburg 1942
Ruy López

White: A. ALEKHINE
Black: P. SCHMIDT

1	e4	e5
2	Nf3	Nc6
3	Bb5	a6
4	Ba4	Nf6
5	0-0	Be7
6	Qe2	b5
7	Bb3	d6
8	a4	

Against Keres in the same tournament I selected the tranquil line resulting from 8 c3 0-0 9 Rd1 etc. But in this game, in honour of my opponent, I preferred to play rather aggressively.

8	...	Bg4
9	c3	0-0
10	Rd1	

As is well known, the moves 10 axb5 axb5 11 Rxa8 Qxa8 12 Qxb5 permit the reply 12 ... Na7 which is rightly considered more than satisfactory.

10	...	b4
11	a5	

The line 11 d4 exd4 12 cxd4 d5

13 e5 Ne4 would not exactly have been to my advantage.

11	...	d5!?

Too risky.

12	exd5	e4!

The right move, for if 12 ... Nxd5 there would follow 13 d4! exd4 14 Qc4! winning a piece.

13	dxc6	Bd6
14	d4!	Re8

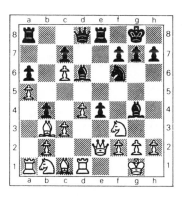

Position after 14 ... Re8

15	Be3	

At this juncture I gave considerable time to the idea 15 Bxf7+ Kxf7

16 Qc4+ with the following possibilities:

(a) 16 . . . Kf8 17 Ng5 Qe7 18 Re1 h6 19 Nh3.

(b) 16 . . . Kg6 17 Nh4+ Kh5 18 f3! Be6 19 Qe2 Kxh4 20 Qe3!

However I am satisfied with my decision.

15	. . .	exf3
16	gxf3	Bh5
17	Nd2	Ne4!
18	Bxf7+	Kxf7
19	Qc4+	Kf8
20	fxe4	

And not 20 Nxe4 Rxe4! 21 fxe4 Qh4 with a strong counter-attack.

| 20 | . . . | Qh4 |

Or 20 . . . Bxd1 21 Rxd1 Qh4 22 Kf1!

21	e5	Bxd1
22	exd6	Qg4+
23	Kf1	cxd6?

It was necessary to play 23 . . . bxc3 bxc3, which would offer Black better chances.

| 24 | d5! | Qh3+ |
| 25 | Ke1 | Bc2 |

25 . . . Bg4 would have been a little better.

26	cxb4	Rxe3+
27	fxe3	Qxe3+
28	Qe2	Qh6

In order to avoid an exchange the Black queen is forced to withdraw quite a way from the battlefield.

| 29 | Ra3! |

Preventing 29 . . . Re8 because of the reply 30 Rf3+ etc.

29	. . .	Bf5
30	Re3	g6
31	Qf2!	Rb8
32	Nc4	Rxb4
33	Nxd6	

Now 33 . . . Rxb2 is not possible owing to 34 Re8+ and mate next move. **Black resigned.**

GAME 6

Second match game, Saragossa 1944
Ruy López

White: A. ALEKHINE
Black: R. REY ARDID

1	e4	e5	5	0-0	Be7
2	Nf3	Nc6	6	Qe2	b5
3	Bb5	a6	7	Bb3	d6
4	Ba4	Nf6	8	c3	Na5

9 d4

This move, so simple, has not yet been tried out in master praxis, but it merits at least a mention in the theoretical manuals. I have played it once and, in spite of the success obtained, I shall not do so again because subsequent analysis persuaded me that Black can easily obtain equality at least. In this game Dr. Rey Ardid falls into an inferior position solely because he allows himself to be influenced by preconceived ideas.

9 ... Nxb3

Very plausible, although not the best. After 9 ... exd4 10 Nxd4 c5 11 Nf3 (or 11 Nf5 Nxb3 12 axb3 Bxf5 13 exf5 Qd7 14 Qf3 0-0 etc.) Nxb3 12 axb3 Bb7, White would be in an unenviable position whether he played 13 Nbd2 or 13 Nfd2.

10 axb3 Nd7

Black's intention can be seen clearly; he is trying at all costs to maintain his centre. Now 10 ... exd4 11 Nxd4 (threatening 12 Nxb5 and 12 Nc6) would give White a good game.

11 Rd1 Bf6

12 dxe5 dxe5

After 12 ... Nxe5 13 Nxe5 Bxe5 14 f4 Bf6 15 e5 Be7 16 exd6 cxd6 17 Re1 Ra7 18 Be3 Rd7 19 Nd2, White's position would have been equally preferable.

13 Na3 c6

The threat of 14 Nxb5 could have been parried by 14 ... Rb8 but this too would lead to troubles (allowing

Nc2-b4). The text move results in a dangerous weakening of the square d6.

14 Nc2 Qe7

15 b4

Demonstrating the inadequacies of Black's queen's side.

15 ... 0-0

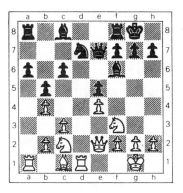

Position after 15 ... 0-0

16 h3!

To my mind this move is the most difficult of the whole game. In fact White, despite his good position, has difficulty in consolidating it. For instance, if he plays 16 Ne3 then 16 ... Nb6, and if 16 Be3 then 16 ... c5 with a good game. The text move threatens by Nh2-g4 to harass the Black king's bishop (conserving his bishop pair is the only satisfaction that Black has to compensate for his weakened position) and thus create a weakness, however slight it may be, on Black's king side.

16 ... Re8

17 Nh2 Qe6

To avoid the exchange of the bishop. But now the square f5 is accessible to the knight and the move . . . g6 becomes unavoidable as a result.

18 Ne3   g6

19 Nf3!

Threatening the exchange of the bishop by means of 20 Ng4 and 21 Nh6+.

19 . . .   Bd8

This move would be good if Black had continued logically with his idea.

20 Ng4   f5?

This move loses. Black allows himself to be influenced by the variation 21 exf5 gxf5 22 Ngxe5? Bf6 and wins, and forgets that at this moment his d6 is not sufficiently well protected. He ought to have played 20 . . . f6 21 Ne1 a5 22 bxa5 Rxa5 23 Rxa5 Bxa5 24 b4 Bc7 25 Nd3 after which he would have excellent chances of resistance.

21 Nh6+

Equally strong was 21 exf5 gxf5 22 Nh6+ Kf8! 23 g4!, with the occupation of f5.

21 . . .   Kg7

With 21 . . . Kf8 22 exf5 etc. Black could reach the variation mentioned above but it too would be without hope. If 21 . . . Kh8, then 22 exf5 gxf5 23 Rd6! and wins.

22 exf5   Qc4

Seeking an exchange of queens which would in fact have granted him some chances of salvation. It is evident that if 22 . . . gxf5 23 Rd6! is decisive.

23 Qc2!   Black resigns

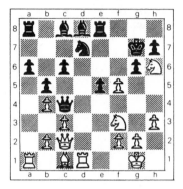

Final position

Black's resignation in this position is justified since he has a lost game. The continuation would have been 23 . . . Nf6 24 Bg5 Nd5! 25 Bxd8 Kxh6 (or after 25 . . . Rxd8 the prosaic win by 26 Nxe5 Qf4 27 Nxc6 Rd6 28 Ng4 Bxf5 29 Qd2 etc.) 26 Rxd5! cxd5 27 Bf6! (threatening 28 Qd2+) gxf5 (if 27 . . . e4 then 28 Qd2+ e3 29 fxe3 Qe4 30 Ng5! Qxe3+ 31 Qxe3 Rxe3 32 Nf7+ Kh5 33 g4 mate) 28 Qd2+ f4 29 Nxe5 and wins.

GAME 7

Cracow 1942
Ruy López

White: A. ALEKHINE
Black: L. ZOLLNER

1	e4	e5
2	Nf3	Nc6
3	Bb5	a6
4	Ba4	Nf6
5	0-0	Be7
6	Qe2	b5
7	Bb3	0-0

This move has been played very often recently instead of the normal variation 7 . . . d6.

8 d4

Also very practicable is 8 c3 d5 9 d3! as I tried with success in a later game against Junge [*Game 9*]. The positional advantage that White would obtain is full compensation for the sacrifice of a pawn that the text move involves.

8 ...   d5

If 8 . . . exd4 (or 8 . . . Nxd4 9 Nxd4 exd4), then 9 e5 Ne8 10 c3! dxc3 11 Nxc3 with an excellent game.

9	dxe5	Nxe4
10	c3	

After 10 Rd1 Be6 11 c4 there would follow 11 . . . bxc4 12 Bxc4 Bc5 13 Be3 Bxe3 14 Qxe3 Ne7 with good defensive chances.

10	...	Be6
11	Nbd2	Nc5
12	Bc2	

More frequently played at this point (since by inversion of moves we find ourselves in a well-known line of the Open Defence 5 . . . Nxe4) is 12 Nd4 Nxb3 13 Nxb3 — and not 13 Nxc6 owing to 13 . . . Nxc1 — Qd7 etc. with almost absolute equality. The text move turns out to be rather deficient, as Black's reply will demonstrate. We are thus at a stage which merits consideration from the point of view of the development of this game.

12 ...   d4

After this the continuation 13 cxd4 Nxd4 14 Nxd4 Qxd4 15 Nf3 Qc4! would scarcely be pleasant for White. Nevertheless by his next move White manages to resolve the situation, giving Black a difficult problem to tackle.

13 Bb1!   dxc3

If 13 . . . d3 White would play 14 Qe3 and the Black pawn would be destined to succumb.

14 bxc3   Qd7

With the idea of disputing the queen's file with White by 15 Rd1 Rad8 etc.

15 Ne4!   Rad8

If now 15 . . . Bc4 there would follow 16 Nxc5 Bxc5 17 Qe4 with great advantage.

16 Nxc5   Bxc5

17 Qe4   g6

A weakening of Black's position that will become fatal. Although not entirely satisfactory, 17 . . . f5 would have been more bearable but after 18 exf6 gxf6 19 Bh6 Rf7 20 Bc2 White has the advantage anyway.

18 Bg5   Be7

19 Qh4!

With the strong threat of 20 Bf6, which obliges Black to create a new weakness.

19 . . .   h5

20 Be4

Threatening 21 Bxc6 Bxg5 22 Bxd7 etc., winning a piece.

20 . . .   Bxg5

21 Qxg5   Bf5

22 Rfe1

Very seductive, but insufficient to win, would be 22 Rad1 Qxd1 23 Bxf5 since after 23 . . . Qd5! White would have to make do with equality by means of 24 Bxg6. Nor would 22 Qh6 Bxe4 23 Ng5 be practical because of the response 23 . . . f5, which shows Black's defensive powers.

22 . . .   Bxe4

If 22 . . . Rfe8 White would secure a decisive material advantage by 23 Bxc6! Qxc6 24 Nd4 Qc5 25 e6 Bxe3 26 Nxe6.

23 Rxe4   Ne7

24 Rae1

Now 25 e6 is threatened with demolishing effect.

24 . . .   Qe8!

With the intention of answering 25 e6 with 25 . . . f6, eluding the *coup*.

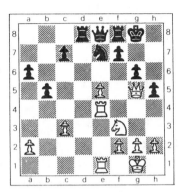

Position after 24 . . . Qe8

25 g4

Up until now White has managed to conduct the attack well, obtaining a winning position. But this move and especially the next are well refuted by Black. A simple and efficacious solution to the problem was 25 Rh4 Kh7 26 Qf6!, winning pawns and increasing the attack until the finish. This would have brought the struggle to an end shortly.

25 . . .   Rd3!

26 Nh4?

Now too White could have attained victory by means of the most natural and logical continuation 26 Nd4! and if 26 . . . c5 then 27 Nf5 Nxf5 28 gxf5 (or 28 e6 or even 28 gxh5). The position of the knight at h4 hinders White's natural attack down the rook's file, at the same time facilitating Black's counter-attack.

26 . . .   hxg4

27	Rxg4	Rd5
28	Qh6	Qd8!

With the intention of replying to 29 e6 with 29 . . . Rd1 30 exf7+ Rxf7.

29	Nf3	Nf5
30	Qc1	

30 Qf4 Ng7 would be useless for White.

30	. . .	Rd3
31	Ng5	

Hoping to play 32 e6 or 32 Ne4.

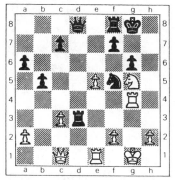

Position after 31 Ng5

31	. . .	Nh6?

A mistake which annuls Black's brilliant resistance and tarnishes the game. Indicated was 31 . . . Re8!, preventing 32 Ne4 and at the same time weakening the effect of 32 e6. The text move was however chosen by Black with the idea of answering 32 e6 with 32 . . . fxe6, to which White would have replied with 33 Ne4! Kg7 (or 33 . . . Kh7) 34 Kh1! and the battle continues with vigour.

32 Ne6!

Forcing the win of the queen through the threat of mate in a few moves.

32	. . .	Qe7

After 32 . . . Nxg4 33 Nxd8 Rfxd8 34 Qf4 White would win the knight as well.

33	Qxh6	Qxe6
34	Rh4	**Black resigns**

GAME 8

Salzburg 1943
Ruy López

White: J. FOLTYS
Black: P. KERES

1	e4	e5
2	Nf3	Nc6
3	Bb5	a6
4	Ba4	Nf6
5	0-0	Be7
6	Qe2	b5
7	Bb3	0-0

The fashionable variation.

8	c3

To be considered is the pawn sacrifice played by me against Zollner at Warsaw 1942: 8 d4 exd4 9 e5 Ne8 10 c3!

8 ...	d5
9 exd5	

Against 9 d3 Black can play 9 . . . d4 and if 10 cxd4 then 10 . . . Bg4 11 d5 Nd4 with good attacking chances.

9 ...	Bg4
10 dxc6	

The continuation 10 h3 Bxf3 11 Qxf3 e4 12 Qe2 Na5 13 Bc2 Qxd5 14 Re1 Rfe8 15 Bxe4 Nxe4 16 Qxe4 Qd7 17 Qf3 c5 would hardly be satisfactory for White.

10 ...	e4
11 d4	exf3
12 gxf3	Bh5
13 Bf4	

As will be seen in the continuation Black, after this move, could force a draw. 13 Nd2 Bd6 14 Ne4 Re8 15 Qd3 etc. offered more possibilities.

13 ...	Re8
14 Be5	Bd6
15 Nd2	Bxe5
16 dxe5	Nd5
17 Ne4	Nf4

After 17 . . . Rxe5 18 Rad1 the pin on the queen's file would have been unpleasant. With the text move Black makes sure of a draw.

18 Qe3	Qh4
19 Ng3	

The only defence against 19 . . . Rxe5.

19 ...	g5

This move which at first sight seems so momentous allows White a clever rejoinder which saves him from peril. Black could force a draw by playing 19 . . . Rxe5 20 Qxe5 Nh3+ 21 Kg2 Nf4+ etc.

White to move

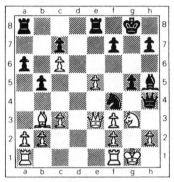

Position after 19 . . . g5

20 Nxh5	Qxh5
21 e6!!	Qh3?

This winning attempt could have had fatal results. Correct was 21 . . . Nxe6 22 Qe4! Nf4 23 Qf5 Re7 24 Qg4. White can deal with the immediate threats but the knight at f4 exerts intense pressure on his position.

22 exf7+	Kg7

If 22 . . . Kf8 then 23 Qc5+ Re7 24 Qxg5 and wins.

23 Qd4+

Perhaps this is sufficient to win but simpler is 23 fxe8(N)+! Kh6 (if 23 . . . Rxe8 then 24 Qd4+ Kg6 25 Bf7+!, followed by 26 Qd7+ and wins) 24 Qxf4 gxf4 25 Rfe1 Qxf3 26 Re6+ Kg5 27 Rae1 and White wins comfortably.

23 ...	Re5!

The only move because if 23 ...
Kg6 then 24 fxe8(Q)+ Rxe8 25
Bf7+ and wins

24	Qxe5+	Kg6
25	Qxf4	gxf4
26	Rfe1?	

After 26 Bd5 Rf8 27 Rfd1, followed
by 28 Rd3 White keeps excellent
winning chances. Now Black is in a

position to draw.

26	...	Rf8
27	Re7	Qxf3
28	Rae1	Qg4+
29	Kh1	

If 29 Kf1 then of course 29 ... f3.

29	...	Qf3+
30	Kg1	Qg4+

Drawn

GAME 9

Cracow 1942
Ruy López

White: A. ALEKHINE
Black: K. JUNGE

1	e4	e5
2	Nf3	Nc6
3	Bb5	a6
4	Ba4	Nf6
5	0-0	Be7
6	Qe2	b5
7	Bb3	0-0
8	c3	

In connection with the following
move this is a safe method of preparing to counter the aggressive
plan of Black which was indicated by
his seventh move.

8	...	d5
9	d3!	dxe4

The opening of the queen's file is to
White's advantage. But 9 ... d4 10

cxd4 Nxd4 11 Nxd4 Qxd4 12 Nc3
followed by 13 Be3 would also have
involved some difficulty for Black.

10	dxe4	Bg4
11	h3	Bh5
12	Bg5	

Preventing 12 ... Na5 which would
be refuted by 13 g4 Bg6 14 Nxe5
simply winning a pawn.

12	...	Ne8
13	Bxe7	Bxf3

If immediately 13 ... Nxe7 then 14
g4 etc.

14	Qxf3	Nxe7
15	Rd1	Nd6
16	Nd2	c6

A better defensive idea would have

been 16 . . . Kh8 in order to be able to answer 17 Bc2 with 17 . . . c6 and 17 Nf1 with 17 . . . f5.

17	Nf1	Qc7
18	a4!	

The opening of the a-file in the Ruy López is, almost without exception, favourable to White.

18	. . .	Rad8
19	Ng3	Nec8
20	axb5	axb5
21	Nf5	

In order to maintain, after the possible exchange, a new weapon of attack in the form of the pawn at f5.

21	. . .	Nb6
22	Qe3!	Nxf5

After 22 . . . Nbc4 White would acquire a decisive positional advantage by means of 23 Bxc4 bxc4 24 Qc5!

23	exf5	c5

It is already the end. To 23 . . . Nd5 White would have replied 24 Qf3

after which Black's position could not be held.

24	f6!	gxf6
25	Qh6	f5

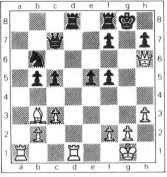

Position after 25 . . . f5

26	Bxf7+!	

An elegant finish. Whether or not he captures the bishop Black loses material.

26	. . .	Qxf7
27	Rxd8	Na4
28	b3!	

If 28 . . . Nxc3 there follows 29 Raa8, **Black resigned.**

GAME 10

Munich 1942
Ruy López

White: A. ALEKHINE
Black: G. BARCZA

1	e4	e5		4	Ba4	Nf6
2	Nf3	Nc6		5	0-0	Be7
3	Bb5	a6		6	Nc3	b5

7	Bb3	d6
8	Nd5!?	

With this interesting move I defeated Bogoljubov in the Munich Tournament last year. The correct continuation for Black is 8 . . . Na5 when White has at his disposal no particularly advantageous line.

8	. . .	Bg4
9	c3	0-0

If Black had played . . . Nxe4 either now or on his previous move the reply d4! would have had a demolishing effect.

10 h3!

Forcing the bishop to declare its plans at this stage is very precise. After 10 . . . Bh5 White would play 11 d3 without the loss of time.

10	. . .	Be6
11	d4	Kh8!

Preparing against 12 Nxe7 which would now be refuted by means of 12 . . . Bxb3 13 Nxc6 Bxd1 14 Nxd8 Bxf3 etc.

12	Re1	Nd7

And not 12 . . . Na5 because of the reply 13 Nxe7 Nxb3 14 Nc6 Qd7 15 axb3, followed by 16 d5.

13	Bc2	f6
14	a4	Na7

If 14 . . . Rb8 then 15 axb5 axb5 16 Ra6 with a good game.

15	axb5	axb5
16	Be3	

Again threatening 17 Nxe7, winning a piece.

16	. . .	c5
17	dxc5	dxc5
18	Ra6!	

With the threat 19 Qa1.

18	. . .	Bxd5
19	exd5	Qc8
20	Qa1	Qb7
21	b4!	

It will no longer now be possible to avoid 22 d6 etc.

21	. . .	Rfb8
22	d6	Bd8
23	bxc5	Rc8
24	Ra2	

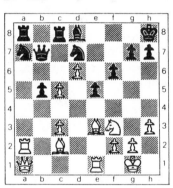

Position after 24 Ra2

24	. . .	e4

Veritable desperation. If 24 . . . Nxc5 there follows 25 Bxc5 Rxc5 26 Be4 etc.

25	Bxe4!	Qxe4
26	Bd4	Qg6
27	Rxa7	Rxa7
28	Qxa7	Ne5
29	Bxe5	**Black resigns**

GAME 11

Prague 1943
Ruy López

White: F. SAMISCH
Black: A. ALEKHINE

1 e4	e5
2 Nf3	Nc6
3 Bb5	a6
4 Ba4	Nf6
5 0-0	d6
6 Re1	

Better would have been 6 Bxc6+, followed by 7 d4.

6 ...	b5
7 Bb3	Na5

The exchange of the White king's bishop gives Black the present of the best prospects of obtaining equality.

8 d4	Nxb3
9 axb3	Nd7

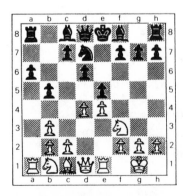

Position after 9 . . . Nd7

More common and perhaps better is 9 . . . Bb7. The text move in any case, provides White with a problem which is not very easy to resolve.

10 dxe5

And — after forty-five minutes' reflection! — Sämisch, dismayed, decides upon a liquidation which hands over to Black a very peaceful game. Schmidt in his game against Keres at Salzburg 1943 played the proper manoeuvre: 10 Bd2!, followed by 11 Ba5. Black had to make considerable efforts to achieve a drawn game.

10 ...   Nxe5

Not 10 . . . dxe5 because of 11 Qd5.

11 Nxe5	dxe5
12 Qxd8+	Kxd8

The two bishops promise Black a few remote prospects but the exploitation of this advantage is not an easy matter.

13 Be3	Bb7
14 Nd2	

14 Nc3 would be simpler.

14 ...	Bd6
15 f3	Ke7
16 Bf2	Ke6
17 Nf1	g6

It is evident that Black must attempt to open up the game in order to leave the field free for his bishops.

18 c3   a5

In order to prevent 19 b4, followed by Nd2-b3-c5.

19 Ra2

This move has no effect. But it is already difficult to indicate a good defensive plan for White.

19 ...   Ra6

20 Ne3   f5

21 exf5+   gxf5

22 Nc2   Kf7!

This prevents 23 Nd4+. In this position f7 is the best square for the king.

23 b4

White, after strenuous efforts, will succeed in exchanging one bishop but in the meantime Black will have secured other advantages.

23 ...   a4

24 Bc5   Rg8

25 Kf2   Rc6!

After this move White must make a decision: yield to his opponent the command of the queen's file or opt for a new restriction on the activity of his pieces after 26 Be3 f4 etc. In this latter case Black would also conserve excellent winning chances.

26 Bxd6   Rxd6

27 Re2?

Losing immediately. In any case even if he had played 27 g3 (definitely not 27 Rxe5 Rd2+ 28 Re2 Rxg2+! winning a piece), which was the best move, he would not have saved the game. For instance, 27 ... Bd5 28 Raa1 Bc4 29 Rad1 Rgd8 30 Rxd6 Rxd6 and the entry of the rook to the seventh rank will be decisive.

27 ...   Bd5

This wins the exchange after 28 Ra1 Bc4, and all further fight is impossible.

28 White resigns

GAME 12

Gijón 1944
Ruy López

White: A. ALEKHINE
Black: A. POMAR

| 1 | e4 | e5 | 3 | Bb5 | a6 |
| 2 | Nf3 | Nc6 | 4 | Ba4 | Nf6 |

5 0-0   d6

6 c3

The only sure way of obtaining a slight advantage in space is 6 Bxc6+, followed by 7 d4 but that day I was in the mood to play with a more complicated structure.*

6 ...   Bg4

7 d4   b5

8 Bb3   Be7

8 ... Bxf3 9 gxf3 would have been disadvantageous for Black.

9 Be3   0-0

10 Nbd2   Re8

11 h3   Bh5

12 d5

This blockading of the position is not bad but it can prove somewhat premature. 12 a4 deserved to be taken into serious consideration.

12 ...   Na5

13 Bc2   Rc8

14 a4

The opening of the a-file corresponds to purely tactical ends but White has no need to conduct the game on both wings (this stratagem has won me many a game but it should be used with discretion and not misapplied), because the natural move 14 b4 would guarantee White an advantage after either 14 ... Nc4 15 Nxc4 bxc4 16 g4 Bg6 17 Nd2 or 14 ... Nb7 15 c4 c6 16 dxc6 Rxc6 17 cxb5 axb5 18 a4 etc.

*Understandable against a twelve-year-old opponent! E.W.

14 ...   c5!

The right move, after which Black will have nothing to fear on the queen's side. But it remains to be seen whether White will be able to work up a sufficiently strong attack against the king's position.

15 axb5   axb5

16 g4   Bg6

17 Nh4   Nd7

Black cannot take the king's pawn. If 17 ... Bxe4? 18 Nxe4 Nxe4 19 Nf5 Nf6 20 g5 Nd7 21 Qd3 Nf8 22 Qxb5 Ra8 23 b4 and wins.

18 Nf5   Bxf5

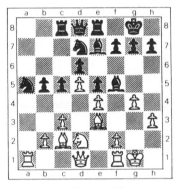

Position after 18 ... Bxf5

19 gxf5?

The attack down the g-file will be sufficient to maintain the equilibrium but that is all. However with 19 exf5 Nc4! 20 Nxc4 bxc4 21 Ba4 Rf8 22 Bxd7 Qxd7 23 Qa4! Qb7 24 Qxc4 Qxb2 25 Rab1 Qa3 26 Rb7 Bd8 27 Rfb1 White would have assured himself of lasting pressure.

19 ...   Bg5!

20 Qe2   c4

21	Kh1	Ra8
22	Rg1	Bxe3
23	Qxe3	Qf6
24	Rg4	Kh8
25	Rag1	Rg8
26	Nf3	Nb7
27	Rh4	Ra6!

With the aim of utilizing the knight at d7 for the defence without having to fear Qb6.

28	Qg5!	Nd8

Obviously he cannot exchange queens.

29	Qh5	Nf8
30	Nh2	

With 30 Ng5 White could force the reply 30 . . . h6 but the attack cannot break through in any case since he has two serious weaknesses: firstly the fact that it is impossible to employ the bishop and secondly Black's latent threat to play . . . Ra2. The text manoeuvre will practically oblige Black to play . . . g6 and will, in a few moves, re-establish a balanced position.

30	. . .	g6
31	Qh6	Qg7
32	Ng4	f6
33	fxg6	

The simplest because if the queen retreats the move 33 . . . Nf7 would give Black a defence that would be more than sufficient. Black is forced to recapture with the queen because 33 . . . Nxg6 would be fatal on account of 34 Nxf6!

33	. . .	Qxg6
34	Qe3?	

But here 34 Qc1 is decidedly preferable, for instance: 34 . . . Qg5 35 Rh6 Rg6 36 Qxg5 fxg5 37 Rxg6 Nxg6 38 Nh6 Kg7 39 Nf5+ Kf6 40 Bd1 and the bishop can at last be used.

34	. . .	Qg5
35	Rh6	Qxe3
36	fxe3	

And not 36 Nxe3 because of 36 . . . Rxg1+ 37 Kxg1 Ra1+ 38 Kh2 Ng6 etc. with advantage to Black.

36	. . .	Nd7
37	Rf1	Ra2

This is good but not the best. Black would have conserved winning chances by protecting the f-pawn with 37 . . . Nf7. For example 37 . . . Nf7 38 Rh5 Rg6 39 Rhf5 Kg7 and White's position would remain seriously threatened.

38	Nxf6	Nxf6
39	Rhxf6	Rxb2
40	Bd1	Rgg2
41	Bf3	Rg3
42	Bg4	Rgg2
43	Ra1	Rh2+
44	Kg1	Rhg2+
45	Kf1	Rh2

Game 12 Ruy López

White to move

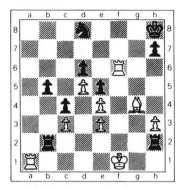

Position after 45 . . . Rh2

Up until here the game has been fairly well conducted by both sides and after 46 Kg1 Black should content himself with a draw. But my next move which avoids such a result is real lunacy and deserves to lose the game.

46 Ke1??

Playing for the advantage in this position is sheer suicide. After 46 . . . Nb7 47 Rf7 Rh1+ 48 Rf1 Rxf1+ 49 Kxf1 Nc5, Black would have achieved a winning position.

46 . . .   b4

Although this advance seems to have all the appearance of something momentous, it actually allows White to extricate himself from his difficult situation.

47 cxb4   c3

48 Rc1   h5!

48 . . . c2 would have been ineffective because of 49 Rf2.

49 Bd1!   Kg7

50 Rf1   c2

51 Be2   Nf7

52 Kd2   Rxb4

White was threatening 53 Kc3, followed by 54 Kb3 and 55 Bd3.

53 Rxc2   Ng5

54 Rc7+   Kg6

55 Kc3   Ra4

56 Bb5?

Out of all danger, White makes a miscalculation after which Black should win easily. The logical continuation was 56 Bd3 Rxh3 57 Rf8 with a certain draw.

56 . . .   Nxe4+

57 Kb3   Raa2

58 Rg1+

When I played 56 Bb5? I thought I could now continue with 58 Bd3 but unfortunately this move is impossible on account of 58 . . . Rhb2+ 59 Kc4 Ra4 mate.

58 . . .   Kh6

59 Rb1   Rad2

He could also win by 59 . . . Nc5+ or 59 . . . Raf2, followed by 60 . . . Rxh3.

60 Bd7   Rxd5

61 Kc4

Black to move

Position after 61 Kc4

61 ...   Rc2+

With a won game and free from any danger, Pomar plays for a draw! This demonstrates his uncertainty and his lack of self-confidence, and he will have to fight to overcome this defect if he desires to achieve

striking successes. In fact 61 ... Rdd2 would be simple and decisive. If 62 Rc6 (to prevent 62 ... d5+) then 62 ... Rhe2 etc.

62	Kxd5	Rxc7
63	Kxe4	Rxd7
64	h4!	d5+!

Otherwise White would, after 65 Kd5, be in an advantageous position, despite being a pawn down.

65	Kxe5	Re7+
66	Kf5	Rxe3
67	Rb6+	Kh7
68	Rd6	Re4
69	Rd7+	Kh6
70	Rd6+	Kg7
71	Rd7+	

Drawn

GAME 13

Munich 1941 (First Brilliancy Prize)
Ruy López

White: A. ALEKHINE
Black: H. ROHACEK

1	e4	e5
2	Nf3	Nc6
3	Bb5	a6
4	Ba4	Nf6
5	0-0	Nxe4
6	d4	b5
7	Bb3	d5

8	dxe5	Be6
9	c3	Be7
10	a4!?	

Preparing for the forthcoming pawn sacrifice. The most energetic of the replies is 10 ... b4 which entails very complicated variations on which the last word has not yet been spoken. In any case the analysis of this position by Dr. Euwe is neither complete nor very convincing.

10 ...   **Rb8**

After this move the sacrifice is fully justified as is shown by the game which, for this reason alone, has a certain theoretical value.

11 axb5   **axb5**

12 Nd4!

As will be seen, this sacrifice assures White of the initiative for a long time.

12 ...   **Nxe5**

13 f3

Now 13 f4 would lead to nothing after 13 ... Bg4 14 Qc2 Nc4!

13 ...   **Nc5**

14 Bc2

Here the attempt to win the exchange would be harmful for White. For example: 14 f4 Nxb3 15 Qxb3 Nd3 16 Nc6 (16 f5 Bd7 would recover the pawn but would leave Black with the advantage of the two bishops) Bc5+ 17 Kh1 Qh4 18 Nxb8 Nf2+ 19 Rxf2 Qxf2 20 Qxb5+ Ke7 21 Nc6+ Kf6 and wins. But now White does threaten 15 f4.

14 ...   **Bd7**

15 b4

With the object of continuing the attack after 15 ... Ne6 with 16 Nf5.

15 ...   **Nb7**

16 Qe2   **Nc4**

17 Re1

Once Black has acquired his first

advantage it becomes clear that he will be obliged to renounce castling.

17 ...   **Kf8**

18 Bf4   **Nbd6**

The threat was 19 Bxc7.

19 Nd2

Black to move

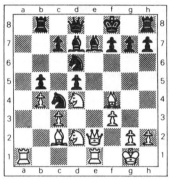

Position after 19 Nd2

19 ...   **g5!?**

This move contains more poison than is apparent. Black, to be sure, will be forced to sacrifice the exchange, but as compensation he will achieve a certain advantageous position on the Black squares. With a peaceful continuation like 19 ... Nxd2 White would not have encountered any difficulty in intensifying his pressure. For instance: 20 Qxd2 Nc4 21 Qe2 Bf6 22 Ra7! Rc8 23 Bd3 and if now 23 ... c5 then 24 Bxc4 cxd4 25 Bxd5 dxc3 26 Bd6+ Kg8 27 Bxf7+ Kxf7 28 Qe6+ Kg6 29 Rxd7 Qb6+ 30 Kh1 with decisive threats.

20 Nxc4!   **gxf4**

Disadvantageous for Black would be 20 ... Nxc4 21 Bxc7 and 20 ... bxc4 (or 20 . . . dxc4) 21 Be5!

21 Ne5!

This threatens in particular the square c6 which Black is in no position to defend effectively (if 21 . . . Rb6 then 22 Ra8 and wins).

21 . . .   **Bf6!**

This is the move which places the most obstacles before his opponent.

22	Ndc6	Bxc6
23	Nxc6	Qc8
24	Nxb8	Qxb8

Black now threatens (after, for instance, the plausible move 25 Qd3) to consolidate his position by playing 25 . . . c6, after which White's advantage — if advantage there be — would in any case be difficult to exploit. His decision to seek a solution by means of a combination is consequently amply justified.

25 Qd2!

Here the complications begin, complications difficult to calculate. The square f4 must be taken at all cost!

25	. . .	Qb6+
26	Kh1	Qc6
27	Bb3!	

The pawn at c3 could not be defended in a direct way. The text move prepares in the main variation for an unexpected rook sacrifice.

Black to move

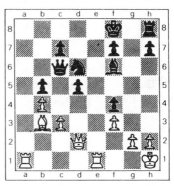

Position after 27 Bb3

27 . . .   **Bxc3**

28 Qc1!

The prosaic continuation 28 Rec1 Bxd2 29 Rxc6 d4 30 Rxc7 Bxb4 would have left Black opportunities of a draw in view of the paucity of material. The text move threatens 29 Bxd5 and at the same time forces the advance of this pawn, which cuts the communication of the bishop with the king's side.

28 . . .   **d4**

After the moves 28 . . . Nf5 29 Bxd5 Ng3+ 30 hxg3 Qh6+ 31 Kg1 the White king would have escaped to e2.

29 Qxf4

This sacrificial combination demanded precise calculation in the following variations:

(a) 29 . . . Nc4 30 Bxc4 (allowing Black to obtain two strong passed pawns) bxc4 31 Qe5! Rg8 32 b5! Qb7 33 Qc5+ Kg7 34 Qg5+ Kf8 35 Qh6+ Rg7 36 Qa6!! Qxa6 37 bxa6 Rg8 38 a7 Kg7 39 Reb1!, followed by 40 Rb8.

(b) 29 . . . Bxe1 30 Rxe1! (tempting but sufficient only for a draw is 30 Qh6+ Kg8 31 Rc1!? with the idea of 31 . . . Bc3 32 Qg5+ Kf8 33 Qf6 Rg8 34 Bxf7! but Black can escape by 31 . . . Qe8! 32 Rc5 Bd2! 33 Qxd2 Qe3! etc.) Qc3 31 Qe5 Rg8 32 Bd5 with a winning attack because on 32 . . . Qxb4 there follows 33 Qe7+ Kg7 34 Bxf7! and on 32 . . . Qc2 33 g4! d3 34 Ra1 and wins.

| 29 | . . . | d3 |

After this move White has an easy task because the pretty liberation imagined by Black has no effect.

30	Rec1	d2
31	Rc2	Qa6!
32	Rd1	Bg7
33	Rxc7	**Black resigns**

GAME 14

Madrid 1945
Ruy López

White: A. POMAR
Black: F.J. PEREZ

1	e4	e5
2	Nf3	Nc6
3	Bb5	a6
4	Ba4	Nf6
5	Nc3	Be7
6	Bxc6	

An original idea of Pomar's, seeking to assure himself of a slight positional advantage and avoid the danger of losing.

6	. . .	dxc6
7	Nxe5	Nxe4
8	Nxe4	Qd4
9	0-0	Qxe5
10	Re1	c5

This is relatively best.

| 11 | d3 | 0-0 |

| 12 | Nc3 | Qd6 |
| 13 | Qf3 | |

With the evident threat of 14 Bf4, followed by 15 Bxc7 and 16 Nd5 etc.

| 13 | . . . | c6 |
| 14 | Be3! | |

This move is more ingenious (and, doubtless, of greater strength) than 14 Bf4. If Black replies 14 . . . b6, then 15 Na4 Bd8 16 Bf4 Qf6 17 Qg3 Be6 18 Bc7 with advantage.

| 14 | . . . | Be6? |

This is a mistake in an already difficult position.

White to move

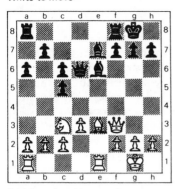

Position after 14 . . . Be6

15 Rad1

A pity! White fails to exploit the advantage he has acquired. With 15 Na4 he could win a pawn and theoretically the game. The text move, played with visions of opening the queen's file and trying an attack against the king's position *which is in no way weakened,* cannot lead to more than equality.

15 . . .	Qc7
16 d4	Bd6
17 Qh5	

Trying to complicate the position without any justifiable motive. How much better and simpler would be 17 h3 cxd4 18 Bxd4 c5 19 Be3 etc.! Black would have been incapable of holding on to the advantage of the two bishops for very long.

| 17 . . . | cxd4 |

More effective would be 17 . . . c4 since the liquidation after 18 d5 would lead only to an equal position.

18 Rxd4?

A grave tactical error after which Black will seize the initiative. After 18 Bxd4 Black would have nothing better than to yield a draw by playing 18 . . . c5 19 Bxg7 etc. because the reply to 18 . . . Be7 would be 19 Rd3, guaranteeing White a real attack.

| 18 . . . | f5! |

The only move, according to Pomar. Without any doubt this is the most powerful response as it suppresses any hope of attack. But 18 . . . Rfe8 was playable too, for example: 19 Rh4 h6 and 20 Bxh6 is impossible because of 20 . . . Bg4!

19 Bc1

A sad retreat after which Black obtains an easy game. White should at least have eliminated one of the bishops by playing 19 Bf4. After 19 . . . Bxf4 20 Rxe6 Be5 21 Rd3 g6 22 Qe2! Black would not have been able to play 22 . . . Bxh2+ 23 Kh1 because the double threat of 24 g3 and 24 Re7 could not be parried.

| 19 . . . | Rae8 |
| 20 Red1 | |

20 Rdd1 would be of greater value but in any case the advantage of the two bishops is already lamentable.

20 . . .	Be5
21 R4d3	f4
22 Ne4	Bf5
23 Qf3	Qe7!

It would have been premature to play 23 . . . Bxb2 on account of 24 Bxb2 Rxe4 25 Qxe4! Bxe4 26 Rd7.

24 Re1

This loses a piece. With 24 R3d2 he could save it but the position after 24 ... Bb8 25 Qb3+ Kh8 26 f3 Bxe4 27 fxe4 Ba7+ 28 Kh1 Qxe4 would also be lost.

24 ...   Bb8

25 Rd4   c5

26 Rd2   Bxe4

27 Qb3+   Qf7!

Otherwise White would recover the piece with 28 f3.

28 Qxf7+   Kxf7!

And not 28 ... Rxf7 because of 29 Rde2, followed by 30 f3.

29 Rd7+   Kg8

and Black wins comfortably.

This game is of double interest. In the first place because Pomar knew how to impose himself on his mighty opponent with a variation invented and analysed by himself. Secondly, after letting slip the winning opportunity on the fifteenth move he proves that at the present moment in his development he lacks the wisdom to understand the latent value of the two bishops. Should it be possible to procure them it would be very profitable for him to study the best games of Janowsky.

GAME 15

Warsaw 1942
Ruy López

White: ROPSTORFF
Black: E. BOGOLJUBOV

1	e4	e5		7	Nc3!	0-0
2	Nf3	Nc6		8	Be3	Ng4
3	Bb5	a6		9	Nd5	f5
4	Ba4	Nf6		10	0-0	Kh8
5	d3	d6		11	Bc2	Bf6
6	c4					

A system which, thirty years ago, enjoyed the favour of the Bohemian champion Duras but which has been demonstrated to be totally inoffensive. In this game too Black manages to get a good position without difficulty.

6 ...   Be7

11 ... f4 was to be considered here as a preparation for a pawn attack. For example: 12 Bd2 g5 13 Bc3 Nh6 14 d4 Nf7 etc. But it was also interesting to maintain the tension and await developments.

12 d4

A correct and very dynamic move.

12 . . .	exd4
13 Bxd4	fxe4

Bogoljubov does not want to submit himself to a cautious line, as in the case of 13 . . . Bxd4 14 Nxd4 fxe4 15 h3! Nf6 16 Nxc6 bxc6 17 Nxf6 Qxf6 18 Bxe4 Rb8, and prefers to launch into the hazardous gain of a pawn.

14 Bxf6

14 Bxe4 would be a mistake owing to 14 . . . Bxd4 15 Nxd4 Qh4 etc.

14 . . .	Nxf6
15 Nxf6	Qxf6
16 Bxe4	Qxb2
17 Ng5!	g6

After 17 . . . h6 there follows 18 Qh5, gaining material.

18 Rb1	Qf6
19 Qd2	h6
20 Nh3	Kg7
21 Rb3	Nd4
22 Rg3	Bf5?

This apparently plausible move is revealed to be a fatal decision. The right move is 22 . . . Nf5 23 Rf3 Qd4 24 Qc2 Re8! with better fighting chances for Black.

White to move

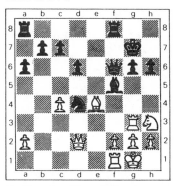

Position after 22 . . . Bf5

23 Nf4	Kh7
24 Bxf5	Nxf5

If 24 . . . gxf5 there would follow 25 Rg6 with decisive effect.

25 Rxg6	Qd4
26 Qc1	

Maintaining the chief threat 27 Ne6.

26 . . .	Rg8
27 Rd1	Qh8?

Now there is no possible hope. It was absolutely essential to play 27 . . . Qe5 28 Re1 Qd4 29 Ne6 with possibly a draw (if 29 Rd1 Qe5) through the continuation 29 . . . Qd3! 30 Rxg8 Rxg8 and now after 31 Nxc7 Qf3 White would even find himself in danger of defeat.

28 Rxg8	Rxg8
29 Qb1	

Decisive.

29 . . .	Rf8
30 Ne6	

30 Rd5 also wins.

30 . . .	Rf7

31	Nd4	Qf6
32	g4	Qg5
33	Nxf5	Qxg4+
34	Ng3+	Kg8
35	Re1	Kf8
36	Qb2	Qg7
37	Qe2	Qd4

38	Qe8+	Kg7
39	Nh5+	Kg6
40	Qg8+	**Black resigns**

A game played with the strong energetic initiative which is characteristic of the representative of Cracow.

GAME 16

Second match game, New York 1942
Ruy López

White: I. KASHDAN
Black: S. RESHEVSKY

1	e4	e5
2	Nf3	Nc6
3	Bb5	a6
4	Ba4	d6

The Steinitz Defence Deferred, which is certainly playable but requires on Black's part exceptionally precise and circumspect play.

5	c3	

An old method which has the tendency of establishing a pawn centre by means of d4. More usual at present is 5 Bxc6+ bxc6 6 d4 f6 or else 5 c4 as played by Kashdan in the fourth match game.

5	...	Bd7
6	d4	Nge7

The alternative is 6 . . . g6. Either one of these moves has its drawbacks: Black either creates weaknesses on his king's side or finds

himself obliged to proceed slowly and laboriously in the advance of his pieces. This allows White to establish his mobilization plan in total security.

7	Bb3!	

With the strong threat of 8 Ng5 which practically forces Black's next move.

7	...	h6
8	Be3	Ng6

If 8 . . . g5? (Ahues-Rubinstein, San Remo, 1930), there follows 9 Bxg5! hxg5 10 Nxg5 with a strong attack for the piece sacrificed. Nor is 8 . . . g6 effective in resolving all Black's difficulties; for example 9 Na3 Bg7 10 Qd2 and Black still has not succeeded in solving the problem of his king.

9	Nbd2	

Position after 9 Nbd2

9 ...   Qf6!

This queen *sortie,* so unusual in this phase of the game, in this case offers, relatively, the best chances of equalizing the game.

10 Qe2   Be7

11 0-0-0

After this move White will have no advantage left. Worth more serious consideration was the move 11 g3 so as to answer 11 . . . Bh3 with 12 0-0-0, followed by 13 Rdg1 and eventually g4. It would have been difficult for Black to maintain his queen's bishop whereas now it is he who will (although certainly for a rather limited period of time) have the advantage of the two bishops.

11 ...   Nf4

12 Bxf4   Qxf4

13 Kb1   Na5

This is not the commencement of an attack but a little trick, the purpose of which is the defence of his d5 square which was gravely threatened by the White knight (Nf1, followed by Bc2 and Ne3 etc.).

14 Bc2   0-0

15 Nf1   Bb5

16 Bd3   f5!

With this move, the logical consequence of the preceding tactics, Reshevsky finally manages to equalize the game. But unfortunately for him he imagines that his position offers chances of playing for a win and this error will quickly lead him into a blind alley.

17 dxe5   Bxd3+

18 Qxd3

Black to move

Position after 18 Qxd3

18 ...   fxe4?

There is no possible explanation for this move as Black has not taken into consideration his opponent's twentieth move. After 18 . . . Qxe4 19 Ng3 Qxd3+ 20 Rxd3 Nc6 the game would have had to end as a draw.

19 Qd5+   Kh8

20 Rd4   dxe5?

A pawn was lost irremediably and

in consequence, *theoretically,* the game. Nevertheless it is incredible that a fighter of Reshevsky's category did not try to take advantage of the practical chances, either in the middle-game after 20 ... Nc6 21 Rxe4 Qf5 22 Ng3 Qg6, or in the ending after 20 ... c6 21 Qxe4! (21 Qxa5 c5!) Qxe4+ 22 Rxe4 d5 etc. Clearly the mistake on the eighteenth move has been fatal for him and has made him lose his equanimity.

21 Nxe5

Threatening, apart from the knight, a deadly check. The rest is an agony that Black could have spared himself:
21 ... Rf6

22 Rxe4 Qxf2 23 Qxa5 Rb6 24 Nd3 Qxg2 25 Ng3 Bd6 26 Re2 Qc6 27 Ne5 Qe8 28 Qd5 Bxe5 29 Qxe5 Qg6+ 30 Qf5 Qd6 31 Rhe1 Rg8 32 Re8 Qg6 33 Rxg8+ Kxg8 34 Qxg6 Rxg6 35 Re7 Rc6 36 Kc2 g6 37 Kd3 h5 38 Ne4 a5 39 Kd4 a4 40 Ke5 Rb6 41 Rxc7 Rxb2 42 Kf6 Rb6+ 43 Kg5 Kf8 44 a3 Rb3 45 Kxg6 Ke8 46 Rxb7 Rxa3 47 c4 Black resigns

GAME 17

Fourth match game, New York 1942
Ruy López

White: I. KASHDAN
Black: S. RESHEVSKY

1	e4	e5
2	Nf3	Nc6
3	Bb5	a6
4	Ba4	d6
5	c4	

A good continuation which assures White of a harmonious development of his pieces.

5	...	Bd7
6	Nc3	Nf6

This simple development of the king's side pieces is not censurable but better prospects are offered here by the fianchetto of the king's bishop: 6 ... g6 7 d4 Bg7 8 Be3 exd4 9 Nxd4 Nge 7.

7	d4	exd4
8	Nxd4	Nxd4?

Why this haste to exchange developed pieces? Indicated was 8 ... Be7, followed by 9 ... 0-0.

9	Bxd7+	Qxd7
10	Qxd4	Be7
11	0-0	0-0
12	b3	

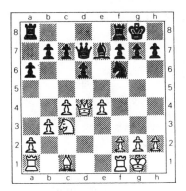

Position after 12 b3

12 ...   **Rfe8**

This is decidedly too passive because withdrawing the bishop to f8 takes away for a long time a strong prospect of activity. In Black's place I would have played 12 . . . c6, creating a weakness more imaginary than real. The denial of the point d5 to the White knight would have increased considerably Black's freedom to manoeuvre. After either 13 Bb2 or 13 Bg5 h6 14 Bh4 Rfe8 etc. he would have had greater chances than in the actual game.

13 Bb2   **Bf8**

14 Rad1   **Re6**

The idea of doubling the rooks on the e-file is hardly a happy one. Logical would be 14 . . . Rad8 and if 15 f3 then 15 . . . c6!

15 Rfe1   **Rae8**

If 15 . . . g6 then 16 e5 and White stands better.

16 f3   **Kh8**

A valueless move but the position is already very difficult. A little better would have been 16 . . . Qc8 with

the intention of . . . c6. Also inferior would be 16 . . . g6 17 Nd5 Bg7 18 Qa7! Qc8 19 Nf4 R6e7 20 c5 etc. with marked superiority.

17 Ne2   **Qc8**

18 Qf2

The knight is going to occupy a formidable position at f5. Black has a strategically lost game but not because of the path chosen in principle. His error consists of a lack of resolution and of any defined plan at the moment of beginning the battle. Fifty years ago this kind of defeat due to insufficient space was very frequent and the present game could easily have been conducted (as White) by Dr. Tarrasch. Nowadays such defeats are less frequent and, in the case of a master of the strength and mettle of Reshevsky, they are an exception.

18 ...   **Nd7**

19 Nd4   **R6e7**

20 Qg3   **f6**

21 Nf5   **Re6**

22 h4

This pawn will guarantee once and for all the position of the knight or else (as occurs in the game) will serve to open up a way against the defence of the Black king.

22 ...   **b5**

A perfectly inoffensive counter-demonstration which, in view of the rooks' lack of action, merely creates fresh weaknesses.

23 cxb5   **axb5**

24 h5   **Qa6**

25	a3	c5
26	Rd5	Ne5
27	Red1	

Threatening 28 Rxd6.

27	...	Nf7
28	Qh4	

Black to move

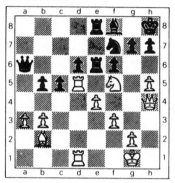

Position after 28 Qh4

28	...	Ne5

Permitting the advance of the h-pawn is an act of desperation entirely justified by the situation. In fact after 28 ... h6 29 Qg4! Black would have been completely paralysed and White would easily have opened up a path with b4, if necessary after one or two preparatory moves. Now Kashdan proceeds to the execution with precision and energy.

29	f4!	Nf7
30	h6	g6

Evidently forced.

31	Bxf6+	Kg8
32	Ng3	Bxh6

33	Bb2	

With the irresistible threat of 34 f5.

33	...	Bg7
34	f5	Bxb2

Or 34 ... gxf5 35 Bxg7 Kxg7 36 Nh5+ Kf8 37 exf5 (even stronger than 37 Nf6) Rh6 38 Qg4 and wins.

35	fxe6	Rxe6
36	Qg4	

Removing from Black his last illusions. On 36 ... Re7 or 36 ... Qc8 the rejoinder 37 Nf5 is at once decisive.

36	...	Re8
37	Qd7	Rd8
38	Qe7	Rf8
39	Rf1	Be5
40	Rd3	Qc8
41	Rdf3	Qe8
42	Rxf7	Qxe7
43	Rxe7	Bxg3
44	Rxf8+	Kxf8
45	Rb7	c4
46	bxc4	**Black resigns**

This game is of great didactic interest. It demonstrates in a very convincing way the dangers of positions with a limited field of action (although without a weakness) and also the way to take advantage of this drawback. It was a defeat (but also a victory) that was well deserved.

GAME 18

Buenos Aires 1939
Ruy López

White: W. CRUZ (*Brazil*)
Black: F. APSCHENEEK
(*Latvia*)

1	e4	e5
2	Nf3	Nc6
3	Bb5	a6
4	Bxc6	

This variation, especially in connection with 5 d4 and the subsequent exchange of queens, has practically been abandoned for some years since it has been shown that Black not only has nothing to fear in the resulting ending but that, thanks to his pair of bishops, he possesses certain winning chances.

4	...	dxc6
5	d4	exd4
6	Qxd4	Qxd4
7	Nxd4	Nf6?

This is an inferior move since White's e4 square can easily be protected while the knight has only very small prospects at f6. The correct plan consists of occupying the two centre files with the rooks, not reducing the forces (particularly maintaining the two bishops) and gradually restricting the enemy pieces. For example 7 ... Bd7, followed by ... 0-0-0, Ne7-g6, Bd6, Rhe8 with a promising game.

8	f3	Bc5?

Now the exchange of one of the bishops is necessary without the slightest positional compensation. Still indicated was 8 ... Bd7, followed by 9 ... 0-0-0.

9	Be3	0-0
10	Nf5	

Of course!

10	...	Bxe3

10 ... Bb4+ would be no better; 11 c3 Bxf5 12 cxb4 etc. with advantage to White.

11	Nxe3	

From now onwards any exchange that does not alter the pawn structure will favour White because it will facilitate the exploitation of his extra pawn on the king's side.

11	...	Be6
12	Nc3	Rad8
13	0-0	Rfe8
14	Rad1	Bc8
15	Rfe1	

15 Rxd8 Rxd8 16 Rd1 etc. would be an excellent manoeuvre in accordance with the above note. But White is anxious to obtain something more than a simple pawn majority and hopes that his opponent will give him opportunities for it. Often such tactics serve only to give the opponent chances of a counterattack.

15	...	g6
16	Kf2	Kg7
17	g4	h5
18	h3	Rh8
19	Kg3	

The exchange of rooks on the queen's file was still indicated. The attempt to advance the central pawns merely results in giving more opportunities to the enemy bishop.

19	...	Nd7
20	f4	Nc5
21	e5	a5
22	Nc4	

With the purpose of exchanging the Black knight which has suddenly found an excellent observation post.

22	...	b6
23	Nd2	hxg4
24	hxg4	Rh7
25	Nde4	Nxe4+

Reasonable chances at least would have been provided by playing 25 ... Rdh8 26 Nf2 etc.

26	Nxe4	Rdh8
27	Nf2	Be6
28	b3	

With the object of answering 28 ... Bd5 with 29 c4.

28	...	a4

The reduction of forces on the queen's flank cannot be condemned, especially as the manoeuvre is related to the possible exploitation of the a-file.

29	Rh1	Rxh1
30	Nxh1	

After 30 Rxh1 Ra8, followed by 31 ... f6 Black would not necessarily be lost either.

30	...	axb3
31	axb3	Ra8?

Now Black overplays his hand and forgets that his king can fall into a mating net. After the attack on White's e5 with 31 ... f6 32 exf6+ Kxf6 the bishop would be superior to the knight and this circumstance would compensate for White's advantage on the king's side.

32	Nf2	Ra2

Logical but fatal. 32 ... Kf8 33 Ne4 Ke7 etc. would offer a better chance of salvation.

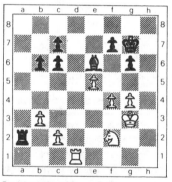

Position after 32 ... Ra2

33	Ne4!	

A correct pawn sacrifice which permits the decisive invasion of the enemy fortress by the White army.

33	...	Bd5

Or 33 ... Rxc2 34 Rd8 with the inevitable threat of 35 Nf6.

34	Nf6	Rxc2
35	Ra1!	

The key to the offensive stratagem which forces the entry of the White rook to the eighth rank.

35	...	Rc3+
36	Kh4	Bg2

The only way of defending against the mate that was looming but White has at his disposal other means of attacking which cannot all be parried.

37	Ra8	Rh3+
38	Kg5	Rh8
39	Ne8+	Kh7

White to move

Position after 39 ... Kh7

40	Kf6?	

White is anxious to play a 'brilliant' move and scorns the easy winning line which was 40 e6! fxe6 41 Rc8 (or 41 Rd8).

40	...	c5

The last mistake. He could have played 40 ... Bd5 with the double threat of 41 ... Bxb3 and 41 ... c5. If then 41 b4 he would play 41 ... c5 42 Rd8 Bc6 etc. and would be saved.

41	Kxf7	

Indirectly protecting the rook by the threat of 46 Nf6+ Kh6 47 g5 mate. Black's reply is forced.

41	...	Rf8+
42	Kxf8	Bxa8
43	Nf6+	Kh8
44	f5	g5

Or 44 ... gxf5 45 g5, followed by 46 g6 and 47 g7 mate.

45	e6	Bc6
46	Nd7	Black resigns

GAME 19

Munich 1941
Ruy López

White: G. KIENINGER
Black: A. ALEKHINE

1	e4	e5	3	Bb5	Bc5
2	Nf3	Nc6	4	c3	Qf6

5 0-0

Better is 5 d4 and if 5 . . . exd4 then 6 e5! Against 5 d4 I had the intention of playing 5 . . . Bd6? but is is evident that in this case too White would have remained with greater freedom of action. On the other hand the text move does not offer more than limited difficulties.

5 . . .   Nge7

6 d3

The continuation given by Bilguer 6 d4 exd4 7 Bg5 Qg6 8 Bxe7 Nxe7 9 cxd4 Bb6 10 Nc3 0-0 11 Bd3 does not, in my view, offer any danger to Black if he continues with 11 . . . d6 12 e5 Qh6 etc.

6 . . .   h6

7 Nbd2   0-0

8 Nc4   Ng6

Position after 8 . . . Ng6

9 d4

As a consequence of the exchanges which result from this move Black obtains a very appreciable advantage in space. Correct would

be 9 b4 Bb6 (if 9 . . . Be7 then 10 Ne3) 10 a4 a6 11 Nxb6 cxb6 12 Bc4 d6 13 Be3 Nf4 and after this White cannot play 14 Bxb6 because of 14 . . . Bh3! 15 Ne1 Qg6 16 Qf3 Bg4 etc. but his position is nonetheless slightly preferable.

9 . . .   exd4

10 Bxc6   dxc6!

11 Nxd4

Necessary because after 11 cxd4 the double pin 11 . . . Rd8 12 Be3 Bg4 would have had very disagreeable consequences.

11 . . .   Re8

But now the direct threat against the e-pawn is more effective than 11 . . . Rd8.

12 Nb3

The lesser of two evils because if 12 . . . Rxe4 then 13 Qd3 etc. But the fact is that now the White knights will have a restricted field of action.

12 . . .   Bf8

13 Qc2

Against the plausible move 13 f3 Black would simply have played 13 . . . Be6 14 Ne3 Rad8 15 Qc2 Nh4 16 Nd4 Bc8 and would have achieved a co-ordination of his forces that would have been full of promise. The text move (which eventually prepares for f4) allows him to hold up more effectively the White queen's side development.

13 . . .   Qe6!

14 Ncd2   Nh4

15 f3   c5!

Neither 15 . . . Qg6 16 Nc4 nor 15
. . . Bd6 (threatening 16 . . . Nxg2)
16 Nd4, followed by 17 Nc4 would
have brought a substantial
advantage. The text move prepares
for . . . Bd6 and at the same time for
an eventual . . . Rd8, followed by
the occupation of the square d3.

16 Rd1

This move — in reality practically
forced in order to give the knight a
square — allows Black to create a
sacrificial combination.

Black to move

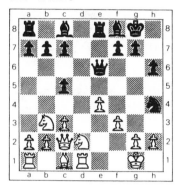

Position after 16 Rd1

16 . . .   Nxg2!

Because otherwise White would
play 17 Nf1 with a defendable
position.

17 Kxg2   Qh3+

18 Kg1

Against 18 Kh1 Bd6 19 f4 (so as to
be able to save himself after 19 . . .
Bxf4 20 Nf1 Qf3+ 21 Qg2 Qxd1
22 Bxf4 etc.) Black had prepared
this pretty variation: 19 . . . Bf5
20 Re1 (if 20 exf5 then 20 . . . Re2)
Bxf4 21 Nf1 Bxe4+ and wins.

18 . . .   Bd6

After 18 . . . Re6 19 Nf1 Rg6+ 20
Ng3 h5 21 Qg2 Qxg2+ 22 Kxg2 h4
23 f4 White would have freed himself without great discomfort.

19 Nf1

To 19 Nc4 Black would have replied
19 . . . Re6, forcing the exchange
sacrifice 20 Rxd6 and after 20 . . .
cxd6 21 Qf2 he would have
continued the attack by 21 . . . f5
without its force being lessened.

19 . . .   Qxf3

20 Rd3

20 Qd3 would be useless on account
of 20 . . . Qxd3, followed by 21 . . .
c4.

20 . . .   Qxe4

21 Rd2   Qh4!

22 Rg2   Bh3

23 Qf2

Black to move

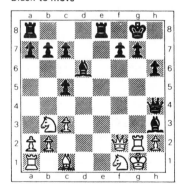

Position after 23 Qf2

23 . . .   Qe4!

Now Black can proceed to the
liquidation because he obtains

sufficient advantage for the ending.
Nevertheless the agility of his rooks,
which accelerate considerably the
dénouement, should be noted.

24	Bd2	Qxg2+
25	Qxg2	Bxg2
26	Kxg2	Re2+
27	Kf3	Rae8

Despite the exchange of queens
Black keeps attacking possibilities.

28	Rd1	b6
29	Nc1	R2e6
30	b3	

This attempt at consolidation will
be refuted convincingly.

30	...	c4!
31	bxc4	Rf6+
32	Kg2	Re4
33	Ne3	Bc5

34	Re1	Bxe3
35	Rxe3	Rg4+
36	Rg3	Rxc4
37	Rf3	Rd6
38	Bf4	

After 38 Rf2 Black wins with the
same ease by playing 38 . . . b5 with
the threat of 39 . . . b4.

38	...	Rd1
39	Ne2	Ra1
40	Kg3	c5
41	Re3	Rxa2
42	h4	b5
43	h5	b4
44	**White resigns**	

In fact there is no way of
stopping the queen's side pawns.

Four Knights Game

GAME 20

Buenos Aires 1939
Four Knights Game

White: E. LUNDIN (Sweden)
Black: P. MICHEL (Germany)

1	e4	e5
2	Nf3	Nc6
3	Nc3	Nf6

4	Bb5	Nd4

Plausible, since the German team
would be satisfied with forcing a
drawn position.

5 Nxe5

It is comprehensible that the Swedish player should avoid the drawing variation 5 Nxd4; but after the analysis of the game Bogoljubov-Rubinstein (match 1920 played in Sweden) why not 5 Ba4, the interesting continuation of which has, relatively speaking, less well-tested complications?

5 ...	Qe7
6 f4	Nxb5
7 Nxb5	d6
8 Nf3	Qxe4+
9 Kf2	Ng4+
10 Kg3	

This king excursion is artificial, appears erroneous and can finally, in fact, lead to equality. One cannot understand what it was that induced Lundin to follow this unfortunate line of play in a game of capital importance since with the defeat of Sweden Germany was assured of the Cup.

10 ...	Qg6
11 Nh4	Qh5

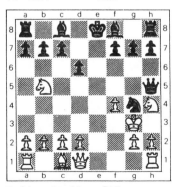

Position after 11 . . . Qh5

12 h3

White does not have anything better. If 12 Nxc7+ Kd8 13 h3 (or 13 Nxa8 g5! with advantage) Nf6 14 Nxa8 then Black can decide the game brilliantly with a queen sacrifice: 14 . . . Qxh4+!! 15 Kxh4 Ne4! etc. All this was discovered in the above match, played twenty years before.

12 ...   Qxb5!

'Theory' recommends 12 . . . Nf6 13 Qxh5 Nxh5+ 14 Kf2 with approximately equal chances. But the simple text move is more convincing because it forces a series of moves which are dangerous for White's position.

13 hxg4   g5!

This refutes for good the strategy employed by White in the opening. One of the points of Michel's move is that the intermediary check 14 Re1+ serves only to increase Black's pressure: 14 . . . Be7 15 fxg5 Qxg5 etc. and White lacks chances.

14 fxg5   Qe5+

As has been said, a draw would be satisfactory for Black. Under other circumstances 14 . . . Qxg5 15 d4 Qg7 could be played, with evident advantage.

15 Kf2	Qd4+
16 Kg3	Qe5+
17 Kh3?	

White should confine himself to the repetition of moves. This unjustified temerity is probably based on the little-analysed advance on the eighteenth move which Michel refutes swiftly and in masterly fashion.

| 17 | . . . | Qxg5 |
| 18 | d4 | Qh5! |

Emphasising the disadvantageous position of the king at h3. If now 19 Kg3 then 19 . . . Rg8 20 g5 Qxd1 21 Rxd1 Be7, followed by 22 . . . h6 and White finally loses his pawn at g5.

| 19 | g3 | Rg8 |
| 20 | Kh2 | Bxg4 |

After achieving a material advantage, winning is purely a question of technique; but the speed of the method used produces a very favourable impression.

21	Re1+	Be7
22	Qd2	Kd7
23	Qh6	

The only temporary salvation.

| 23 | . . . | Qd5! |

Black avoids the direct exchange of queens in order to exploit the frail position of the enemy king.

| 24 | Be3 | Rae8 |

| 25 | Bf2 | Bg5! |

Giving back the extra pawn to force the opening of the h-file with the plan of a direct attack on the enemy king.

26	Qxh7	Rh8
27	Qd3	Reg8
28	c4	Qf3

Now simplification assists Black's victory since the queen is the only piece protecting White's position.

| 29 | Qxf3 | Bxf3 |
| 30 | Rg1 | |

Forced, owing to the threat of 30 . . . Bxh4 etc.

| 30 | . . . | f5 |
| 31 | a4 | Rh7 |

The rapid advance 31 . . . f4 would also be conclusive.

32	Ra3	Be4
33	Raa1	f4
34	Kh3	fxg3
35	White resigns	

Three Knights Game

GAME 21

Berlin 1942
Three Knights Game

White: PAHL
Black: WERKMEISTER

1	e4	e5
2	Nf3	Nc6
3	Nc3	Bb4
4	Nd5	Ba5

4 . . . Nf6 is better.

5	Bc4	d6
6	0-0	Nge7
7	d4	Bg4
8	dxe5	Nxe5

A very typical mistake, well punished by White as will be seen. After 8 . . . dxe5 White would not have had any appreciable advantage.

White to move

Position after 8 . . . Nxe5

9 Nxe5!

A sacrifice of great strength and beauty.

9	. . .	Bxd1
10	Nf6+	Kf8

It is easy to see that if 10 . . . gxf6? there follows 11 Bxf7+ Kf8 12 Bh6 mate.

11	Ned7+	Qxd7
12	Nxd7+	Ke8
13	Rxd1	Rd8

[In a game probably unknown to Alekhine (J. Corzo-Capablanca, Havana 1909) Black played 13 . . . Kxd7 14 Bxf7 Raf8 15 Bh5 Bb6 and drew after many vicissitudes. E.W.]

14	Nc5!	dxc5
15	Rxd8+	Kxd8
16	Bxf7	

After the hard struggle White has emerged with an excellent pawn structure. On this circumstance is based the victorious *dénouement* which offers only the natural technical demands.

16	. . .	Rf8
17	Bh5	g6
18	Be2	a6
19	Bg5	Ke8
20	Rd1	Nc6
21	c3	Ne5
22	Rd8+	Kf7
23	Rd5	

Winning at least a second pawn.

23	. . .	Re8
24	f4	Nc6
25	Rd7+!	**Black resigns**

If 25 . . . Ne7 then 26 Bc4+, winning a piece.

Philidor's Defence

GAME 22

Buenos Aires 1939
Philidor's Defence

White: L. PIAZZINI (Argentina)
Black: S. TARTAKOWER (Poland)

1	e4	Nf6
2	Nc3	e5
3	Nf3	d6
4	d4	Nbd7

After beginning as an Alekhine's Defence and changing gradually into the Vienna Game and the Three Knights Game, the contest now has the definite character of Philidor's Defence.

5	Bc4	h6
6	h3	

This preparation to activate the king's side (which is facilitated by the fact that Black has already compromised the future residence of his king) is certainly more promising than an immediate liquidation of the tension in the centre as played, for instance, by Tylor against Dr. Tartakower at Nottingham, 1936.

6	...	c6
7	Be3	Qc7
8	Bb3	

A characteristic retreat to prevent Black from playing 8 . . . b5 (because of the possibility of the reply 9 d5).

8	...	Be7
9	g4!	

Quite in accordance with his overall plan of mobilization. Now Black must try *nolens volens* to obtain some freedom for his pieces in the centre before he can dare to expose his king to a wing attack.

9	...	exd4
10	Bxd4	

Better than 10 Nxd4 Nc5 with the elimination of the powerful White king's bishop.

10	...	c5?

Abandoning the d5 square is decidedly too risky and will have tragic consequences. Necessary, and fairly natural, would be 10 . . . Ne5 with a defensible game.

11	Bxf6	Nxf6
12	Qe2	

Preparing to castle long and threatening not only 13 g5 but also an eventual e5! Black has very little choice.

12	...	0-0
13	0-0-0	

Evidently he does not appreciate fully Black's ingenious fourteenth move. Otherwise he would have played the consistent 13 g5 without loss of time. After 13 . . . hxg5 14 Nxg5 or 13 . . . Nh5 14 Nd5 Qa5+ 15 c3 there would be very little hope for Black.

13	. . .	Be6!
14	g5	

Much less strong than on the previous move but, in the circumstances, best.

Black to move

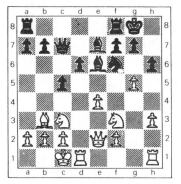

Position after 14 g5

The first crisis: Black not only escapes from his opening difficulties but even gains the initiative.

14 . . . **c4!**

An interesting and exactly calculated tactical resource.

15	gxf6	Bxf6
16	Nd5	

Besides this continuation White would have had to give consideration principally to the alternative 16 e5 which would have been answered by 16 . . . Bxe5 since 16 . . . cxb3 17

exf6 bxa2 18 Nxa2 Bxa2 19 fxg7 Rfe8 20 Qd2, threatening 21 Qxh6 etc. would be to White's advantage. But after 16 . . . Bxe5 17 Nxe5 dxe5 18 Ba4 a6 19 Bd7! Bxd7 20 Nd5 Qd6 21 Rhg1 Kh8 White's temporary initiative would not compensate for his material deficit. White's sixteenth move was thus more or less dictated by necessity.

16	. . .	Bxd5
17	Rxd5	cxb3
18	axb3	a5

Clearly this is the best attacking plan. But its technical execution will entail various difficulties, particularly in the event of an exchange of queens, which would practically assure White of a draw.

19	Nd4	Rfe8!

If now 19 . . . a4 then 20 Qc4! and Black would be compelled to exchange queens (if 20 . . . Qd7 then 21 Qb5) or else allow White to consolidate with 21 bxa4.

20	Nb5	Qc6

Now 21 Rxd6 (not 21 Nxd6 Qxd5) Rxe4! 22 Qd3 Qe8 etc. would be agreeable for Black. But 21 Qd3 a4 22 b4 could have been tried.

21 Qc4

Again threatening 22 Nxd6, a possibility that Black should have avoided by 21 . . . Red8. Although the following advance seems tempting it leads only to a drawn rook ending.

21 . . . **a4!?**

Game 22 Philidor's Defence

White to move

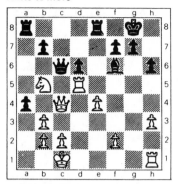

Position after 21 . . . a4

The second crisis: White, dangerously threatened, avoids defeat with a move of great ingenuity.

22 Nxd6!   **axb3**

Nor would other moves be successful against the correct replies. For example, firstly: 22 . . . Bg5+ 23 Rxg5! Secondly 22 . . . Re6 23 Qxc6 bxc6 24 Rd3 axb3 25 Kb1. Thirdly 22 . . . Rad8 23 Nf5! axb3 24 Rxd8 Bxd8 25 Qxc6 bxc6 26 Kb1, still with a draw in prospect.

23	Qxc6	bxc6
24	Nxe8	cxd5
25	Nxf6+	gxf6
26	Rg1+	Kf8
27	Rg3	Ra1+
28	Kd2	bxc2
29	Kxc2	dxe4

Black's great effort has been translated into the gain of a pawn. But as this pawn is doubled and his king cannot stop White's free b-pawn in time, a draw is the definite conclusion.

30 Re3!

It is absolutely essential to eliminate the advanced king's pawn; it would be pointless for Black to try to defend it, for instance 30 . . . f5 31 f3 Ra4 32 Kb3 Rd4 33 Kc3 etc.

30	...	Rf1
31	Rxe4	Rxf2+
32	Kc1	

The king is cut off only momentarily since White, before sacrificing the h-pawn, will always be in a position to propose an exchange of rooks.

32	...	f5
33	Rd4	Rf3
34	h4	Ke7
35	b4	Ke6
36	Kc2	Ke5
37	Rd3	

To a certain extent this is the simplest way, but 37 Rd7 would also have saved the half point.

37	...	Rf4
38	b5	Rxh4
39	Rb3	Rc4+

Or 39 . . . Rh2+ 40 Kd1 Rg2 41 b6 Rg8 42 b7 Rb8 43 Ke2 with the same result.

40	Kd3	Rc7
41	b6	Rb7
42	Ke3	Kd5
43	Rb5+	Kc4
44	Rxf5	Rxb6
45	Rxf7	Rg6

46	Kf3	Kd5
47	Re7	h5
48	Ra7	

Drawn

A splendid effort by the Argentinian master.

GAME 23

Düsseldorf 1908
Philidor's Defence

White: C. VON BARDELEBEN
Black: A. ALEKHINE

Recently I was glancing through one of my old notebooks that I had not looked at for many years when I found the following game. It was the first game of a short championship that I disputed and 'won' in Düsseldorf in 1908 against the former champion C. von Bardeleben by four wins and one draw. This championship took place shortly after the German Chess Federation Congress and just before the battle for the world championship between Lasker and Tarrasch. Although I was then only fifteen years of age and unable to judge my true strength, or rather weakness, it was very clear to me that I should not become too conceited over this success since my opponent, an elderly* and kindly gentleman, was quite lacking in fighting ambition and, what was worse, in any real class as a chess-player.

Anyway, I believe that this game, which until now has never been published, has perhaps some small

*Alekhine, writing in February 1941, forgets that White was in fact only forty-seven. E.W.

historical importance for chess and is not wholly lacking in interest.

1	e4	e5
2	Nf3	d6
3	d4	Nd7

Nimzowitsch's proposal to replace this innovation of the American Hanham by 3 . . . Nf6 seems to be refuted by the continuation 4 dxe5 Nxe4 5 Qd5! etc.

4	Bc4	c6
5	dxe5	

Neither useful nor necessary. Indicated is Schlechter's continuation (played against me at Hamburg, 1910) 5 Nc3 and if 5 . . . Be7 (somewhat better than 5 . . . h6) then 6 dxe5 dxe5 7 Ng5! Bxg5 8 Qh5 with the advantage of the pair of bishops.

5	. . .	dxe5
6	Be3	

To prevent 6 . . . Nc5.

6	. . .	Be7
7	Nc3	Qc7

At this moment the text was not

necessary and could have been replaced by the developing move 7 . . . Ngf6, followed by castling, which would undoubtedly have been more logical and more convenient for Black.

8 a4   Nc5

8 . . . Ngf6 would still have been more natural and better.

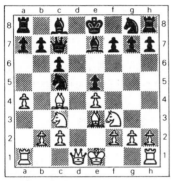

Position after 8 . . . Nc5

9 b4?

A double mistake which allows the initiative to pass into Black's hands. Firstly, with this move White compromises his pawn structure on the queen's side without any compensation and secondly he fails to take advantage of the opportunity to acquire the better position by 9 Ng5 Nh6 10 h3! etc.

9 . . .	Ne6
10 Rb1	**Nf6**
11 0-0	**0-0**
12 Ne1	

Probably with the idea of being able to play 13 Nd3 against 12 . . . Rd8. But if White had foreseen the expanding move that follows he

would have preferred to be on his guard by means of 12 Be2 (or 12 Bd3), in which case, however, Black's position would have been preferable after 12 . . . Rd8, followed by 13 . . . Nd4.

12 . . .   b5!

Together with the next move, this is without doubt the best way of exploiting the weakness of White's ninth move which left the queen's knight in a precarious position.

13 Bd3   a5!

14 axb5

There hardly exists an alternative since after 14 bxa5 b4, followed by 15 . . . Qxa5 the White pawn would be without protection.

14 . . .   axb4

15 b6

Black would have remained with an extra pawn if permitted to play 15 . . . cxb5.

15 . . .   Qb7

16 Ne2   c5

This is the position that I had been seeking on my twelfth move, in the hope of obtaining a decisive advantage. Nonetheless the truth is that White still has at his disposal several hidden possibilities.

17 c3!

Not only is the weakness of the c-pawn hereby eliminated but the harmful possibility of 17 . . . Nxe4 is prevented because of 18 cxb4 cxb4 19 Nc2 with a fairly good game for White.

17 . . .   Bd7

Best, as this prudent manoeuvre will contribute to the threat (in case of 18 f3, for example) 18 . . . Ba4 19 Nc2 Rad8 with the better game. Consequently White has to protect his e-pawn with the knight and to do this he must undertake an unprofitable exchange at b4.

| 18 | cxb4 | cxb4 |
| 19 | Ng3 | Nc5 |

Threatening two pawns at the same time. White prefers, not without reason, to protect his free pawn.

| 20 | Bc4 | Ncxe4 |

20 . . . Qxb6 is not possible owing to 21 Nd3 with good compensation.

| 21 | Nxe4 | Nxe4! |

Much better than 21 . . . Qxe4 22 Qd3! with compensatory chances.

| 22 | Bd5 | |

This simplification favours Black. The most convincing move was 22 Qd5, not only with 22 . . . Bc6 23 Qxe5 Bd6 24 Qf5 Rfe8 but also with 22 . . . Qxd5 23 Bxd5 Nc3 24 Bxa8 Nxb1 25 Bb7 etc., after which the battle would not yet have been resolved by any means.

22	. . .	Bc6
23	Bxc6	Qxc6
24	Qh5	

This is veritable desperation but if 24 Qf3 then 24 . . . Qc4 with clear superiority.

| 24 | . . . | Nc3 |
| 25 | Rb2 | |

If 25 Rc1 then 25 . . . g6, followed if necessary, by . . . f5, . . . e4 and

finally . . . Ne2+ with decisive advantage.

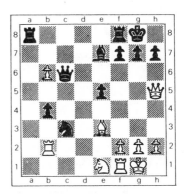

Position after 25 Rb2

| 25 | . . . | Qb5! |

Again threatening . . . g6, . . . f5 etc., gaining the exchange. If White prevents this line by 26 g3 then there would follow 26 . . . Ra1 and the victorious advance of the infantry.

| 26 | Nf3 | |

Whether he cares to or not, Black must accept this sacrifice since the use of more complicated offensive methods would have led to a similar end with moves of inferior quality. For example, 26 . . . f5 27 Ng5? Qxf1+, followed by mate in two moves. But against 26 . . . f5 White's reply should be 27 Re1.

26	. . .	Ne2+
27	Rxe2	Qxe2
28	Qxe5	Bf6
29	Qc5	b3
30	Bf4	

The last hope.

| 30 | . . . | Rfe8! |

Threatening 31 . . . Qxf1+, which White fails to notice.

31	b7?	Qxf1+
32	Kxf1	Ra1+
33	Bc1	b2
34	White resigns	

Looking back at old games and examining the level of our knowledge in time gone by undoubtedly produces a certain emotion, perhaps because in this way we experience again the memories of our youth, at once so distant and so close.

Scotch Gambit

GAME 24

Madrid 1943
Scotch Gambit

White: A. MEDINA
Black: P. KERES

Up until the thirteenth move the variation is well known and considered favourable to Black. Is the simple bishop retreat (instead of 14 b4 as played in a previous game) capable of changing this view? It is doubtful. For instance Keres could, instead of the plausible move 14 . . . 0-0-0, play 14 . . . Qd5 and if 15 Bxc7 then 15 . . . Rc8 16 Bd6 h5! with advantage. Besides he later let slip several chances of at least equalizing.

1	e4	e5
2	Nf3	Nc6
3	d4	exd4
4	Bc4	Nf6
5	0-0	Nxe4
6	Re1	d5
7	Bxd5	Qxd5
8	Nc3	Qa5
9	Nxe4	Be6
10	Bg5	h6
11	Bh4	Bb4
12	Re2	g5
13	a3	Be7
14	Bg3	0-0-0
15	b4	Qd5
16	Qe1	h5
17	h4	Bg4
18	c4!	

Well played! If 18 . . . Qxc4 then simply 19 Ned2 and White

wins two pieces for the rook.

18	...	Qf5
19	b5	Bxf3

Again Black lacks any option. If 19 ... Nb8 then 20 Qa5 Rd7 21 Nxd4 etc.

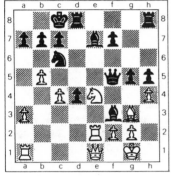

Position after 19 ... Bxf3

20 bxc6!

The point of White's combination. If 20 ... Bxe2? then 21 Qb1! wins the queen because of the threat of 22 Nd6+.

20	...	d3
21	cxb7+	Kb8
22	Bxc7+	Kxc7
23	Ng3	dxe2
24	Nxf5	Rd1
25	Nxe7	Rxe1+
26	Rxe1	Bxb7
27	Rxe2	gxh4

28	Kh2	Rd8
29	Nf5	Bc8
30	Re5	Rd2
31	f3	h3
32	Kxh3	

Thus all the ingenious combinations conceived by White have at last yielded him a pawn, which should have brought him victory, although not easily. Lack of technique lets the win escape; a pity, as this would have been a sensational game.

32	...	Rd3
33	a4	Bd7
34	a5	Rc3
35	Rc5+	Kd8
36	Kh4	Bxf5
37	Rxf5	Rxc4+
38	Kxh5	Ke7
39	Rb5	Kf6
40	g3	Ra4
41	f4	Ra3

Drawn

What would White have risked by continuing the game? After 42 Kh4 Keres told me that he would have found it extremely difficult to obtain a draw. It was a great surprise to him when, after the adjournment, his opponent declared himself satisfied with a draw.

GAME 25

Match Spain v Portugal 1945
Scotch Gambit

White: RIBEIRO
Black: A. POMAR

1 **e4**	**e5**
2 **Nf3**	**Nc6**
3 **d4**	**exd4**
4 **Bc4**	

Ribeiro was certainly ill-advised to opt for this opening against Pomar who has adopted it (and defended it) several times in serious play.

4 ...	**Bc5**
5 **Ng5**	**Nh6**
6 **Nxf7**	**Bb4+**

The normal continuation is 6 . . . Nxf7 7 Bxf7+ Kxf7 8 Qh5+ g6 9 Qxc5 d6 (it is also possible to play 9 . . . d5, followed by 10 . . . Re8 with advantage in development). However Pomar's move is equally good.

7 **c3**	**dxc3**
8 **bxc3**	**Nxf7**
9 **Bxf7+**	

Had he played 9 cxb4 then 9 . . . Qf6.

9 ...	**Kxf7**
10 **Qb3+**	

This is a grave and perhaps decisive loss of time. Necessary was 10 cxb4 because 10 . . . Qf6 was not to be feared in view of 11 Qb3+, followed by 12 Bb2. Best for Black would have been 10 . . . d5! with a good, but not decisive, game.

10 ...	**d5**
11 **cxb4**	

If 11 exd5 then undoubtedly 11 . . . Nd4.

11 ...	**Re8**
12 **Nd2**	

Because of the threat of 12 . . . Nd4 White has no satisfactory move at his disposition. If 12 Nc3 then 12 . . . Be6! 13 0-0 dxe4.

12 ...	**Nd4**
13 **Qc3**	**dxe4**
14 **Bb2**	

Black to move

Position after 14 Bb2

14 ...	**e3 !**

This looks decisive because 15 Qxd4 would deprive White of hope after 15 . . . exd2+ 16 Kxd2 (if 16 Kd1 Qg5 is strong and if 16 Kf1 then 16 . . . Qxd4 17 Bxd4 Rd8 and

wins) Qg5+ 16 Kc3 Bf5 with a
winning attacking position.

15 Nf3!

Nevertheless this move offers White
defensive resources unsuspected at
first sight.

15	...	Nxf3+
16	gxf3	Qg5

16 ... exf2+ leads to no result: 17
Kxf2 Qh4+ 18 Kg1 Qg5+ 19 Kf2
and in view of the threat of 20 Rhg1
Black has nothing better than 20 ...
Qh4+.

| 17 | h4 | Qg2 |

Pomar confesses that he forgot here
that his opponent could castle. With
17 ... Qh6 he could prevent
castling and 18 Rg1 would be fatal
because of 18 ... exf2+ 19 Kxf2
Qxh4+ 20 Rg3 Re2+, followed by
21 ... Qxg3. But 18 Ke2! would
have allowed White to continue the
fight.

| 18 | 0-0-0 | exf2 |
| 19 | Rhf1 | Bf5! |

The f-pawn could not be saved but
the strong position of this bishop,
quite apart from the extra pawn,
assures Black of the upper hand.

20	Rxf2	Qg6
21	Rfd2	Re7
22	h5	

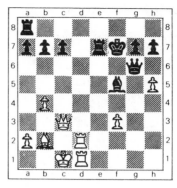

Position after 22 h5

| 22 | ... | Qc6! |

More effective than 22 ... Qh6 23
Rg1 Kg8 24 Qf6! Qxf6 25 Bxf6
Rf7 26 Be5, followed by 27 f4 and
White is in a better position than
in the actual game.

| 23 | Qxc6 | bxc6 |
| 24 | Rg1? | |

However this eases Black's task. 24
Bd4 was necessary, after which
Black's best chance would have
consisted of 24 ... a5 25 a3 axb4
26 axb4 Ra3 etc.

| 24 | ... | g6 |
| 25 | h6 | |

25 hxg6+ Bxg6 would also have
been insufficient.

| 25 | ... | a5! |
| 26 | a3 | |

Or 26 bxa5 Rxa5 27 a3 Rc5+ 28
Kd1 Re3, followed by 29 ... Be6.

26	...	axb4
27	axb4	Rb8
28	Rd4	c5!

Decisive.

29	**Rc4**	**Rxb4**	**34**	**Rg8+**	**Kd7**

Simpler than 29 . . . cxb4 "which would evidently have been adequate" (Pomar).

			35	**Rg7+**	**Kc6**
			36	**Kd1**	**Rh2**
30	**Rxc5**	**Re2**	**37**	**Bc1**	**Rd4+**
31	**Rxf5+**	**gxf5**			
32	**Rg7+**	**Ke8**	**38**	**White resigns**	
33	**Ba3**	**Ra4!**			

An excellent game by Pomar, worthy of the great opportunities.

PART TWO: SEMI-OPEN GAMES

French Defence

GAME 26

Cracow 1942
French Defence

White: E. BOGOLJUBOV
Black: A. ALEKHINE

1	e4	e6
2	d4	d5
3	Nc3	Nf6
4	Bg5	Be7
5	e5	Nfd7
6	h4	

This interesting attack was introduced by me at Mannheim in 1914 and since then has been incorporated into master praxis.

6	...	c5

One of the numerous replies which are possible but which do not present White with any difficulties. Much more promising is 6 . . . f6.

7	Bxe7	Kxe7

If 7 . . . Qxe7 there follows 8 Nb5.

8	Qg4	Kf8
9	Nf3	Nc6

With the offer of an exchange of queens by 9 . . . cxd4 10 Qxd4 Qb6

Black could obtain approximate compensation.

10	dxc5	Nxc5

Sharper would have been 10 . . . Ndxe5 11 Nxe5 Nxe5 12 Qg3 f6.

11	0-0-0	a6
12	Rh3	h6?

Usually Black does not worry about the king's side and seeks counterplay on the queen's flank. This move is not correct and, as will be seen, White manages to take possession of and exploit the strong strategic point d4. The opportune move would have been 12 . . . Qc7 13 Rg3 f6 14 exf6 gxf6 with chances of a counterattack.

13	Rg3	Rg8
14	Bd3	Nxd3+
15	Rxd3	Qb6
16	Rd2	Qc7
17	Qf4	Bd7

18	Ne2!	Rc8
19	Ned4	Na5
20	Rd3	Nc4
21	b3	

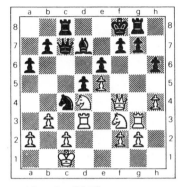

Position after 21 b3

21	...	Qa5

A blow which is based on a tactical calculation. With ... Na5-c6 Black would have been able to defend himself for some time but I had already lost my taste for this position and also my confidence in the resistance I would be able to offer.

22	bxc4	dxc4
23	Re3!	c3

Too late I realized that 23 ... Qxa2 is refuted by 24 Nd2! with the double threat of 25 Ra3 and 25 Ref3.

24	Nb3!	Qa3+
25	Kd1	a5
26	Nfd4	Ke7
27	Ref3	Be8
28	Ne2	Qb2
29	Nxc3	Rd8+
30	Rd3	Bc6

In case of 30 ... Qxc3 there would follow 31 Rxd8, attacking the queen.

31	Qc4!	Rxd3+
32	Rxd3	Rc8
33	Qc5+	Ke8
34	Qxa5	Bxg2
35	f3	Bf1
36	Qb5+	Kf8
37	Qxb7	Re8
38	Rd7!	Kg8
39	Qc7	Rf8
40	Rd8	Rxd8
41	Qxd8+	Kh7
42	Kd2	

I resigned a few moves later. Bogoljubov exploited my mistakes very well, winning the game in elegant style.

GAME 27

Buenos Aires 1939
French Defence

White: D. YANOFSKY* (Canada)
Black: A. DULANTO (Peru)

1	e4	e6
2	d4	d5
3	Nc3	Nf6
4	Bg5	dxe4

For a long time I felt a preference for this variation, but the experience of numerous games (mine and those of other masters) over the last decade has induced me to revise my point of view regarding this matter and I am now convinced that White's spacial advantage is more than enough compensation for the potential value of the two Black bishops.

5	Nxe4	Nbd7

Comparatively better would be the immediate 5 . . . Be7 so that, after 6 Bxf6 (best) Bxf6, he can maintain the choice between the two possible developments of the queen's knight, at d7 or at c6.

6	Nf3	Be7
7	Nxf6+	Nxf6

If 7 . . . Bxf6 then 8 Qd2, followed by 9 0-0-0 with the better game.

8	Bd3

Capablanca's move 8 Ne5, which has been in fashion for a quarter of a century, can be refuted by 8 . . . Qd5! (Spielmann's discovery). But White does not need to make such exaggerated efforts to maintain the

*Aged fourteen. E.W.

pressure. Besides the text move, he could play 8 c3, avoiding for the moment the following manoeuvre by Black.

8	. . .	c5
9	dxc5	Qa5+
10	c3	Qxc5
11	0-0	0-0
12	Re1	

A more effective way of limiting Black's chances is 12 Qe2, whereby he would have prevented 12 . . . b6 owing to 13 Bxf6 Bxf6 14 Qe4.

Position after 12 Re1

12	. . .	Rd8

Now, or at the latest on his next move, he should have played . . . h6, eliminating combinations connected with the pseudo-sacrifice at h7. The pinning of White's king's bishop is decidedly ineffective;

besides, White's next move will prevent 13 . . . Bd7 because of 14 Bxf6 Bxf6 15 Nxd7, followed by 16 Bxh7+.

| 13 Ne5 | b6? |

This move would not even be satisfactory after 13 . . . h6 14 Bf4 on account of the reply 15 Qf3 Qd5 16 Nc6 etc. But 13 . . . h6 14 Bf4 Bd7 would have prevented temporarily the characteristic catastrophe that follows.

14 Bxf6

Simpler than the strong alternative 14 Qf3.

| 14 . . . | Bxf6 |

15 Bxh7+

Naturally this bishop is untouchable since 15 . . . Kxh7 16 Qh5+ Kg8 17 Qxf7+ Kh8 18 Re3 finishes the game immediately.

15 . . .	Kf8
16 Qh5	Bxe5
17 Rxe5	Qc7
18 Be4	Bb7

Likewise after 18 . . . Rb8 19 Qh8+, followed by 20 Qxg7 White would have won easily. With the text move Black has the hope of protecting his g-pawn because of the possibility (after 19 Bxb7 Qxb7 20 Qh8+ Ke7 21 Qxg7) of 21 . . . Rg8. But White destroys this last hope with a pretty *coup*.

19 Bxb7	Qxb7
20 Qh8+	Ke7
21 Qxg7	Rg8

White to move

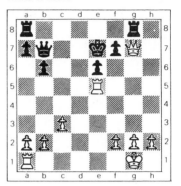

Position after 21 . . . Rg8

22 Rxe6+!

Not complicated, of course, but neat and decisive. The whole little game is characteristic of the incisive style of the young Canadian who was practically the only revelation of the Buenos Aires Team Tournament.

22 . . .	Kxe6
23 Re1+	Kd6
24 Qf6+	Kc5

If 24 . . . Kd7 then 25 Re7+ or 25 Qxf7+ wins at once.

25 Re5+	Kc4
26 b3+	Kd3
27 Qd6+	Kc2

Or 27 . . . Kxc3 28 Re3+ Kb2 29 Re2+, followed by mate in two moves.

| 28 Re2+ | Black resigns |

GAME 28

Buenos Aires 1939
French Defence

White: E. LUNDIN (Sweden)
Black: I. RAUD (Estonia)

1	e4	e6
2	d4	d5
3	Nc3	Nf6
4	e5	Nfd7
5	Nce2	

An old line of play (instead of the more usual 5 f4) which has of late been successfully adopted by Spielmann. For my taste this knight move is rather artificial.

5	...	c5
6	c3	f6

As the continuation will demonstrate, this move is premature and could eventually be played after 6 ... Nc6 7 f4 etc. The following tactical complications are characteristic of this type of position and are therefore quite instructive.

7	Nf4	Qe7
8	Bd3	

The first indirect protection of e5. If now 8 ... fxe5 9 dxe5 and Black cannot play 9 ... Nxe5 because this would bring him great discomfort after 10 Qh5+ Nf7 11 Bxh7 Qg5 12 Qh3!

8	...	fxe5
9	dxe5	Nc6

Planning to obtain a strong central position, on the basis of the surrender of the exchange, in the line

10 Qh5+ Qf7! 11 Bg6 hxg6 12 Qxh8 Ndxe5, followed by ... Bd7 and ... 0-0-0 with excellent fighting prospects.

10 Nf3!

Much more logical than the variation indicated above. Black's chances of development are very limited since 10 ... g5?, for example, would be fatal owing to 11 Ng6. The alternative 10 ... Ncxe5 11 Nxe5 Nxe5 12 Qh5+ Nf7 13 Bxh7 Qg5 14 Qxg5 Nxg5 15 Bg6+ Nf7 (if 15 ... Kd8 16 Nxd5) 16 0-0 would leave White with a clear positional advantage.

10	...	Nd8

This improves very little the variation indicated in the previous note because after the following tactical *intermezzo* the queens will still remain on the board and the Black king will be subjected to renewed inconvenience.

White to move

Position after 10 . . . Nd8

11 Ng6!

This does not win material but it does create weaknesses in Black's position and, what is even more important, it prevents for a long time the effective co-operation of the enemy forces. On the other hand 11 Bg6+ Nf7 would have been pointless.

11	. . .	hxg6
12	Bxg6+	Nf7
13	Bg5	Nf6
14	exf6	gxf6
15	Ne5!	

The true essence of the offensive idea.

| 15 | . . . | fxg5 |
| 16 | Bxf7+ | |

After 16 Nxf7 Rg8 17 Bh5 Kd7 18 Ne5+ Kc7 Black would have obtained an important tempo compared with the text continuation.

| 16 | . . . | Kd8 |
| 17 | Bh5 | Rg8 |

18	0-0	Bg7
19	Re1	Kc7
20	Qd3!	

With the aim of refuting the move 20 . . . Qd6 (which would be possible in the case of 20 c4) by the reply 21 Qh7.

20	. . .	Bxe5
21	Rxe5	Qd6
22	Rae1	Bd7
23	c4!	

Decisive since after the (practically forced) reply Black will not be in a position to defend simultaneously the three weaknesses at e6, g5 and c5.

23	. . .	d4
24	Bg4	Rae8
25	Qa3	

Also very strong is 25 b4 cxb4 26 c5, followed by 27 Qxd4 but the text move is more in accordance with the type of campaign developed by White.

| 25 | . . . | Kb8 |
| 26 | Rxc5 | |

This is somewhat stronger than 26 Qxc5 Qxc5 27 Rxc5 Rc8 28 Rxc8+ Rxc8 29 b3 b5 30 cxb5 Bxb5 since in this case White would not have a passed pawn on the king's side as he has in the actual game.

| 26 | . . . | Qf4 |
| 27 | Qg3 | Rc8 |

After 27 . . . Qxg3 28 hxg3 Rc8 29 Rxc8+ Rxc8 30 b3 b5 31 cxb5 Bxb5 White would force a quick victory with 32 a4! Bd7 33 Rd1 etc.

28	Rxc8+	Rxc8
29	Qxf4+	gxf4
30	b3	b5
31	h4	

This immediate utilization of the passed pawn is more convincing than the inactive 31 cxb5 Bxb5 32 a4 Bd3! after which Black would still have resources to continue the struggle.

31	...	bxc4
32	bxc4	Rxc4
33	h5	Kc7

Evidently there is not time for the counter-attack 33 ... d3.

34	Re4!	f3

Simple desperation since the plan 34 ... Rc6 would be useless owing to 35 h6.

35	Bxf3	Bc6
36	Rh4	Rc1+
37	Kh2	Bxf3
38	h6	Rb1

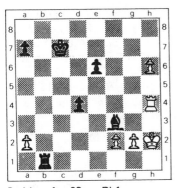

Position after 38 ... Rb1

39 gxf3!

Avoiding the last trap 39 h7 Rb8 40 h8 (Q) Rxh8 41 Rxh8 d3! Now White continues with a two-pawn advantage in a rook ending and therefore there can be no doubt about the result, despite Black's heroic resistance.

39	...	Rb8
40	Rxd4	Rh8
41	Rh4	Kd6
42	Kg3	Ke5
43	Kg4	Kf6
44	Kh5	e5
45	Ra4	Rh7
46	f4	e4!
47	Rxe4	Rc7
48	Ra4	Rc5+
49	Kg4	a5
50	Rd4	Rc2
51	Rd6+	Kf7
52	a4	Rxf2
53	Ra6	Rg2+
54	Kf5	Rh2
55	Ra7+	Kg8
56	Kg6	Rg2+
57	Kf6	Rh2
58	h7+	Kh8
59	Rxa5	Black resigns

GAME 29

Buenos Aires 1939
French Defence

White: I. PLECI (Argentina)
Black: L. ENDZELINS (Latvia)

1	e4	e6
2	d4	d5
3	Nd2	c5
4	Ngf3	

This move, which generally leads to very complicated positions, was introduced by me in an exhibition game against the Champion of Bolivia, Sánchez at Bogotá in March 1939. This game had the following drastic continuation: 4 . . . Nc6 5 Bb5 Bd7 (?) 6 exd5 Nxd4 7 Nxd4 cxd4 8 dxe6! Bxb5 9 Qh5! Qe7 10 Qxb5+ Kd8 11 0-0 and White wins quickly by a direct attack.

| 4 | . . . | dxe4 |

Doubtless inferior to 4 . . . Nc6 or 4 . . . Nf6 but playable.

| 5 | Nxe4 | Nd7(?) |

Allowing White to obtain the advantage of the pair of bishops. 5 . . . cxd4 is better.

| 6 | dxc5 | Nxc5? |

The decisive error. Instead of this, 6 . . . Bxc5 7 Nxc5 Qa5+ 8 c3 Qxc5 9 Be3 Qc7 etc. is necessary. Now we witness the execution of an attack in the style of Morphy.

7	Qxd8+	Kxd8
8	Bg5+	f6
9	0-0-0+	Ke8
10	Bb5+	Kf7

All these Black moves have been practically forced. If 10 . . . Bd7 then simply 11 Nxc5 Bxb5 12 Nxe6 winning easily.

White to move

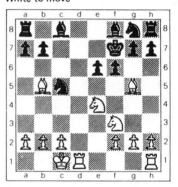

Position after 10 . . . Kf7

11 Rd8!!

A truly brilliant conception which makes this game a pearl from the Buenos Aires Tournament. The two attacked pieces are now immune because if 11 . . . fxg5 then 12 Ne5+ Ke7 13 Re8 mate. After 11 . . . Nxe4 12 Ne5+ Ke7 (12 . . . fxe5 13 Be8 mate) 13 Re8+ Kd6 14 Nf7+ Kc5 15 Rxf8 Nxg5 16 Nxh8 etc. White would remain with a material advantage.

11 . . .   Be7!

At first sight it seems as though White has made a mistake because 12 Be8+ Kf8 leads to nothing. But his next two moves clarify the situation once and for all.

12	Ne5+!	fxe5
13	Nd6+!	

If now 13 . . . Bxd6 then 14 Be8+, followed by mate. Black must yield the exchange, after which he will be practically lost.

13	. . .	Kg6
14	Bxe7	Nxe7
15	Rxh8	a6
16	Be2	e4

17	f4	b5
18	Re8!	

The precise way to prevent 18 . . . Bb7.

18	. . .	Kf6
19	Rf8+	Kg6
20	h4	Bb7

This is one of those cases when suicide is amply justified.

21	h5+	Black resigns

GAME 30

Buenos Aires 1939
French Defence

White: P. KERES (Estonia)
Black: G. STAHLBERG (Sweden)

1	e4	e6
2	d4	d5
3	Nd2	c5
4	Ngf3	Nc6

The alternative 4 . . . c4?, played by Ståhlberg against the same opponent in the final section, is of doubtful value since after 5 g3 Nc6 6 Bg2 Bb4 7 0-0 Nge7 8 c3 Ba5? Keres, instead of the time-consuming manoeuvre that he initiated with 9 Ne5, could have conserved his advantageous position by continuing the development of his pieces: 9 Re1 0-0 10 exd5 exd5 11 Nf1, followed by 12 Ne3 or 12 Bf4 first.

5	exd5	exd5
6	Bb5	c4

Although not as bad as 6 . . . Qe7+? played by Capablanca against Keres in the AVRO Tournament of 1938, this move is not entirely satisfactory, as the continuation demonstrates. It seems better to prepare immediately for castling with 6 . . . Bd6 7 0-0 Ne7 etc.

7	0-0	Bd6
8	b3	

The positional refutation of Black's sixth move, eliminating the blockading pawn and at the same time opening up the important a-file.

8	. . .	cxb3
9	axb3	Ne7
10	Re1	0-0
11	Nf1	

Game 30 French Defence

White is in no hurry to accomplish the profitable exchange of the black-squared bishops since he is able to prove that in the long run his opponent cannot prevent the move Ba3.

11	...	Bg4
12	c3	Qc7
13	Ba3	Rfd8
14	Bd3	Bxa3
15	Rxa3	Qf4

Position after 15 ... Qf4

At first sight it appears that Black has overcome his initial difficulties and that he will not have much trouble in liquidating the 'explosive' material on the e-file, with a draw in prospect. But in reality his problem is not as simple as that since the majority of exchanges will weaken even more his isolated d-pawn. Also, the constellation on the a-file is far from reassuring (the pawn at a7, for example, may become compromised by the advance b4-b5 etc.). The following attempt by Black to create threats on the king's flank, which will be dealt with by Keres with extreme

exactitude, is therefore strategically incomprehensible.

16	Be2	Ng6

A relatively better route for this knight would be 16 ... Nf5, eventually followed by ... Nd6. Since White does not intend exchanging queens at this moment the reply g3 that the text move provokes is, in fact, part of his general plan.

17	Ne3	Be6
18	g3	Qd6
19	Ra2	h6

In order to avoid 20 Ng5, followed by 21 f4.

20	Bd3	Bh3

But this fresh demonstration by the bishop is merely a loss of time since the possibility of 21 Bxg6 fxg6 22 Nh4 g5 23 Nhf5 Qf8 etc. could not be considered a serious threat. It would have been better to utilize this time by playing, for instance, 20 ... a6, 20 ... Rac8, or 20 ... Rde8.

21	Nd2	

With the clear plan, which cannot be prevented, of establishing this knight at e5.

21	...	Nce7
22	f4	

Also threatening 23 f5, followed by 24 Qh5.

22	...	Bd7
23	Nf3	b5

The possibility of c4, establishing a White passed pawn in the centre, had

to be kept in mind, but after the
text move Keres is able to take
control of the Black squares,
practically forcing . . . a5, and to
create a new and decisive weakness
at Black's b5.

| 24 | Ne5 | Nxe5 |
| 25 | fxe5 | Qb6 |

If 25 . . . Qc6 then 26 Qa1.

| 26 | b4 | a5 |

After 26 . . . a6 White would finally
have brought his knight to c5 (via
c2, a1, and b3 or f1, d2, and b3)
with decisive effect.

27	bxa5	Rxa5
28	Qb3	Rxa2
29	Qxa2	

Black will soon be incapable of
defending the two squares b5 and
d5. His only chance of salvation
will therefore consist of another
try on White's king's side which has
been slightly weakened by 18 g3.
The last part of this game is a model
of play with respect to the two
opponents.

| 29 | . . . | Qc6 |

Also after 29 . . . Bc6 30 Qa3 Qb7
31 Rb1, followed by 32 Qc5 Black
would have lost material forthwith.

30	Qa3	Ng6
31	Rb1	Rb8
32	Qb4	

Now White threatens Bf1-g2,
followed by c4. An attempt by
Black to deal with this threat by
Nf8-e6-c7 would be refuted by the
following double attack on d4.

32	. . .	Nf8
33	Qb3!	Be6
34	Kf2	

Not immediately 34 Bxb5
because of 34 . . . Rxb5 35
Qxb5 Qxc3 with good fighting
chances.

| 34 | . . . | b4 |

A much better line would be 34 . . .
Rc8 35 Nd1. White's square d4
would then be in a state of
permanent unease.

35	cxb4	Qb6
36	Qb2	Nd7
37	b5	f6!

By eliminating the e-pawn and
opening the f-file Ståhlberg now
obtains a real counter-attack.

| 38 | exf6 | |

Instead of 38 Rc1 which would
not suffice because of 38 . . .
fxe5 39 Rc6 Qxd4.

38	. . .	Nxf6
39	Rc1	Bd7
40	Kg1	Re8

Of course not 40 . . . Bxb5 on
account of 41 Bxb5 Qxb5 42 Rc8+.

| 41 | Ng2 | Ne4 |

The beginning of an opportune
demonstration against White's f3.
It is evident that after 42 Bxe4
Rxe4 White's winning chances
would have swiftly vanished.

42	Nf4	Ng5!
43	Kg2	Bg4
44	Rf1	Rf8

Each move increases Black's
pressure but his counter-attack
is condemned to failure owing to
the fact that his queen is virtually
pinned down because of the
obligation to block the powerful
passed pawn.

45 h4!

Compelling his opponent to execute
his threats in the correct belief
that they can successively be
parried.

45 ...   Nf3

This knight is immune for the
moment because of the possibility
of 47 ... g5 after 46 Rxf3 Bxf3+
47 Kxf3. But White's next move
brings the matter to its critical
point.

46 Be2

Black to move

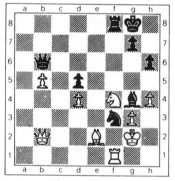

Position after 46 Be2

46 ...   Rxf4!

Evidently planning several moves
ahead. In fact the acceptance of the
sacrifice would have led White into
a dangerous position, since after 47
gxf4 Nxh4+ the move 48 Kg3 would

have been answered by 48 ... Nf5+
(49 Kxg4? Qg6+, followed by mate)
and to 48 Kh2 Black would have
replied 48 ... Qg6 (49 Rg1? Nf3+
etc. with advantage to Black).

47 Bxf3!

Such a refutation, in appearance
effortless, of a sacrificial combination is not uncommon in the
games of Keres, and is more
characteristic than so-called
brilliancies. White returns his
material advantage and finally is
crowned with success by demonstrating the perpetual vitality of his b-
pawn. The ending has a clear artistic
air.

47 ...   Rxd4

If 47 ... Bxf3+ 48 Rxf3 Qxd4 (if
48 ... Rxd4 49 Qc2 with advantage)
49 Qxd4 Rxd4 50 Rb3 with a won
rook endgame.

48 Bxg4   Rxg4

49 Qe5

A formidable move which starts up
a mating attack. The chief threat
is of course 50 Qe8+, followed by
51 Rf8.

49 ...   Qg6

50 b6!

Were this pawn captured the
execution of the threat mentioned
above would win at once.

50 ...   Rb4

51 Qxd5+   Kh7

52 Rf8   Qc2+

If 52 ... Qg4 then 53 Qg8+ Kg6
54 h5+ Kxh5 55 Qf7+ with mate

or the gain of the queen in a few moves.

53	Kh3	Rb2

54	Qg8+	Kg6
55	h5+	Kxh5
56	Qf7+, followed by mate.	

GAME 31

Prague 1943
French Defence

White: A. ALEKHINE
Black: M. BARTOSEK

1	e4	e6
2	d4	d5
3	Nd2	c5
4	Ngf3	Nc6
5	Bb5	

White's inclination is to maintain the tension in the centre for as long as possible. Black's next move, although fairly plausible, is nonetheless a mistake which is perhaps decisive. Relatively better would be 5 . . . cxd4 whereupon White can castle since the defence of the pawn at d4 would only create difficulties for Black.

5	...	Bd7
6	exd5	exd5
7	0-0	Nxd4

It is quite clear that Black will not manage to castle on the king's side. Through the exchanges arising from the text move one perceives that he is trying to prepare to castle long, which furnishes him — although only comparatively so — with the best chance of resistance.

8	Nxd4	cxd4
9	Qe2+	Be7
10	Nf3	Bxb5
11	Qxb5+	Qd7
12	Qe2	0-0-0

If 12 . . . Nf6 then, naturally, 13 Re1 and Black cannot castle.

13 Bf4!

Virtually forcing the exchange of bishops and at the same time eliminating a very useful defensive piece.

13	...	Bd6
14	Bxd6	Qxd6
15	Nxd4	Nf6

White to move

Position after 15 . . . Nf6

The problem of creating an attack is not very easy to resolve. Neither 16 Nf5 Qf4! nor 16 Nb5 Qb6 would have any result. On the other hand Black is going to occupy the e-file with his rooks, which will procure a counter-attacking advantage. White's next move is the only one likely to give him a lasting initiative.

16 Qf3!

This threatens 17 Nf5 and at the same time 17 Nb5.

16	...	Qb6
17	Rfd1	Rhe8

It is clear that the capture of the b-pawn, either now or on the following moves, would have deadly con-sequences for Black.

18	a4	Re4
19	a5	Qc5

For example, if 19 . . . Qxb2 then 20 c3!

20	c3	Rde8
21	h3!	

Making use of a moment's respite to open up an escape square for the king. This move will be found in analogous positions in many of my games.

21	...	Qc7
22	a6	b6
23	c4!	

23 Nb5 Qc5 24 Nxa7+? Kb8 would be premature but the move played is very effective because against 23 . . . dxc4 White responds with 24 Nb5 winning the exchange.

23	...	Qc5
24	Nf5	

Threatening to win by 25 Nxg7.

24	...	Qb4
25	cxd5	Rf4
26	Qd3	Re5
27	Rac1+	Kd7

If 27 . . . Kb8 then 28 d6 etc.

28	Ne3	Ne4
29	Ng4!	Re8

White to move

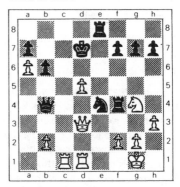

Position after 29 . . . Re8

30 g3

This wins at least the exchange since the rook cannot retreat because of 31 Rc4. But 30 Rc4 played immediately would constitute an error owing to 30 . . . Nxf2!

30 . . .   Nc5

This move allows an even more rapid finish.

31	Rxc5	Re1+
32	Rxe1	Qxe1+
33	Kg2	Rxg4

34 Qf5+, followed by mate in a few moves.

GAME 32

Buenos Aires 1939
French Defence

White: P. KERES (Estonia)
Black: R. FLORES (Chile)

1	e4	e6
2	d4	d5
3	Nd2	Nf6
4	e5	Nfd7
5	Bd3	c5
6	c3	Nc6
7	Ne2	Qb6
8	Nf3	cxd4
9	cxd4	Bb4+

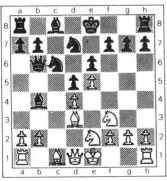

Position after 9 . . . Bb4+

This position is well known on account of the match between Spielmann and Stoltz at Stockholm in 1930 and my encounter with Capablanca in the AVRO Tournament of 1938. On both occasions White answered the check with 10 Kf1 in order to avoid the exchange of queens that Black could force after 10 Bd2. Keres demonstrates that the position resulting from this simplification is decidedly favourable to White and that the alternative chosen by him is thus, because of its simplicity, even more convincing than the more or less artificial king move.

10	Bd2	Bxd2+
11	Qxd2	Qb4
12	Rc1	Qxd2+
13	Kxd2	Nb6
14	b3	

In order to bring the bishop back to

b1 without having to worry about
. . . Nc4+.

14 . . .	Ke7

White to move

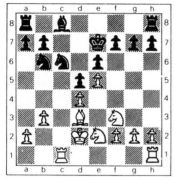

Position after 14 . . . Ke7

15 h4!

The principle of an attack on the
king's side is entirely justified from
the positional point of view as it
can be sustained by nearly all the
White pieces. The venture has a
very good chance of succeeding
completely, particularly since the
concentration of Black pieces on the
queen's side is scarcely useful for
active counter-play and still less for
defence, as the continuation
demonstrates.

15 . . .	Bd7
16 Rh3	Nb4
17 Bb1	a5
18 a3	Na6
19 a4	

This stops once and for all any
serious counter-attack, firstly
because Black's control of b4 has
only an aesthetic and not a
strategic value; and secondly

because the preparations for Black's
irruption will make him lose a great
deal of time and even if realized it
would have very little effect.

19 . . .	Rac8
20 Rg3	g6
21 h5	Rxc1
22 Nxc1	

White does not have to worry
about this new reduction of material
since the presence of an active rook
on the king's side is sufficient.

22 . . .	Nc8
23 Rh3	gxh5

Practically forced, as after 23 . . .
Rg8 24 hxg6 hxg6 25 Rh7 Be8 26
Ng5 Black would have no satisfactory
defence against Ne2-f4 etc.

24 Rxh5	h6

Position after 24 . . . h6

25 Nh2

The knight will come very strongly
to f6 and after Black has made the
effort to eliminate it its colleague
will promptly occupy the same
square, this time with deadly effect.
A simple plan but an irresistible one.

25	...	Kf8
26	Ng4	Kg7
27	Nf6	Bc6
28	Rh3	Nc7
29	Nd3!	

At this moment the manoeuvre 29 Rg3+ Kf8 30 Nh7+ Ke7 31 Rh3 would be premature owing to the troublesome reply 31 . . . b5.

29	...	Ne8
30	Nxe8+	Bxe8
31	Nf4	Bc6
32	Nh5+	Kf8
33	Nf6	Nb6

Or 33 . . . Ne7 34 Rg3. The h-pawn is doomed.

34	Nh7+	Ke7
35	Rxh6	Nd7
36	Bd3	Rb8

If 36 . . . Nf8 then 37 Nf6.

37	Ng5	Rg8

Or 37 . . . b5 38 Rh7 winning.

38	f4	Rg7
39	Rh7	Rxh7
40	Nxh7	Nb6

After 40 . . . f5 the game would probably have lasted a few moves more but this would have been an unnecessary torture.

41	g4	Nc8

This knight has tried very hard to make an impression but without any success, since the squares it controls have no influence over the battle lines.

42	f5	exf5
43	gxf5	Na7
44	f6+!	

This pawn gets through, since 44 . . . Ke6 would be answered by 45 Nf8 mate and 44 . . . Kd8 by 45 e6 Be8 46 Bg6.

Black resigns

GAME 33

Madrid 1945
French Defence

White: A. POMAR
Black: A. ALEKHINE

1	e4	e6
2	d4	d5
3	exd5	

The exchange variation is very far from being as innocent as it appears.

This, of course, providing that one of the protagonists plays for the advantage. Here, as we shall see, it was Black who took it upon himself to complicate the game, and not without danger, it must be confessed.

3	...	exd5
4	Bd3	Nc6
5	c3	Bd6
6	Nf3	Nge7
7	0-0	Bg4
8	Re1	Qd7
9	Bg5	f6

This move was not obligatory now. He could perfectly well have continued with 9 ... 0-0-0 and if 10 Bb5 then 10 ... f6 11 Bh4 Qf5 12 Nbd2 Ng6! 13 Bg3 Nce7 with better chances than in the actual game.

10	Bh4	0-0-0
11	Nbd2	h5

I did not play 11 ... Ng6 12 Bg3 Nf4 because of the pin 13 Bb5 which seemed to me unpleasant.

12	Bg3	h4
13	Bxd6	Qxd6

13 ... cxd6 deserved to be taken into consideration, suppressing any danger of attack against Black's castled position. In a general way Black, whose whole interest is in winning, does not examine carefully the details of the position and he will soon be faced with a dilemma which is hardly pleasing.

14	h3	Bh5
15	Qe2	Bf7

In order to be able to play to win Black must withdraw his bishop to a square without a future. Preferable is 15 ... Bg6 16 Bxg6 Nxg6 17 Qe6+ Qxe6 18 Rxe6 Nf4 19

Re3 g5 with a good game but with minimal chances of achieving victory on account of the paucity of material.

16	Nb3	Rde8
17	Nc5	Nd8
18	Qc2	b6

White to move

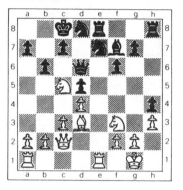

Position after 18 ... b6

19 Nb3?

There are positions in which a combination is obligatory. In order to evade the necessary mental effort the player lets slip his chances and little by little finds himself reduced to the defensive and ends up by suffering a defeat which, logically, is well merited. In this particular case the offer of the knight by 19 b4 bxc5 and then either 20 bxc5 (considered by me) or 20 dxc5 (analysed by Pomar) would have secured White an irresistible attack, the Black pieces not being well arranged for the defence of his king. It was not my intention to take the knight. I calculated 19 b4 Kb8 20 Reb1 Ka8 21 Na6 c6 and Black can defend himself but it will be difficult

for him to organize an attack on the
other wing.

19 ...   g5

20 Nh2

As no direct threat existed, the
demonstration 20 a4 would be the
right move. Against 20 ... Rhg8
White would have had sufficient
time available to play 21 Nh2.

20 ...   Ne6

21 c4

White's position starts becoming unpleasant and Pomar perceives that
he must undertake something. But
the price he pays for the opening of
the c-file (the weakness of the
central pawn and the square d5 for
the Black pieces) is decidedly too
high. 21 a4 a5! 22 Nd2 still offered
some possibilities.

21 ...   dxc4

22 Bxc4   Kb8

But not 22 ... Nd5 23 Qf5!

23 Rac1   Nd8

24 Bxf7   Nxf7

Now Black has a specific objective
for the endgame, the d-pawn, and
he no longer has to attempt direct
attacks against the king.

25 Qc4   Nd5

26 Qb5

As will be seen, the e-file here has
no more than a relative value.

26 ...   Rxe1+

27 Rxe1   c6

28 Qe2   Nh6

29 Nd2   Nf4

30 Qe4   Qd5!

31 Nhf3

If 31 Qxd5 cxd5!, followed by 32
... Rc8 etc., since 32 Rc1 is impossible on account of 32 ... Ne2+.

31 ...   Nf5

32 Kh1

With the object of being able to play
33 Rc1, but the king is badly placed
for the endgame.

32 ...   Rd8

33 Rc1   Kb7

34 b3   Qxe4

35 Nxe4   Nd5

36 Re1   Kc7

White to move

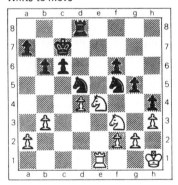

Position after 36 ... Kc7

37 Ned2?

It is obvious that White has a very
difficult game but with 37 a3 he
could still have defended himself.
The plan foreseen by Black for this
case was 37 ... Re8, followed by
... Re6 and ... Nf4.

37 ...   Nb4!

38 Re6   Rd6

39	Re8	Nxa2
40	Ne4	Rd8
41	Rxd8	Kxd8
42	Nxf6	Nc1
43	b4	

Otherwise after the capture of this pawn the Black a-pawn would advance straight to its queening square.

43	...	Nd3
44	d5	

The last attempt.

44	...	Ke7
45	Nh7	cxd5
46	b5	g4!
47	hxg4	Nxf2+
48	Kg1	Nxg4
49	**White resigns**	

There is no defence against 49 ... Kd6, followed by 50 ... Kc5.

GAME 34

Buenos Aires 1939
French Defence

White: F. APSCHENEEK (Latvia)
Black: A. ALEKHINE (France)

1	e4	e6
2	d4	d5
3	exd5	exd5
4	Bd3	Nc6
5	c3	Bd6
6	Ne2	Qh4

Introduced by me at Nottingham, 1936 against W. Winter who replied 7 Nd2 and after 7 ... Bg4 had some difficulty in equalizing. Apscheneek's move is more in accordance with the tendency of 3 exd5. In fact after a very few moves he achieves a perfectly satisfactory position and I had to take considerable chances in order to give the game the semblance of a fight.

7	g3	Qh5

After 7 ... Qe7 White's threats on the open e-file would have compensated for the relative weakness of his king's position.

8	Nf4	Qxd1+
9	Kxd1	Nf6

More natural and, in fact, much more promising would be 9 ... Bg4+ 10 Kc2 0-0-0. In choosing the text continuation I underestimated White's developing manoeuvre on the twelfth and thirteenth moves.

10	Re1+	Ne7
11	f3	Bd7
12	b3!	0-0-0

Clearly there is no way of protecting the king's bishop.

13	Ba3	Nf5
14	Bxd6	Nxd6
15	Nd2	

Thus a perfectly equal position has been attained and Black's efforts to give the battle some life will be shown to be incapable of unsettling the balance.

15	...	g5

With the aim of controlling the e-file, Black wishes to open the f-file (on which he will have an isolated pawn) for his opponent; this is certainly no small price to pay.

16	Ng2	g4
17	Nh4	

If 17 f4 then 17 . . . Nde4 18 Bxe4 dxe4 19 Ne3! (but not 19 Nxe4 because of 19 . . . Nxe4, followed by 20 . . . Bc6 winning) and White's chances would not be inferior.

17	...	gxf3
18	Ndxf3	Nfe4
19	Kc2	f6!

Occupation of e4 and control of e5 has been Black's idea for the moment. But unfortunately the coming exchange is unavoidable.

20	Re3	Nf2
21	Bf1	Rde8
22	Rae1	Re4
23	Nd2	Rxe3
24	Rxe3	Ng4
25	Re2	Bb5

This has no effect. The same would have been the case after 25 . . . Nf5 26 Nxf5 Bxf5+ 27 Kc1. The position is decidedly sterile.

26	Re6	Bd7
27	Re2	Rg8
28	Bh3	Kd8
29	Bxg4	Bxg4
30	Re1	h5
31	c4	c6
32	Rf1	Ke7
33	c5	Nb5
34	Kd3	Nc7
35	Nf5?	

The previous blocking of the queen's side would have been justified only by the pawn advances b4 and a4. The premature exchange gives Black the opportunity he has awaited for so long.

35	...	Bxf5
36	Rxf5	

Black to move

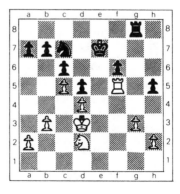

Position after 36 Rxf5

36 ...   **h4!**

This eliminates Black's weakness, creates one in the enemy position and also opens up a very important file for the rook. Could any more be asked of a modest pawn move, especially in the endgame?

37 Nf1

37 gxh4 would be advantageous to Black: 37 . . . Ne6 38 Nf3 Ng7 39 Rf4 Nh5 40 Rf5 Rh8, threatening 41 . . . Ke6.

37 . . .	**Rh8**
38 Ne3	**hxg3**
39 hxg3	**Ne6**
40 Rf1	**Rh3!**

And not 40 . . . Rh2 because of 41 Rxf6, but in the long run White will not be able to avoid the rook's intrusion to the seventh or eighth rank.

41 Nf5+	**Kf7**
42 Ke3	**Rh2**
43 Rf2	**Rh1**

After this the next problem will be to organize an attack on the White pawns without allowing the enemy rook to intrude effectively via h5.

44 Kd3   **b6!**

With a double purpose; to clear the second rank of pawns and at the same time to provoke another White pawn to an exposed square.

45 b4   **Rb1**

As will be seen, the forced move of the White king will allow Black to gain an important tempo.

46 Kc3   **Rg1!**

Now . . . Ng5-e4+ becomes a strong threat.

47 Rh2

The only possible counter-play.

| **47 . . .** | **Ng5** |
| **48 Rh8** | **Ke6!** |

An important preparation for the capture of the g-pawn! At this moment 48 . . . Ne4+ 49 Kd3 Nxg3 would be premature.

| **49 Ng7+** | **Kf7** |
| **50 Nh5** | |

In view of the inevitable loss of material this is a desperate manoeuvre. I was hoping for the natural continuation 50 Nf5 and then 50 . . . Ne4+ 51 Kd3 bxc5! (at the right moment; White cannot reply 52 dxc5 because of 52 . . . a5 etc.) 52 bxc5 Nxg3 53 Nd6+ Ke6 54 Re8+ Kd7 55 Ra8 f5 56 Rxa7+ Ke6 57 Rc7 f4, followed by the victorious march of the passed pawn.

50 . . .	**Ne4+**
51 Kd3	**bxc5**
52 bxc5	**Nxg3**
53 Nf4	

The rook ending would be clearly hopeless for White.

Black to move

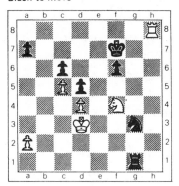

Position after 53 Nf4

53 . . .   Rf1?

It is not very often that I overlook a tactical trap. 53 . . . Rd1+ 54 Kc2 Rxd4 55 Rh7+ Kg8 56 Rg7+ Kh8! would quickly have decided the game in Black's favour.

54 Nxd5

This pseudo-sacrifice works in two variations: (a) 54 . . . cxd5 55 c6 Nf5 (55 . . . Rc1 56 c7 is evidently suicidal) 56 c7 Nd6 57 Rd8 Rc1, and (b) 54 . . . Kg7 55 Ne3 Kxh8 56 Nxf1 Nxf1? 57 d5 winning. Black's reply is the only possible winning method.

| 54 . . . | Rd1+ |
| 55 Kc2 | Rxd4 |

56 Nb6!

This second surprising knight move is stronger than 56 Ne3 Ra4 etc., and with correct play subsequently it would have saved the game.

56 . . .   Ne4

Other moves would be bad: I. 56 . . . axb6? 57 cxb6 Rb4 58 b7 winning. II. 56 . . . Ke6 57 Re8+

Kf5 58 Kc3. III. 56 . . . Kg7 57 Rb8 axb6 58 cxb6 Rb4. With the continuation actually chosen Black achieves a material advantage.

57 Rh7+	Ke6
58 Rxa7	Nxc5
59 a4	Nd7

The following rook ending will in effect offer White the greatest technical difficulties. If 59 . . . f5, however, then the simple advance of the a-pawn would have been sufficient to simplify the position into a draw.

60 Nxd7	Rxd7
61 Ra8	f5
62 a5	Kd5
63 a6	Rf7
64 Kd3	

After 64 a7 Kc5 etc. the White pawn would have been overcome. The plan to stop the f-pawn by the intervention of the king is correct.

64 . . .	f4
65 Ke2	Kc4
66 Kf3	

But here he does not realize the significance of Black's last move. He could have obtained a more or less accidental draw by 66 Rb8! Ra7 (66 . . . f3+ 67 Kf2 would not have changed anything) 67 Rf8 Rxa6 68 Rxf4+ Kc3 69 Rf3+ Kc2 70 Rf6 after which Black would not be able to move his king, which would permit the White king to take up an impregnable position on the c-file.

66 . . .   Kb5!

After this White will gradually be led into a blind alley.

67	Rc8	Kb6
68	Ra8	

If 68 a7 Rxa7 69 Kxf4 Re7 winning.

68	...	Rf6
69	Ke2	f3+
70	Kf2	Ka5!

The winning triangular manoeuvre.

71	Ra7	Kb5!
72	Ra8	Kb6
73	a7	Kb7
74	Rb8+	Kxa7
75	Rb1	

If 75 Rb3 Ka6 76 Rxf3 Rxf3+ 77 Kxf3 Kb5 winning.

75	...	Ka6
76	Ra1+	Kb5
77	Rb1+	Kc4
78	Rc1+	Kd3
79	Rc5	Kd4
80	Ra5	c5
81	White resigns	

Caro-Kann Defence

GAME 35

Buenos Aires 1939
Caro-Kann Defence

White: P. KERES (Estonia)
Black: V. MIKENAS (Lithuania)

1	e4	c6
2	d4	d5
3	Nc3	dxe4
4	Nxe4	Nf6
5	Nxf6+	exf6
6	Bc4	Bd6
7	Qh5	

A method of playing for a quick attack rather than slowly concentrating the forces by 7 Qe2+ Be7 8 Nf3 0-0 9 0-0 Be6 10 Re1 etc. The best proof of the ineffectiveness of the experiment of the text is the fact that White, despite all Keres's ingenuity, succeeds only in maintaining the balance throughout the greater part of the game and finally wins solely because of a grave error by his opponent.

7	...	0-0
8	Ne2	g6

With the double purpose of developing the rook and placing the queen's
bishop at f5. The small weakness of
the king's side is of minimal importance here because the four pawns
are a good enough protection.

9	Qf3	Re8
10	Bh6	Bf5
11	0-0-0	Be4
12	Qb3	Qc7
13	f3	

White forces the following simplification because otherwise Black will
obtain supremacy with 13 . . . b5,
followed by 14 . . . Bd5.

13	. . .	Bd5
14	Bxd5	Rxe2

And not 14 . . . cxd5 15 Nc3.

15 Rhe1!

Taking control of the central file.
But it will not be for long.

15	. . .	Rxe1
16	Rxe1	Na6

After 16 . . . Bf4+ 17 Bxf4 Qxf4+
18 Kb1, 18 . . . cxd5 could not be
played because of 19 Qxb7.

17 Bc4   b5

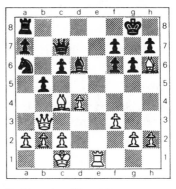

Position after 17 . . . b5

18 Qe3!

White certainly takes advantage
of the unusual position of his
queen's bishop. The text move not
only threatens 19 Qe8+ but also
prevents 19 . . . Bf4+ and frees the
b3 square for the bishop.

18	. . .	Qd7
19	Bb3	Nc7
20	Qf2	a5

Also fairly good is the simple 20 . . .
Rd8 but Black is ambitious and, in
fact, decides upon this advance
which offers certain possibilities.

21	a4	bxa4
22	Bxa4	Nd5
23	Qh4	

White begins to play with fire. The
safe alternative would be 23 Bd2 but
this would have required a wholly
different strategy, an admission that
could hardly be expected from a
player of the temperament and
calibre of Keres. He prefers to
sacrifice a pawn; without much
danger, it is true, but also without
much hope of winning.

23	...	g5

Forced but, as the continuation demonstrates, perfectly safe.

24	Qe4	Bxh2
25	c4	

This was planned with 23 Qh4. White manages to infiltrate to e7, but at a high price.

25	...	Nb4
26	Qe7	Bf4+

An important intermediary check.

27 Kb1

Black to move

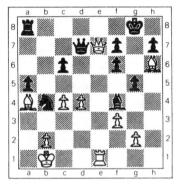

Position after 27 Kb1

27	...	Qf5+??

This suicidal check is even less comprehensible if it is assumed that Black was short of time. The most natural thing would be to avoid complications by exchanging queens and remain with an extra pawn. In fact after 27 ... Qxe7 28 Rxe7 Bd6 White would only have a choice between the retreat of the rook to e3 (or e1) followed by 29 ... Bf8 30 Bxf8 Kxf8 after which he would have no compensation for the pawn, and 29 Rd7 which allows Black to force a draw quickly by means of 29 ... Re8! 30 Kc1 (best) Bf4+ 31 Kd1 Nd3! 32 Kc2 (32 Bxc6 would be a mistake not because of 32 ... Re1+ 33 Kc2 Nb4+ 34 Kb3 Nxc6 35 d5 etc., but on account of 32 ... Nxb2+ 33 Kc2 Nxc4) Nb4+ 33 Kd1 Nd3 etc. The unfortunate check of the text move loses a piece and puts an end to all possible fight.

28	Ka1	Be5

There is no other defence against the threat of mate. Black would have done better to resign.

29	dxe5	Nd3
30	Bc2	fxe5
31	Rd1	Qg6
32	Bxg5	h6
33	Bf6	e4
34	fxe4	Nb4
35	Rd8+	**Black resigns**

GAME 36

Bilbao Championship 1945
Caro-Kann Defence

White: A. POMAR
Black: RICO

1	e4	c6
2	d4	d5
3	Nc3	dxe4
4	Nxe4	Bf5
5	Ng3	Bg6
6	Nf3	Nd7
7	Bd3	

More usual is 7 h4 with the aim of forcing the exchange of the bishops after 7 . . . h6 8 Bd3. But Pomar plans to castle on the king's side.

7	. . .	e6
8	0-0	Qc7
9	Re1	Ngf6
10	b3	

Inviting Black to exchange his dark-squared bishop. The move is not to be condemned but it is very modest. Although more risky, more chances would be offered by the procedure 10 Ne5 and if 10 . . . Bd6 then 11 Bxg6 hxg6 12 Qe2 etc.

10	. . .	Bb4
11	Bd2	Bxd2
12	Qxd2	Bxd3
13	Qxd3	0-0-0

This move is not justified by the position, as Black has no real possibility of attacking the enemy's castled position. Safe and good would be 13 . . . 0-0 14 c4 Rfd8,

followed by 15 . . . c5 with more or less identical prospects.

14	c4	

More exact of course would be 14 b4 because after the text move there remained Black's last opportunity to divert his opponent in the centre with 14 . . . c5.

14	. . .	h5

Rico launches into an attack that cannot come to a good end as White's king's side offers no weaknesses. It is easy to see that White must win.

15	b4	h4
16	Ne4	Rh5
17	c5!	Nxe4
18	Qxe4	Nf6
19	Qe2	g5
20	Qb2!	

This defends the d-pawn and at the same time prepares for 21 Ne5 or 21 b5. Black's plan of defence is not satisfactory.

20	. . .	g4
21	Ne5	Rg8

Black tries to suggest to his adversary that he has a counter-attack but Pomar, undaunted, does not let himself be intimidated.

22	b5	cxb5
23	a4	

23 Qxb5 would be an intelligent move, but the text cannot be censured because the advance of the a-pawn could eventually be useful for the attack.

23	...	b4
24	Qxb4	Nd5
25	Qb3	g3

Otherwise White would increase his pressure decisively by playing 26 a5 and if 26 ... a6 then 27 Rec1.

26	fxg3	hxg3
27	h3	f6
28	Nc4	

Black to move

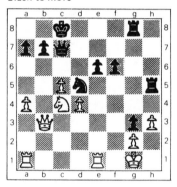

Position after 28 Nc4

| 28 | ... | Nf4 |

After this move White wins simply by attacking the knight. With 28 ... Qf4 he could present his opponent with a tactical problem because 29 Nd6+ Kd8! leads in this case to unclear variations, for instance: 30 Qb2 Qf2+ 31 Qxf2 gxf2+ 32 Kxf2 Nf4 33 Rg1 Rxh3. The solution lies in 29 Qb2! against which Black would have no better move than 29 ... Qf2+ 30 Qxf2 gxf2+ 31 Kxf2 Nf4 32 Ne3 and White would have achieved a securely won endgame. 29 ... Nc3 would be refuted by 30 Re3!

29	Nd6+	Kd7
30	Re4!	Rh4
31	Rf1	

Black could resign here with an easy conscience but he preferred to persist with a few more moves which were, of course, without interest after 31 ... b6 32 Rfxf4 etc. An excellent game by Pomar, who proves that his failure at Bilbao was solely due to fatigue. His powers are continuing intact and are following their normal course of development.

GAME 37

Cracow 1940
Caro-Kann Defence

White: K. RICHTER
Black: G. KIENINGER

| 1 | e4 | c6 | 3 | Nc3 | dxe4 |
| 2 | d4 | d5 | 4 | Nxe4 | Bf5 |

5 Bd3

An interesting pawn sacrifice which has not yet been properly examined by theory.

5 ...	Qxd4
6 Nf3	Qd8
7 Qe2	Nf6

7 ... Nd7 is not possible owing to 8 Nd6 mate.

8 0-0	Bxe4
9 Bxe4	Nbd7
10 Bg5	Nxe4

In view of the material advantage more chances would probably be offered by the continuation 10 ... e6, followed by 11 ... Be7.

11 Qxe4	Nc5
12 Qe2	Ne6
13 Rfd1	

Better is 13 Rad1 for if then 13 ... Qa5 there follows the strong move 14 Bc1 Qxa2 15 Ne5.

13 ...	Qc7
14 Bh4	g6
15 Bg3	Qc8
16 Be5	Bg7
17 Bxg7	Nxg7
18 Rd3	Ne6
19 Qe3	Qc7

After 19 ... 0-0 there would naturally follow 20 Rad1 and Black's defence would be exceedingly difficult.

20 Ne5	Rd8
21 Rxd8+	Nxd8?

Better is 21 ... Qxd8 22 Qxa7 Qd4! 23 Qb8+ Nd8 24 c3 Qd6 with a probable draw.

22 Rd1	a6

22 ... 0-0 is impossible because of 23 Nd7, followed by 24 Nxf8.

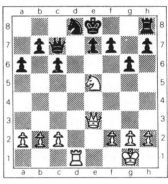

Position after 22 ... a6

23 Rd7

Decisive, since if 23 ... Qa5 there follows 24 Rxe7+. Nor is 23 ... Qc8 possible, owing to 24 Qc5 0-0 25 Qxe7 etc.

23 ...	Qxd7
24 Nxd7	**Black resigns**

GAME 38

Madrid 1945
Caro-Kann Defence

White: A. POMAR
Black: J. SANZ

1	e4	c6
2	d4	d5
3	Nc3	dxe4
4	Nxe4	Nd7

A good move rarely adopted today. A question of fashion! The idea is obvious: prepare the way for the king's knight without fear of modifying the pawn configuration after Nxf6+.

5 Qe2

This threatens 6 Nd6 mate but 5 . . . Ndf6 easily prevents this.

5	. . .	Qc7

Theoretically one cannot censure this move, nor the one that follows, because they do not put the game in danger. But in fact the former champion of Spain should have tried to *fight* with more eagerness against his young rival.

6	g3	Ngf6
7	Bf4	Qa5+

White to move

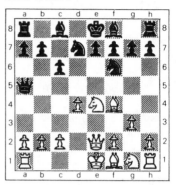

Position after 7 . . . Qa5+

8 b4!

The alternative 8 Bd2 Qd5 9 Bg2 Nxe4 10 Bxe4 Qxd4 11 0-0-0 certainly gives White a fine development in exchange for the sacrificed pawn, but the result cannot be seen clearly. Pomar opts for an immediate draw against his powerful opponent, and he is right to do so.

8	. . .	Qxb4+
9	c3	Qa3
10	Nd6+	Kd8
11	Nxf7+	Ke8
12	Nd6+	

It is quite evident that perpetual check is agreeable to White.

Drawn

GAME 39

Buenos Aires 1939
Caro-Kann Defence

White: A. ALEKHINE (France)
Black: E. ELISKASES (Germany)

1	e4	c6
2	d4	d5
3	exd5	cxd5
4	c4	Nf6
5	Nc3	e6

After 5 . . . Nc6 6 Bg5 Black
would have nothing better than 6
. . . e6 (7 Bxf6! is the reply to 6 . . .
dxc4); so it is evident that this pawn
move immediately gives Black more
options in the future.

6	Nf3	Be7
7	cxd5	

White contents himself with a
minimal advantage in development
and a symmetrical pawn position in
the centre. This would be obtained
after 7 . . . exd5 8 Bb5+ Nc6 9 Ne5
or 8 . . . Bd7 9 Bxd7+ Nbxd7 10
0-0 0-0 11 Bf4 etc.

7	. . .	Nxd5
8	Bb5+	Bd7

After 8 . . . Nc6 I intended to
continue simply with the development of my pieces by 9 0-0 0-0 10
Re1 with numerous possibilities
based on the advantage in space.

9	Bxd7+	

Position after 9 Bxd7+

9	. . .	Nxd7

A more lively game would result
from 9 . . . Qxd7 10 Ne5 Nxc3 11
bxc3 (but not 11 Qf3, suggested by
Dr. Euwe and faithfully reproduced
in a dozen chess magazines, on
account of 11 . . . Qxd4 12 Qxf7+
Kd8 and White, because of the
threat of mate at d1, has no means
of continuing his attack with
sacrifices) Qb5 12 c4 Qa5+ 13 Bd2
Bb4 14 Rb1 or 11 . . . Qd5 12 0-0
Nc6 13 Re1 and White has obtained
greater space, but at the cost of a
possible weakness in his central
position.

10	Nxd5	exd5
11	Qb3	Nb6

If 11 . . . 0-0 White would not
accept the pawn sacrifice but
would simply reply 12 0-0 which
would practically force the text

continuation.

12	0-0	0-0
13	Bf4	Bd6

The desire to exchange the well-placed White bishop is easy to understand and cannot be considered one of the reasons for the subsequent deficiencies in Black's position. The mistake comes later.

14	Bxd6	Qxd6
15	Rfe1!	

With the aim of replying to 15 . . . Nc4 with 16 Ne5.

15	. . .	Rac8
16	Rac1	

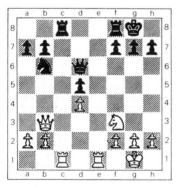

Position after 16 Rac1

16	. . .	h6?

This not only fails to prevent 17 Ne5 but also accentuates the weakness of Black's g6. Despite some considerations against it (for example the weakness of e6) the radical 16 . . . f6 — which has not been suggested by any annotators — would have made it possible to maintain the equilibrium for some time. My most favourable reply to

this would have been 17 g3, followed by 18 Nh4.

17	Ne5	Rc7

Now this is the only way of relieving the knight of its servile task of defending b7.

| 18 | g3! | |

As will soon be seen, the formation of pawns at f2, g3, and h2 (or h4) is much more appropriate for the battle of the rooks on the queen's side than the formation f2, g2, and h3.

18	. . .	Rfc8
19	Rxc7	Rxc7

If 19 . . . Qxc7 the reply 20 Qa3! would have restricted Black's position much more.

| 20 | Qb5 | |

In playing this move I hoped for the natural answer 20 . . . Re7, trusting that after 21 Qa5! f6 22 Ng6 Rxe1+ 23 Qxe1 Kf7 24 Nf4 I would be in a position to play for a win despite the reduced material.

20	. . .	Nd7

This eliminates the disagreeable White knight but at the cost of the e-file and the security of the position of his king.

21	Nxd7	Rxd7
22	Re8+	Kh7
23	h4!	

Since the queen at b5 attacks a number of important points she will move only if obliged to do so.

23	. . .	a6

Contrary to the opinion of learned

commentators, it would not be
good to play the otherwise natural
move 23 . . . h5 because White
would reply 24 Ra8 and if 24 . . .
a6 then 25 Qe2!, threatening 26
Qxh5+ and 26 Qe8

24	Qe2	Rd8
25	Re7	Rd7
26	Re5	g6

26 . . . Qg6 27 h5 Qb1+ 28 Kg2 etc.
would be less promising.

| 27 | h5 | Qf6 |
| 28 | Qd3 | |

Planning the diversion 29 Qb3 and
also in some cases Re8.

| 28 | . . . | Rd6 |

In order to answer 29 Re8 with 29
. . . Re6.

| 29 | Qb3! | Rb6 |
| 30 | hxg6+ | |

Forcing Black to retake with the
queen because 30 . . . fxg6 would be
answered by 31 Qxd5, threatening
32 Qd7+ and 30 . . . Kxg6 by 31
Qc2+, followed by 32 Rxd5.

30	. . .	Qxg6
31	Qxd5	Rxb2
32	Rf5	

Black to move

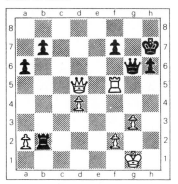

Position after 32 Rf5

| 32 | . . . | Rb5? |

Now White secures an easy rook
ending. Nor would he have any
difficulties after 32 . . . Kg7,
because he would gain a necessary
tempo for d5 by means of 33 Qe5+.
The only good move, 32 . . . Kg8!,
would have given White unclear
technical problems, the solution
to which would begin with 33 Rf4!,
protecting the passed pawn and
freeing the queen to undertake
various attacks. The final phase of
this well-played game promised in
that case to be as instructive as the
middle-game.

33 Rxf7+!

Eliskases was obviously relying upon
33 Qxf7+ Qxf7 34 Rxf7+ Kg6 with
a drawn ending.

33	. . .	Kg8
34	Rf6+	Rxd5
35	Rxg6+	Kh7
36	Rb6	Rxd4

Also after 36 . . . Rd7 the endgame
would be hopeless because of the

dominant position of the White rook.

37	Rxb7+	Kg8
38	Rb6	Ra4
39	Rxh6	Rxa2
40	Kg2	a5
41	Ra6	a4
42	Ra7	

The game is decided and Black could quickly resign.

42	...	a3
43	g4	Ra1
44	Kg3	Rg1+
45	Kf4	Ra1
46	g5	Kf8
47	Kf5	Black resigns

GAME 40

Munich 1942
Caro-Kann Defence (by transposition)

White: A. ALEKHINE
Black: K. RICHTER

1	e4	d5
2	exd5	Nf6
3	c4	c6
4	d4	

After 4 dxc6 Nxc6 5 Nf3 e5, followed by 6 . . . Bc5 Black would obtain a game full of promise thanks to White's weakness on the queen's file. Thus the selection of this good variation of the Caro-Kann by White is fully justified.

4	...	cxd5
5	Nc3	Nc6
6	Bg5	

Good but probably not superior to the old move 6 Nf3.

6	...	e6

Against 6 . . . dxc4 White can advantageously offer a pawn sacrifice by means of 7 Bxc4! For example: (a) 7 . . . Qxd4 8 Qxd4 Nxd4 9 0-0-0, or (b) 7 . . . Nxd4 8 Nf3 Nxf3+ 9 Qxf3, in both cases with a development that is ample compensation for the slight material disadvantage.

7	Nf3	Be7
8	Bd3	

The blockading attempt 8 c5 would be a double-edged weapon. For instance, 8 c5 0-0 9 Bb5 Ne4! 10 Bxe7 Nxe7 11 0-0 Ng6 with a balanced position. The text move leads to a line of the Queen's Gambit Accepted in which White will have to resolve the problem of the isolated d-pawn.

8	...	0-0

9	0-0	dxc4
10	Bxc4	b6
11	a3	

In order to remove the worry of the reply 11 . . . Nb4.

| 11 | ... | Bb7 |
| 12 | Qd3! | |

White is now threatening, after 13 Rad1, to bring his bishop via a2 to b1, provoking a weakness in his opponent's king's side. Black's next move which simplifies the position by exchanges is therefore well justified, although, as will be appreciated, it does not allow him to equalize the game *completely*.

| 12 | ... | Nd5 |

Black cannot try 12 . . . Na5 13 Ba2 Bxf3 14 Qxf3 Qxd4 on account of 15 b4 Nc4 16 Rad1 etc.

| 13 | Bxd5 | Bxg5 |

After 13 . . . exd5 14 Bxe7 Nxe7 15 Re1 White's position would be slightly preferable, chiefly because of the lack of future for the Black bishop at b7. Once Black has played the text move he will be induced to create a weakness at e6, although in return for the possibility of finding compensation in White's at d4. The battle moves towards a tactical phase.

| 14 | Be4 |

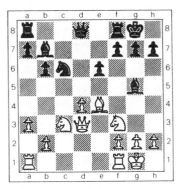

Position after 14 Be4

| 14 | ... | f5 |

Besides this move, apparently the most energetic, two other lines had to be considered:

(a) 14 . . . g6 with the continuation 15 Qb5! Bf6 16 Bxc6 a6 17 Qc4 (stronger than 17 Qa4 b5 etc.) Rc8 18 Ne5 Bxe5 19 dxe5 Rxc6 20 Qf4 (threatening 21 Ne4) Rc7 21 Rad1 Rd7 22 Rd6 with advantage to White.

(b) 14 . . . h6 which White would answer simply by 15 Rad1 and if now 15 . . . f5 then 16 Nxg5 Qxg5 17 Bf3 or 16 . . . hxg5 17 Bxc6 Bxc6 18 Rfe1, with hardly a promising result for Black in either case.

| 15 | Nxg5 | Qxg5 |
| 16 | Bf3 | Kh8 |

Here Richter lets slip the possibility of a pretty trap by playing immediately 16 . . . Rad8! for if White executes his threat, which consists of 17 Qc4 Kh8 18 Bxc6 Rac8 19 Qxe6, Black wins brilliantly with 19 . . . Rxc6 20 Qd7 Qxg2+!! 21 Kxg2 Rg6+ 22 Kh3 Bg2+ 23 Kh4 Rg4+ 24 Kh5 Bf3! since White would have no adequate defence against the discovered check by the rook moving to any square along the fifth rank and 26 Kg5 h6+ 27 Kg6 Rf6 mate. But by simply answering with 17 Qe3! White would assure himself of a slight positional advantage without any danger.

17 Rfe1

Preparing for the astonishing queen manoeuvre that we shall see forthwith.

17 ...   Rad8

Threatening not only the d-pawn but also the strong advance 18 ... e5. Clearly 18 Rxe6 loses the exchange after 18 ... Nxd4. White's position seems critical.

White to move

Position after 17 ... Rad8

18 Qf1!!

The idea of this move is to force Black to occupy d4 with the rook and at the same time to make possible the attack Qb5 which at once would be a mistake because of 18 ... Nxd4. If Black does not take the pawn then White simply plays 19

Rad1, maintaining his pressure on the e-file with an excellent game.

18 ...   Rxd4

19 Qb5!   Rd6

Black does not resign himself to the variation 19 ... Nd8 20 Bxb7 Nxb7 21 Rxe6* Nc5 22 Re8 which would leave him in a manifestly inferior position although, at the same time, it would offer him chances of resistance. He mistakenly decides upon a complicated variation which will be refuted by the sacrifice of the White queen. The ending that follows is of technical interest; White must proceed very meticulously in order to make his material advantage tell.

20 Ne4   Qg6

21 Nxd6!

The move 21 Bh5 was tempting since the sacrificial variation 21 ... Qxh5 22 Nxd6 Nd4 23 Qd3 Nf3+ 24 gxf3 Bxf3 25 Re3 etc. would be incorrect. But by playing 21 ... Rd5! 22 Qxd5 exd5 23 Bxg6 fxe4 24 Bh5 Ne5 25 Be2 d4 Black, with a pawn for the exchange, would have obtained excellent fighting chances on account of his dominant position in the centre.

21 ...   Nd4

22 Bxb7   Nxb5

23 Nxb5

---

*The notes to this game appeared in *Ajedrez Hipermoderno*. In *Gran Ajedrez* Alekhine recommends 21 Qe5! Rg4 22 g3 Nc5 23 Rad1 'with the better prospects for White'. E.W.

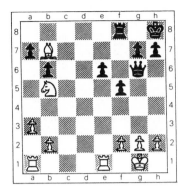

Position after 23 Nxb5

23 . . .   Qf6!

White's minor pieces are now a little displaced and Black exploits this circumstance in order to advance the pawn to e4, a co-ordination point of the White forces.

24 Nc3   e5

25 Rad1   e4

26 Rd7   h5

It would be in Black's interest to exchange his rook, which, as we shall see, plays only a passive role. But unfortunately for him 26 . . . Rd8 is at this moment impossible because of 27 Nd5! Qg5 28 Rxd8+ Qxd8 29 Rc1 and wins.

27 h3   h4

Nor is 27 . . . Rd8 possible now, on account of 28 Nd5 Qg5 29 h4! Qxh4 30 Ne7! With this manoeuvre White has avoided for good the exchange of rooks.

28	Red1	Kh7
29	Ba6	Rf7
30	R7d6	Qg5
31	R6d5	Qf4
32	Ne2	Qg5
33	Nd4	Rf6
34	Be2!	

In order to reply to 34 . . . Rg6 with 35 Bg4.

34	. . .	Qf4
35	Nc2	Rf7
36	Ne3	Kh6
37	Bc4	g6
38	Rd6	Rc7
39	b3	Kh7
40	a4	Qe5
41	Re6	Qc3
42	Nd5	Qc2
43	Rf1	Rg7
44	f3!	

The elimination of the pawn at e4 puts an end to all resistance.

44	. . .	exf3
45	Rxf3	Kh6

Or 45 . . . Qc1+ 46 Kh2 Qg5 47 Nf4 winning.

| 46 | Ne3 | **Black resigns** |

GAME 41

Frankfurt 1942
Caro-Kann Defence

White: A.BRINCKMANN
Black: H. HEINICKE

1 e4	c6	
2 d4	d5	
3 exd5	cxd5	
4 c4	Nf6	
5 Nf3	e6	
6 Bg5	Be7	
7 Nc3	0-0	
8 Bd3		

8 c5 would offer better chances.

8 ...	dxc4
9 Bxc4	Nc6
10 0-0	Nd5

Against me at Munich Richter first played 10 . . . b6, followed by 11 . . . Bb7 after which the diagonal h1-a8 turned out to be fatal for Black. The text move is more appropriate in order to seek equality.

11 Bxd5	exd5
12 Bxe7	Nxe7
13 Ne5	

Much more energetic would be 13 Qb3, maintaining the pressure. The text move facilitates Black's defence.

13 ...	Qb6!
14 Qd2	Be6
15 Rfe1	Rac8
16 Rac1	Ng6
17 Nxg6	

It would be far more practical to leave the choice of this exchange to the opponent, confining himself to playing 17 h3.

17 ...	hxg6
18 Re3	Qc6
19 Rce1	b5

Black mounts his attack, and with good reason.

20 a3	a5
21 Ne2	Qc2
22 Qxa5	Qxb2
23 Nf4	Qxd4
24 Nxe6	fxe6
25 Qxb5	e5!

The strength of the central pawns now manifests itself in all its efficacy.

26 Qe2	e4
27 Rd1	

This is like bringing coal for the opponent's fire. Still necessary was the precautionary measure 27 h3.

27 ...	Qc5
28 Qg4?	

Losing rapidly. But in any case 28 h3 Rf5, followed by 29 . . . Rcf8 would hardly be a solution.

Black to move

Position after 28 Qg4

28	...	Rxf2!
29	Kxf2	Rf8+
30	Ke2	

Or 30 Kg1 Qxe3+ 31 Kh1 Rf6!, the simplest way to win.

30	...	Qb5+!
31	Kd2	

Nor would 31 R3d3 exd3+ 32 Rxd3 Re8+ etc. offer any hope.

31	...	Qb2+

Mate next move.

GAME 42

Buenos Aires 1939
Caro-Kann Defence

White: J.R. CAPABLANCA (Cuba)
Black: M. CZERNIAK (Palestine)

1	e4	c6
2	d4	d5
3	exd5	cxd5
4	c4	Nc6

This move is rarely adopted and is of great theoretical importance because of 5 Nc3, when Black *nolens volens* would be obliged to play the usual variation 5 ... Nf6 6 Bg5. The alternative 5 ... dxc4 6 Nf3 Bg4 7 Bxc4 is decidedly favourable to White.

5 Nf3

This move gives the opening a particular character. Black obtains good fighting chances, many more than may be the general impression after White's rapid victory in the present game.

5	...	Bg4
6	cxd5	Qxd5
7	Be2	

7 Nc3 Bxf3 8 Nxd5 Bxd1 9 Nc7+ Kd8 10 Nxa8 Bh5 11 Be3 (or 11 d5 Nb4) e6 etc. would have been risky. With the text move White allows the fixing of his isolated pawn, hoping to find compensation for this weakness in superior development.

7	...	e6
8	0-0	Nf6
9	Nc3	Qa5

At this point this is preferable to 9 . . . Qd8 because he had to take into consideration the reply 10 Qa4 by White.

10	h3	Bh5
11	a3	

An astute move whose true value Black evidently does not appreciate.

| 11 | . . . | Rd8? |

Decidedly too optimistic since Black's vital preoccupation should be castling quickly. On the other hand the square d8, as will be seen, was a possible refuge for the Black queen. For these two reasons 11 . . . Be7 would have been good and if 12 g4 Bg6 13 b4 then 13 . . . Qd8 followed by castling, with many chances of counter-play.

12	g4	Bg6
13	b4!	

A profound conception, the consequences of which are much more effective than 13 Be3 Be7 14 b4 Qc7 etc.

Black to move

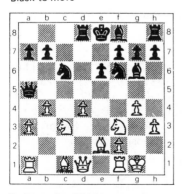

Position after 13 b4

| 13 | . . . | Bxb4 |

Czerniak imagines that he has found a refutation of White's combination and happily accepts the sacrifice. But even if Black had been less optimistic he would not have found a satisfactory continuation since 13 . . . Qb6 would have been answered by 14 Be3 and 13 . . . Qc7 by 14 Qa4! Nd7 15 Bg5.

14	axb4	Qxa1
15	Qb3	

Threatening 16 Bb2.

| 15 | . . . | Rxd4 |

If now 16 Bb2 then 16 . . . Rxb4 and if 16 Nxd4 then 16 . . . Nxd4 17 Qc4 Qxc3(!), both lines being in Black's favour. But there exists a third possibility.

| 16 | Ba3 | |

And after Black's last effort . . .

| 16 | . . . | Bc2 |

. . . the liquidation of the tension with:

17	Qxc2	Qxa3
18	Nb5!	Qxb4
19	Nfxd4	Nxd4
20	Nxd4	

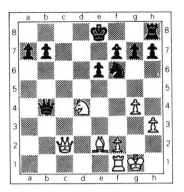

Position after 20 Nxd4

If now 20 . . . Qxd4 then 21 Rd1
Qe5 22 Qc8+ Ke7 23 Qxh8 Qxe2 24
Qd8 mate. This represents a combination of twelve moves beginning with
13 b4!, a very rare instance in
modern chess of a master having to
calculate so far ahead.

20 ...   0-0

The three pawns obtained for the
piece are not sufficient compensation while they have no possibility
of being promoted.

21 Rd1   Nd5?

It must be admitted that here and
later Black facilitates White's game.
Instead of this useless knight
manoeuvre it would have been
better to choose 21 . . . h6 in connection with . . . Rd8, or the
immediate 21 . . . a5

22 Bf3   Nf4

23 Kh2   e5?

Why? As there was no immediate
threat an escape square for the
king (23 . . . h5) would be preferable.

24 Nf5   g6

25 Ne3

The knight is now very well placed
while d5 has become weak for
Black. White is ready to attack
(26 Rb1).

25 ...   Ne6

26 Nd5   Qa3

27 Rd3   Qa1

28 Qd2

Intending 29 Qh6.

28 ...   Kg7

29 Qe2

More precise is the immediate 29
Qe3, threatening 30 Ra3.

29 ...   f6

30 Qe3   a6

31 Rd1   Qb2

A comparatively better square
would be a5.

32 Nc3   Nd4

33 Rb1   Qc2

34 Be4   Black resigns

The adventurous lady has not
escaped her destiny.

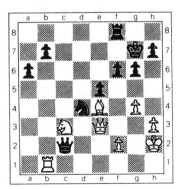

Final position

GAME 43

Simultaneous exhibition, Madrid 1941
Caro-Kann Defence

White: A. ALEKHINE
Black: I. NAHARRO

After the moves 1 e4 c6 2 Nc3 d5
3 Nf3 dxe4 4 Nxe4 one arrives at
a position analogous to the normal
variation (with 2 d4) and Black
might be tempted to continue in the
same way, that is to say by playing
4 . . . Bf5. In reality this move is
an important loss of time here and
frequently leads to a swift
catastrophe.

1	e4	c6
2	Nc3	d5
3	Nf3	dxe4
4	Nxe4	Bf5
5	Ng3	Bg6?

The lesser evil would be 5 . . . Bg4.

| 6 | h4 | h6 |
| 7 | Ne5! | |

Herein lies the difference from the
variation which begins with 2 d4:
White can at once attack the bishop,
which can choose only between
the square h7 and an exchange
which weakens the pawn structure
in a decisive way.

7	. . .	Nd7
8	Nxg6	fxg6
9	d4!	

This prevents 9 . . . Ne5.

9	. . .	e5
10	Qg4	Qf6
11	Be3!	

The best. Less effective would have
been 11 Bg5 Qf7 etc. But if Black
castles then 12 Bg5! is played.

| 11 | . . . | Ne7? |

Position after 7 Ne5

Position after 11 . . . Ne7

Black should not lose so quickly, although strategically and in the long run his game could not be defended.

12 Ne4

Winning the queen.

Black resigned
(at move 16, in fact. E.W.)

Sicilian Defence

GAME 44

Buenos Aires 1939
Sicilian Defence

White: P.S. MILNER-BARRY
(England)
Black: J. FOLTYS (Czechoslovakia)

1	e4	c5
2	Nf3	Nc6
3	d4	cxd4
4	Nxd4	Nf6
5	Nc3	d6
6	Be2	

Milner-Barry is one of the best connoisseurs of the Dragon Variation (. . . g6) and he does not wish to avoid this line of play. There would be no serious objection to 6 Bg5, especially since White, in reply to 6 . . . h6, could go back with the bishop to e3 and try to exploit the weakness of d6.

6	. . .	g6
7	Be3	Bg7
8	Nb3	0-0
9	f4	Be6

10 0-0

10 g4 appears to lead only to a draw after 10 . . . d5 11 f5 Bc8 12 exd5 Nb4 etc. (Alekhine-Botwinnik, Nottingham, 1936).

10 . . .   Na5

A better line is 10 . . . Qc8, followed by 11 . . . Rd8 and eventually . . . d5, gaining control of that square.

11	f5	Bc4
12	g4	

An important improvization, instead of the alternative 12 Bd3 which has been exclusively adopted, without convincing success, for some time.

12	. . .	Nd7
13	Nxa5	Bxe2
14	Qxe2	Qxa5

15 Nd5   **Rfe8**

After this f7 becomes weak. Black
should play 15 . . . Rae8 and if
16 Bg5 then 16 . . . Nf6 with
defensive chances.

16 Qf2   **Ne5**

16 . . . Nf6 would be unsatisfactory
for Black because of 17 fxg6,
followed by 18 Bd4.

17 fxg6   **hxg6**

This will finally lose a pawn without compensation. Necessary was
17 . . . fxg6 and if 18 Bd4 then 18
. . . Rf8 19 Nxe7+ Kh8 20 Qg3 Nf3+
21 Rxf3 Bxd4+, followed by 22 . . .
Bxb2 with a possible defence.

18 Bd4   **Nf3+**

The likely attempt 18 . . . f6 would
have been successfully countered
by 19 g5!

19 Qxf3   **Bxd4+**

20 Kh1   **Rf8**

20 . . . f6 21 g5! would only have
given White new possibilities.

21 Nxe7+   **Kg7**

22 c3   **Be5**

23 Rf2   **Qd8**

24 Nd5   **Qh4**

A counter-attack based on the open
h-file is Black's only hope of
salvation.

25 Raf1   **Rae8**

But now he could have freed his
rook from the defence of f7 by
playing 25 . . . f6 and if 26 Rg2 (26
Nf4 Rad8) then 26 . . . Rf7, followed
by 27 . . . Rh8, offering fair
resistance.

26 Rg2

Threatening not only 27 g5 but also
(after 26 . . . f6 for example) a forced
exchange of queens by 27 Qf2!

26 . . .   **Qg5**

27 Ne3   **f6**

After this the Black queen will be
caught in spectacular fashion. 27 . . .
Kh7 would have helped only for a
short time after 28 Qe2, followed
by 29 Rf3 and 30 Rh3+.

28 Nf5+   **Kf7**

29 h4   **Rh8**

Hoping to sacrifice the exchange at
h4 after 30 Kg1. But White has a
more convincing reply.

White to move

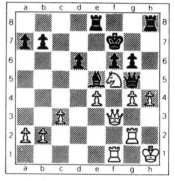

Position after 29 . . . Rh8

30 Rh2!   **gxf5**

Or 30 . . . Qf4 31 Qxf4 Bxf4 32
Rxf4 gxf5 33 gxf5 winning.

31 hxg5   **Rxh2+**

32 Kg1   **Reh8**

33 Qxf5   **Rxb2**

Clearly 33 . . . Rh1+ leads to nothing.

34 Qd7+   **Kg6**

35 Rxf6+

From beginning to end White's play has been full of energy and determination.

35 ...   Bxf6

36 Qf5+   Black resigns

If 36 ... Kg7 then 37 Qxf6+ Kg8 38 g6.

GAME 45

Buenos Aires 1939
Sicilian Defence

White: B. ROMETTI (France)
Black: C. DE RONDE (Holland)

1	e4	c5
2	Nf3	Nc6
3	d4	cxd4
4	Nxd4	Nf6
5	Nc3	d6
6	Be2	g6
7	Be3	Bg7
8	0-0	0-0
9	f4	

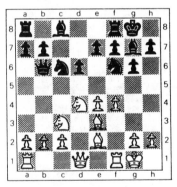

Position after 9 . . . Qb6

The usual move here is 9 Nb3 and the text advance has been considered dubious by theory because of the following reply. After this game, this opinion will need to be reviewed.

9 ...   Qb6

Seeking risks and, in fact, giving White the opportunity to make a strong pawn sacrifice. 9 . . . Bd7 would have left his opponent with an appreciable advantage in space.

10 e5!

I do not know whether this move has been played before. The latest edition of *Modern Chess Openings,* revised by Fine, mentions here only 10 Qd3 (!) and continues 10 . . . Ng4 11 Nd5 Bxd4 with equal chances. The idea of the sacrifice in the text is to forestall the response 10 . . . Qxb2 which would have been played after 10 Nf5.

10	...	dxe5
11	fxe5	Nxe5
12	Nf5	Qe6

If 12 ... Qd8 then simply 13 Qxd8 Rxd8 14 Nxe7+ Kf8 15 Bc5 or 14 ... Kh8 Bg5 etc. And if 12 ... Qxb2 then 13 Nxe7+, followed by 14 Bd4 with a won game.

13	Nxg7	Kxg7
14	Qd2	Neg4

As the continuation demonstrates, this loses by force. After 14 ... Ng8 15 Bd4 f6 16 Nb5 White would have full compensation for the pawn sacrificed.

15	Bd4	Qd7

There are no satisfactory moves. If 15 ... Nh6 then 16 Nd5 etc. with a quick decision.

White to move

Position after 15 ... Qd7

16 Qf4

As a reward for his tenth move White has rapidly obtained a won position, but he should have found the best way of forcing immediate resignation. This final manoeuvre consisted of 16 Bxg4 Qxg4 17 Rxf6! exf6 18 Nd5 with numerous deadly snares, the most direct one being 19 Bxf6+ Kg8 20 Ne7 mate. The queen manoeuvre in the text merely puts off the inevitable execution.

16	...	Qf5
17	Qg3	Qe6
18	Rae1	Nh6
19	Bd3	Qg4
20	Qe5	Ng8

Realizing that the pursuit of the White queen would be in vain. For example: 20 ... Qe6 21 Qf4 Qg4 22 Bxf6+ exf6 23 Qxf6+ Kg8 24 Nd5 winning.

21	Nd5	Bd7
22	Rxf6	

The simple 22 Nxe7 would also be sufficient.

22	...	exf6
23	Nxf6	Qxd4+
24	Qxd4	Nxf6
25	Rf1	Bf5
26	Bxf5	Rad8
27	Bd7	Rxd7
28	Qxf6+	Black resigns

A game of appreciable theoretical value.

GAME 46

Championship of Lithuania 1942
Sicilian Defence

White: W. HASENFUSS
Black: TETERIS

1	e4	c5	15	Bd4	Nf8
2	Nf3	d6	16	Qe3	Qc6
3	d4	cxd4	17	h5	Be6

If 17 . . . Ne6 there follows 18 hxg6 hxg6 19 f5.

4	Nxd4	Nf6	18	0-0-0	f5
5	Nc3	g6	19	exf6	exf6
6	Be2	Bg7	20	hxg6	hxg6
7	Be3	0-0	21	f5!	Bf7
8	g4				

Although the attack initiated by this move may be premature, it certainly presents Black with difficult problems and threatens a strong offensive.

8	. . .	d5

Clearly this is not an acceptable solution. 8 . . . Nc6 seems better.

If 21 . . . gxf5 22 gxf5 Bxf5 23 Rdg1.

9	e5	Ne4	22	Rh3	Re8
10	f4	Nxc3	23	Qd2	g5
11	bxc3	a6			

23 . . . Nd7, followed by 24 . . . Ne5 would have been much better.

The alternative was 11 . . . Nc6 or 11 . . . Nd7.

12	h4	Qc7	24	Rdh1	Qc7
13	Qd3	Nd7			
14	Nb3	Rd8			

He should still have played 24 . . . Nd7 which offered better resistance. Evidently White's combination was not suspected.

Black's weaknesses stand out more and more clearly. The idea of liberation by means of a sacrifice is not possible; for example, after 14 . . . Bxe5 play would go 15 fxe5 Nxe5 16 Qd1 Nxg4 17 Bxg4.

White to move

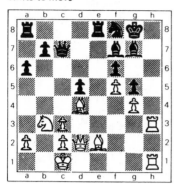

Position after 24 . . . Qc7

25 Qxg5!

Of course it is not possible to take the queen on pain of mate in two moves (26 Rh8+).

25 . . .	Bg6
26 fxg6	Rxe2
27 Bxf6	Nxg6
28 Qxg6	Black resigns

Since he cannot play 28 . . . Qxc3, naturally.

GAME 47

Munich 1942
Sicilian Defence

White: P. KERES
Black: J. FOLTYS

1 e4	c5
2 Nf3	d6
3 d4	cxd4
4 Nxd4	Nf6
5 f3	

In this move there is more venom than effectiveness. Black of course selects the most logical and promising line.

5 . . .	e5
6 Bb5+	Bd7
7 Bxd7+	Nbxd7

Less common is 7 . . . Qxd7 8 Nf5 d5 9 Bg5 d4! 10 Bxf6 gxf6 with apparent equality.

8 Nf5	Nb6
9 Bg5	d5
10 Qd3	

In order to reply to 10 . . . dxe4 with 11 Qb5+.

10 . . .   g6?

This weakens Black's pawn structure, which will definitely occasion material loss. Indicated was 10 . . . a6 11 Bxf6 gxf6, eventually followed by . . . d4.

11 Ne3	d4
12 Ng4	Be7
13 Nxe5	0-0
14 Bh6?	

This offers Black the chance of material compensation. Thus 14 0-0 is preferable.

14	...	Bb4+

But Black does not take advantage of this good opportunity to save his game. He ought to have played 14 ... Re8 with haste, after which White, in order to obtain control of the centre, would have had to give away a pawn. For example: 15 0-0 Bd6 16 f4! Bxe5 17 fxe5 Ng4 18 Bf4 Nxe5 19 Bxe5 Rxe5 20 Nd2 etc. After the unfortunate text move Black's game is clearly inferior.

15	c3!	Re8
16	cxb4	Rxe5
17	0-0	Rc8
18	Nd2	Re6
19	Rac1	Rec6
20	Rxc6	Rxc6
21	Nb3	Rc4
22	Rc1!	Qc7

If 22 ... Rxb4 there would follow 23 a3 Ra4 24 Nc5 winning the exchange.

White to move

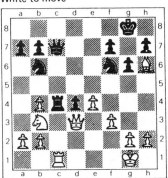

Position after 22 ... Qc7

23 Qxd4!

After this excellent move what follows is simple.

23	...	Rxd4
24	Rxc7	Rd7
25	Rc1	Ne8
26	Nc5	Re7
27	a4	f6
28	Bf4	Kf7
29	Kf2	Na8
30	Bb8	b6
31	Na6	Rb7
32	Rc8	Ke7
33	Bg3	**Black resigns**

This game, which was so important for Foltys, was very unsafely played by him.

GAME 48

Munich 1942
Sicilian Defence

White: J. FOLTYS
Black: G. STOLTZ

1	e4	c5
2	Nf3	e6
3	Nc3	d6
4	d4	cxd4
5	Nxd4	a6
6	a4	

Preventing Black's planned 6 . . . b5.

6	...	Nf6
7	g3	Bd7
8	Bg2	Nc6
9	0-0	Be7
10	Kh1	0-0
11	f4	Qc7
12	Nf3	Nb4
13	Be3	Rac8
14	a5!	d5
15	Bb6	Qb8
16	e5	Ne8
17	Nd4	

White has assured himself of a very considerable advantage through his exemplary handling of the opening. Nonetheless, in the next few moves he lets an opportunity pass by.

17	...	Nc7
18	f5	Ne8

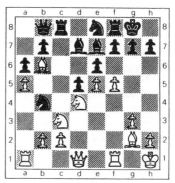

Position after 18 . . . Ne8

19 fxe6?

Much better is 19 Bh3! with the following possible continuation: 19 . . . Qxe5 20 Re1 Qf6 (20 . . . Qd6? 21 fxe6 fxe6 22 Rxe6!) 21 fxe6 fxe6 22 Nxe6 Rf7 23 Bg4! with numerous threats, the main one being 24 Bd4 etc.

19	...	fxe6
20	Rxf8+	Bxf8
21	Qe2	Nc7!

After 21 . . . Nc6 White would be able to continue 22 Nxd5 with advantage.

22	Bh3	Nc6
23	Qe3	Nxd4
24	Qxd4	Nb5

More prudent would have been 24 . . . Re8 first.

25	Nxb5	axb5
26	Ba7	Qc7
27	c3	b4?

A deplorable mistake which quickly loses the game. The way to proceed was 27 ... Ra8 28 Bb6 Qc8 and Black would have good defensive means at his disposal.

28	cxb4	Qc4? ?

Black's last hope could have been 28 ... Qc2.

29 Qxc4 Rxc4 30 b5 Kf7 31 a6 bxa6 32 bxa6 Bb4 33 Bb8 Bc6, 34 a7 Ba8 35 Bd6! Bxd6 36 exd6 Rc6 37 Rf1+ Ke8 38 d7+ Kxd7 39 Rf8 Rc1+ 40 Kg2 Rc2+ 41 Kf3 Bb7 42 Rb8! Kc7 43 a8(Q) Bxa8 44 Rxa8 Rxh2 45 Bxe6 h5 46 Bxd5 Rxb2 47 Rh8 Rh2 48 Kf4 Kd6 49 Bf3 h4 50 Rxh4 Rxh4+ 51 gxh4 Black resigns

GAME 49

Buenos Aires 1939
Sicilian Defence

White: A. ALEKHINE (France)
Black: A. TSVETKOV (Bulgaria)

1	e4	c5
2	Nf3	d6
3	c3	

The idea of this unusual move is to construct a pawn centre with 4 d4 if Black does not play 3 ... Nf6 immediately. After the knight move White, with the advance of the e-pawn, has the chance of obtaining a favourable position, particularly since the line has not been analysed like other variations of the Sicilian.

3	...	Nf6
4	e5	dxe5
5	Nxe5	Nc6!

Consenting to impair his pawn structure with the aim of eliminating White's only developed piece.

6	Nxc6	bxc6
7	Bc4	Bf5

The play against White's backward queen's pawn will compensate for the weakness created on the queen's side.

8	d3	e6
9	Qf3	Qd7
10	h3	

With the object of answering 10 ... Bd6 with 11 Nd2 (and then Ne4 or Nb3) and 10 ... Rd8 with 11 0-0 etc. In reply to immediate castling Black would have played 10 Bd6, followed eventually by ... Ng4.

10	...	Be7
11	Nd2	

In this way the following transaction will secure White a slightly preferable ending; however it would perhaps have been more promising to play 11 0-0 Rd8 12 Rd1 Nd5 13 Be3, eventually followed by Nd2-e4.

11 ...   Rd8

12 0-0

And not 12 Ne4 Nxe4 13 dxe4 Bxe4.

12 ...   Bxd3

13 Bxd3   Qxd3

14 Qxc6+   Qd7

15 Qa6?

By simply playing 15 Qxd7+ Rxd7 16 Nc4 White would have achieved the same advantage as in the game. The text move is inconsequential because Black's middle-game chances are now equal.

15 ...   0-0

16 Nc4   Qc7

17 Qa5

Trying to rectify his previous queen move.

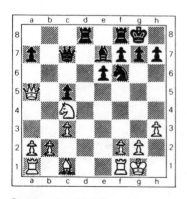

Position after 17 Qa5

17 ...   Qxa5?

Fortunately for White, Black here shows evidence of a lack of initiative and decision; by avoiding the exchange of queens he would have obtained a middle-game which might perhaps have yielded a different result. For example: 17 ... Qb7 18 Be3 Nd5! 19 Bxc5 Nf4 or 18 Bf4? Qe4 19 Bc7 Rc8 etc. and Black's development is compensation for the weakness on the queen's flank. The endgame that follows is highly instructive, despite the apparent simplicity of the means employed by White, and represents a typical example of a consistent exploitation of the double weakness of two pawns on the same side of the board.

18 Nxa5   Rd6

19 Be3   Ra6

20 Nb3

White does not need to prevent the advance of the Black c-pawn because this would turn out to be to his own advantage after 20 ... c4 21 Nd2 Rc8 22 b3 Nd5 23 Bd4 Bf6 24 Nxc4 Nxc3 25 Bxc3 Bxc3 26 Rac1 with a strong knight and a pawn majority on the queen's side.

20 ...   Rc8

21 c4!

Depriving the Black knight of its best square, d5. It is interesting to observe how Black, without committing any errors, will be first reduced to complete passiveness and then obliged to give up material without being able to improvize anything in his position.

21 ...   Kf8

22 Rfd1   Rd6

The reduction in forces is welcome to the side which has its movements restricted — as is Black's case since his pieces are paralysed by the necessity of protecting his c-pawn. But as the continuation shows, the combination of three pieces (rook, bishop, and knight) supported by the king is all that is required to exercise decisive pressure on the queen's side.

23 Rxd6   Bxd6

24 Rd1   Ke7

25 Na5   Be5

Parrying the strong threat 26 Nb7.

26 Rd3!

Solely because of the possibility of manoeuvring this active rook does Black's position (which would have been fairly pleasant after, say, 26 Rd2 Ne4 or 26 b3 Bc3) gradually become critical.

26 . . .   Rc7

And not 26 . . . Bxb2 27 Rb3 Be5 28 Rb7+ Rc7 because of 29 Nc6+ winning a piece.

27 Rb3   Nd7

28 f4

Just at the right moment because 28 . . . Bd4 loses a pawn after 29 Bxd4 cxd4 30 Rd3. After 28 . . . Bf6 the bishop is unable to co-operate in the defence of the queen's wing.

28 . . .   Bd6

29 Kf2   Nb6

30 Kf3   Kd7

31 Rd3

The immediate 31 Rb5 would perhaps have shortened the game but as Black is from now on condemned to complete inactivity White really has no need to hurry.

31 . . .   Ke7

32 g4

This and the following pawn moves have a very clear purpose; White is preparing the most favourable position on the king's flank for the moment when he breaks through on the other side.

32 . . .   f6

33 h4   Na4

34 Rb3   Nb6

35 Rb5   Kd7

36 h5   Ke7

37 a3   Kd7

38 Ke4

The initial move of the winning plan. The king will be provisionally reserved for the protection of the c-pawn, which will allow for the knight to go from a5 to b5 with decisive effect.

38 . . .   Ke7

39 Kd3   Kd7

40 Nb3   Na4

41 Nd2   Kc6

41 . . . a6 42 Rb8 would also be hopeless.

42 b3   Nb6

43 Ne4   Nd7

44 Ra5   Be7

Black has managed to defend his c-pawn adequately, but now it is the a-pawn's turn!

45	Nc3!	Rb7
46	Nb5	Kb6
47	b4	a6
48	Nc3	Kc7

White planned 49 Na4+ etc. The pawn can no longer be protected and the alternative of abandoning it by 48 . . . Rc7 would have proved that Black is without hope: 49 Ne4! Kb7 (or 49 . . . f5 50 gxf5 exf5 51 Nc3, followed by 52 Nd5+, winning) 50 bxc5 Nb8 51 Nd6+.

49	Rxa6	cxb4
50	Nb5+	Kd8
51	axb4	Bxb4
52	Rxe6	Bc5
53	Bd2!	

Intending a decisive simplification: 54 Ba5+ Bb6 (or 54 . . . Nb6 55 Rc6) 55 Rxb6 Rxb6 (or 55 . . . Nxb6 56 c5) 56 Kd4.

53	. . .	Nf8
54	Rc6	Nd7

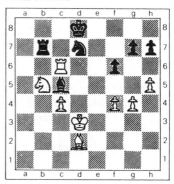

White to move

Position after 54 . . . Nd7

55 Ke4!

The weakness of Black's e6 permits the White king to start up a mating attack, thereby bringing the game to an end more rapidly than by any other exploitation of his material advantage.

55	. . .	Ke7
56	Kd5	Bg1
57	Bb4+	Kd8
58	Ke6	

Threatening 59 Be7+, followed by mate next move and thus forcing the win. **Black resigned.**

GAME 50

Prague 1943
Sicilian Defence

White: A. ALEKHINE
Black: J. PODGORNY

1	e4	c5
2	c3	

In reply to this relatively little-played move (which is in no way inferior to the other systems of combating the Sicilian Defence), Black can play: (a) 2 . . . e6 3 d4 d5 4 exd5 etc. (b) 2 . . . d6, after which White would, of course, continue with 3 d4. (c) 2 . . . Nf6 3 e5 Nd5 4 d4 e6 etc., a form of Alekhine's Defence. In fact the text move can result in Black's queen finding herself in an exposed position. But, on the other hand, White will have to seek, by means of tactical manoeuvres, compensation for the isolation of his central pawn.

2	...	d5
3	exd5	Qxd5
4	d4	Nc6
5	Nf3	

Equally possible would be 5 dxc5 Qxc5 6 Be3 Qa5 etc., but White has no wish to avoid the isolation of the pawn since he desires to demonstrate that Black will not have available the necessary time to exploit this weakness.

5	...	Bg4
6	Be2	cxd4

If 6 . . . e6 immediately then 7 h3! Bh5 8 c4, followed by castling, with complications advantageous to White.

7	cxd4	e6
8	Nc3	Bb4

This aggressive move, in conjunction with the following one, leads to complicated tactical problems.

9	0-0	Qa5

White to move

Position after 9 . . . Qa5

We are already at the critical point in the game. If White does not find the line of play appropriate to the position he will not only lose his advantage in development (which rests especially in the fact that his king is in absolute safety whilst the future of that of his rival is uncertain) but will also find that the eventual weakness of his isolated pawn may occasion him serious trouble. If, for example, he plays 10 Bd2 Nf6 11 a3 then the continuation 11 . . . Bxc3 12 bxc3 Ne4 13 Be1! would, to be sure, give him full satisfaction were it not for the fact that Black, instead of such a line, would answer 11 a3 with 11 . . . Be7! 12 Nb5 Qd8, followed by 13 . . . 0-0 and White would have achieved absolutely nothing. Also tempting at first sight is 10 d5 since 10 . . . 0-0-0 would be punished by 11 Ng5!; but — apart from the consequences of 10 . . . Rd8 11 Ng5 Bf5 etc., which would leave nothing clear on the horizon — Black can simply play 10 . . . exd5 11 Qxd5 (if 11 Nxd5 0-0-0 with advantage)

and now either 11 . . . Qxd5 12
Nxd5 Bd6 or 11 . . . Bxc3 12 Qe4+
Be6 13 bxc3 Nf6, followed by
castling on the king's side, with a
satisfactory game for Black in both
cases. Consequently White is
obliged, on account of the very
position, to seek a combinative
continuation which, in some lines,
will involve implicit sacrifices. The
objectives that White will pursue
are (1) the Black king and (2) the
Black queen. The following move
requires a very thorough analytical
examination of the position.

10 a3!!

The difficulty of this move lies
firstly in the fact that it does not
appear to threaten anything (an
exchange of the two rooks for the
Black queen would be of doubtful
value in this position — see the note
to White's next move) and it permits Black to play an important
developing move. Secondly, not
only does it fail to parry the threat
10 . . . Bxc3 11 bxc3 Qxc3 but, so
to speak, it actually invites Black
to put this plan into operation.
Therefore the consequences of 10
. . . Nf6 and 10 . . . Bxc3 had to be
examined with particular care.

10 . . . Nf6

If 10 . . . Bxc3 11 bxc3 Qxc3 the
continuation would have been 12
Rb1! (unconvincing on the other
hand would be 12 Bd2 Qb2 13 Rb1
Qxa3 14 Rxb7 Nge7 and Black will,
at least, be able to consolidate his
position by castling) 12 . . . Nge7
(if 12 . . . 0-0-0 then 13 Qa4!
(threatening 14 d5) Bxf3 14 Bxf3

Nge7 15 Qb5 Rd7 16 Bf4! with a
winning position in view of the
threat, after 16 . . . Qxd4 or 16 . . .
Qa5, of 17 Bxc6 Nxc6 18 Qxc6+!)
13 Rxb7 0-0 14 Qa4! and one cannot see how Black can parry the
multiple threats of his adversary.

11 d5!

This move alone (and not the
exchange mentioned above 11 axb4
Qxa1 12 Qb3 Bxf3 13 Be3 Qxf1+
14 Bxf1 Bd5 15 Nxd5 Nxd5 16 b5
Nce7, followed by 17 . . . 0-0 with
a defensible game for Black) con-
stitutes one of the most important
objectives of the combinative play
begun with 10 a3!!

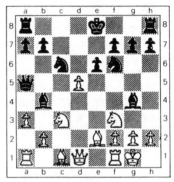

Position after 11 d5

11 . . . exd5

Besides this move, the following
were to be considered: (a) the inter-
polation of 11 . . . Rd8 (or 11 . . .
0-0-0), which would have been
triumphantly refuted by 12 Qb3!,
threatening 13 axb4, followed by 14
Be3 winning the queen; (b) 11 . . .
Nxd5 which would have received the
reply 12 Nxd5 exd5 13 axb4 Qxa1
14 Qb3 Bxf3 15 Bg5! Qxf1+ 16

Bxf1 Be4 17 f3! and Black, not having managed to castle, will succumb, given the dislocation of his pieces (the knight will be expelled by b5). After the text move White will force a liquidation that will guarantee him a slight material advantage.

12	axb4	Qxa1

13 Nd2!

Threatening 14 Nb3 and thus forcing the exchange that follows.

13	...	Bxe2
14	Qxe2+	Ne7

If 14 ... Kf8 then 15 Nb3 Qa6 16 b5 Qb6 17 Na4 Nd4 18 Qd1 and wins.

15 Re1!

More attractive but insufficient would be 15 Qb5+ Nd7 16 Re1 on account of the reply 16 ... Kd8!

15	...	0-0

Evidently this is the only chance of avoiding an immediate catastrophe.

16	Nb3	Qa6
17	Qxa6	bxa6
18	Rxe7	Rab8

Likewise after 18 ... Rfb8 19 Na2! Re8 20 Rxe8+ Rxe8 21 h3 White's material advantage would gradually impose itself.

19 b5

Now this advance prevents for good the entry of the Black rooks into enemy territory.

19	...	axb5
20	Rxa7	b4
21	Ne2	Rfc8
22	f3	Ra8
23	Rxa8	Rxa8
24	Kf2	Nd7
25	Nf4	Nb6
26	Ke3	Rc8
27	Kd3	g5

A desperate try since there exists no defence against the threat of 28 Be3 Nc4 29 Bd4.

28	Nh5	Black resigns

In fact after 28 ... h6 29 Be3 Nc4 30 Nf6+ Kf8 31 Bc5+ Kg7 32 Bd4 etc., Black's whole position crumbles away.

Alekhine's Defence

GAME 51

Buenos Aires 1939
Alekhine's Defence

White: E. REED (Chile)
Black: G. DANIELSSON (Sweden)

One of the very few revelations of the 1939 Buenos Aires Olympiad was Ernst Reed, the young Chilean (of German ancestry) whose style was distinguished by its clear energy and daring attacking conception. The following game is a specimen characteristic of his understanding of the game.

1	e4	Nf6
2	e5	Nd5
3	d4	d6
4	Nf3	Nc6

When one chooses a pattern of play which is in itself dubious, as is the case with Alekhine's Defence, it is absolutely vital to know in depth at least the most important lines derived therefrom. After this incorrect move (4 . . . Bg4 would have been better) White obtains a strong, perhaps already decisive, attack.

5	c4	Nb6
6	e6!	fxe6

Naturally there is no alternative. Black's greatest disadvantage is the difficulty of developing his two bishops, and he will not succeed in doing so without returning the pawn that he has 'won'.

7 Bd3

This simple developing move is more convincing than 7 Ng5 after which 7 . . . e5 8 Qf3 Nxd4 9 Qf7+ Kd7 would solve Black's problem without any imminent danger.

7	. . .	Nd7

8 0-0

White, convinced that he has the superior development and the better game, quite rightly prefers not to force events. With 8 Ng5 he could have won the exchange, for example: 8 . . . Nf6 9 Bxh7 Nxh7 10 Qh5+ Kd7 11 Nxh7 Nxd4 12 Na3 Qe8 (there is nothing better) 13 Nf6+ exf6 14 Qxh8 but after 14 . . . Qg6 Black would nonetheless have obtained good fighting prospects.

8	. . .	Nf6
9	Re1	e5?

His opponent's quiet developing moves have made Black nervous and he hurriedly gives back the pawn. It would have been better to play 9 . . . g6, after which White would have had to increase the pressure with another pawn sacrifice (10 d5 exd5 11 cxd5 Nxd5 12 Ng5!). But would he have decided to play this line? It is doubtful. On the other hand, after the text move White not only maintains his attack but does so with material equal.

10	dxe5	Nxe5
11	Nxe5	dxe5
12	Rxe5	Qd6

If 12 . . . Bg4 then the reply 13 Qb3 would be disturbing.

13	Bf4	Bg4
14	Qd2	

Preventing 14 . . . 0-0-0 since 15 Rd5 would then win at once.

14	. . .	Qd7
15	Nc3	

It is remarkable that this move could have led to a considerable and unnecessary tangle. The simple technical solution to the problem was 15 h3 and if 15 . . . 0-0-0 then 16 Qa5!! Qxd3 17 Rc5 winning.

15	. . .	Rd8?

The Swedish champion was certainly not on form this day, since otherwise he would have decided to castle, with the following possibilities: 16 Nd5 e6 and if 16 Re3 e5 17 Bxe5 Bb4 etc., leaving White with insufficient to win. Only the sacrifice of a piece 16 Nb5! Qxd3 17 Qa5 (and if 17 . . . Qxc4 18 Rc5 or 17 . . . Kd7 18 Re3 Qc2 19 Qxc7+ Ke8 20 Rae1) would have invigorated the attack. But in any case instead of 16 . . . Qxd3 Black could play the quieter 16 . . . c6, sustaining the position for some time.

16	Nd5	c6

Truly forced, as 16 . . . e6 would be fatal owing to 17 Nxc7+, followed by 18 Rxe6+ etc. The following final attack is exemplarily elegant.

White to move

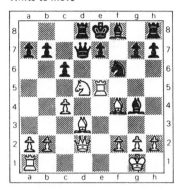

Position after 16 . . . c6

17 Qc2!

An intermediary move of great importance which prepares for the following bishop attack. The immediate 17 h3 would not have brought success after 17 . . . cxd5 18 hxg4 dxc4.

17	. . .	Kf7

Forced because of the threat of 18 Bg6+.

18	h3	cxd5

Again forced because if 18 . . . Be6 19 Rxe6! Qxe6 20 Bf5.

19	hxg4	Qxg4

This loses at once but it is certain that Black's fate was already decided.

20 Bf5!!

In the purest and most lucid attacking style!

20	. . .	Qxf4

21	Be6+	Ke8	24	Rxd7	Nxd7
22	Qa4+	Rd7	25	Rd1	Black resigns
23	Rxd5	Qc7			

King's Pawn, Nimzowitsch Defence

GAME 52

Buenos Aires 1939
King's Pawn, Nimzowitsch Defence

White: E. ROJAHN (Norway)
Black: M. CZERNIAK (Palestine)

1	e4	Nc6
2	d4	d5
3	e5	Bf5
4	g4!	

White adopts, not without success, a stratagem common in a similar variation of the Caro-Kann Defence 1 e4 c6 2 d4 d5 3 e5 Bf5 4 g4 with the object of taking advantage of the exposed position of the Black bishop. The idea is particularly enticing since Black will find difficulty in undertaking a counter-attack in the centre because his c-pawn is blocked by the knight and his f-pawn is immobilized by the necessity of protecting the e-pawn against the White knight at f4.

4	...	Bg6
5	Nh3	e6
6	Nf4	

However this is a slight inexactitude which would have hampered the effect of his plan. 6 Be3 first was the right move, and only then Nf4.

| 6 | ... | Be4 |
| 7 | Rg1 | Nh6 |

Not taking into account the possibility of 7 ... Nb4 8 Na3 c5 which would have assured him of a game full of promise.

| 8 | Be3 | Be7 |
| 9 | Nd2 | Bh4? |

Of the two mistakes this is decidedly the greater, since after the exchange of the Black queen's bishop the chances are in White's favour. Better is 9 ... Bg6, followed eventually by ... Qd7, ... 0-0-0, and ... f6.

| 10 | Nxe4 | dxe4 |
| 11 | Bg2 | Qe7 |

He tries to protect his e-pawn

indirectly but this would not have
been successful had White selected
the simply reply 12 c3! and if 12
. . . 0-0-0 (or 12 . . . Rd8) then 13
Bxe4 Nxe5 14 Qa4 with advantage
to White.

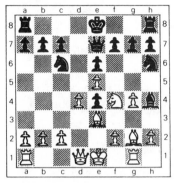

Position after 11 . . . Qe7

12 Bxe4!?

In no way an error, but a counter-
combination by which he hopes to
win more material than by a tranquil
plan. In fact the plausible variation
12 . . . Nxe5 13 g5! Bxg5 14 Rxg5
Qxg5 15 dxe5 Qxe5 16 Bxb7 Rd8
17 Bc6+ Ke7 18 Nd3 Qxh2 19 Bc5+
would be advantageous for him.
But Czerniak, who is a tactician
par excellence, discovers an
interesting way of complicating
things.

12 . . .   Nxe5

13 g5!   Nc4!

An ingenious resource which, however, could hardly have produced
the desired effect after 14 gxh6
Nxe3 15 Qe2! g5! 16 Nh5 Nd5 (or
16 . . . Nf5 17 Bxf5 exf5 18 Ng7+,
followed by 19 Qxe7+ and 20 Nxf5+)
17 Bxd5 exd5 18 Nf6+ Kf8 19 Qxe7+

Kxe7 20 Nxd5+ Kd6 21 Nf6 with
advantage to White.

14 gxh6   Nxe3

15 hxg7?

Totally fulfilling Black's hopes and
desires.

15 . . .   Bxf2+

A powerful intermediary check
which tilts the balance in Black's
favour.

16 Ke2

Clearly forced.

16 . . .   Rg8

17 Qd3   Bxg1

Black has no other choice, as his
bishop is now truly caught.

18 Qb5+   c6!

Again a well calculated finesse. If
immediately 18 . . . Kd8 then 19
Rxg1 Nf5 20 Qxb7 Rc8 21 Bxf5
exf5+ 22 Kd3 and White has the
advantage.

19 Bxc6+   Kd8

20 Bxb7!

Insufficient would be 20 Rxg1 Nf5!
21 Qa5+ Qc7 and Black stands
better.

20 . . .   Nxc2!

Now Black seems, at last, to be free
from all anguish; he not only has an
extra rook but the other White rook
and the queen (indirectly) are
attacked. Apparently there is no
perpetual check; for example: 21
Qa5+ Qc7 22 Qg5+ Ke8 23 Qb5+
Qd7 and 24 Bc6 is impossible
because of 24 . . . Nxd4+. Nonethe-

less White saves his position with a combinative miracle.

21 Qa5+   Qc7

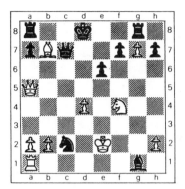

Position after 21 ... Qc7

22 Nxe6+!!

The idea of this sacrifice is to permit a queen check at h5 each time the Black king goes to e8; in addition the king cannot escape to c7 (in the position that is reached after move

33) because of the reply 34 Rc1 which would give White an attack that would rapidly be decisive. The following moves demonstrate convincingly that it is impossible for Black to avoid the draw.

22 ...	**fxe6**
23 Qg5+	**Qe7**
24 Qa5+	**Kd7**
25 Qb5+	**Kd8**
26 Qa5+	**Qc7**
27 Qg5+	**Ke8**
28 Qh5+	**Ke7**
29 Qg5+	**Kd7**
30 Qb5+	**Kd8**
31 Qg5+	**Qe7**
32 Qa5+	**Kd7**
33 Qb5+	

Drawn

This encounter can certainly take its place in an anthology of thrilling games.

PART THREE : CLOSED GAMES

Queen's Gambit Declined, Orthodox Defence

GAME 53

Buenos Aires 1939
Queen's Gambit Declined

White: R. GRAU (Argentina)
Black: E. ELISKASES (Germany)

1	d4	Nf6
2	c4	e6
3	Nc3	d5
4	Bg5	Be7
5	e3	h6
6	Bh4	0-0
7	Nf3	Ne4
8	Bxe7	Qxe7

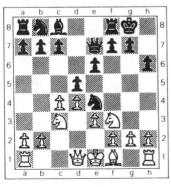

Position after 8 . . . Qxe7

9 cxd5

If 9 Qc2 Nxc3 10 Qxc3 the new method 10 . . . dxc4 11 Bxc4 Nd7 (possibly also 11 . . . b6) offers a satisfactory defence. Characteristic of Black's chances in this variation, especially if White plays passively, is the game Lundin-Raud played in the preliminary section, which continued as follows (after 11 . . . Nd7): 12 0-0 b6 13 Rfd1 Bb7 14 Rac1 Rfd8 15 Be2 c5 16 Qa3 a5 17 Nd2 e5! 18 dxc5 Nxc5 19 Nc4 Qg5 20 g3 Qf6 21 Rxd8+ Rxd8 22 Rd1 Rxd1+ 23 Bxd1 Ba6 24 Nd2 Qd6 25 Qc3 Ne4! and White resigned.

9	. . .	Nxc3
10	bxc3	exd5
11	Qb3	Qd6

For the move 11 . . . Rd8 see the game Ståhlberg-Piazzini (Game 54).

12	c4	dxc4
13	Bxc4	Nc6

14	Qc3	Bg4
15	Nd2	

Since the game Euwe-Eliskases, Noordwijk 1938, 15 0-0 has been considered too daring, principally because (as is usually the case) White lost that game. But as the withdrawal of the knight in the text gives Black easy equalizing chances, Euwe's doubtful move probably requires a more detailed analysis.

15	. . .	Rad8
16	0-0	

The natural reply and at the same time a little trap; the attempt 16 . . . Nxd4 17 exd4 Qxd4 would now be refuted by 18 Nb1!

16	. . .	Ne7
17	Rfc1	

Allowing the following emancipation. 17 h3 Bf5 (or Bc8) 18 Rfd1 was to be considered although Black would have found adequate counter-play in any case.

| 17 | . . . | c5! |

Exactly calculated. The principal variation after 18 Ne4 would be 18 . . . cxd4 19 Nxd6 dxc3 20 Nxb7 Rd7 21 Na5 Nd5! 22 f3 Be6 23 e4 Nf4 24 Rxc3 Bxc4 25 Rxc4 Rd2 with advantage to Black.

18	Nb3	cxd4
19	Nxd4	Nf5!?

The centralization of the White knight was truly strong and its elimination is thus desirable. But why not try to achieve this without losing a pawn? In fact there would be no objection to 19 . . . a6

20 h3 Bc8 21 a4 Nc6. If in this case 22 Nxc6 Qxc6 25 a5 then simply 25 . . . Be6 with a certain draw.

20	Nxf5	Bxf5
21	Qa5!	

Rightly recognizing that the couple of attacking moves that Black will play after losing the pawn can easily be neutralized.

21	. . .	Be4
22	Qxa7	

And not 22 f3 b6!, saving the pawn.

22	. . .	Qg6
23	Bf1	Rd2
24	Qa5	

Intending to exchange a pair of rooks by 25 Rc8 if Black plays 24 . . . Rfd8.

24	. . .	Rd5
25	Qb4	Rfd8

White to move

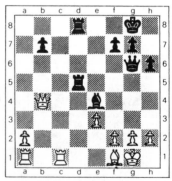

Position after 25 . . . Rfd8

26 Rc4?

An elementary error which is even more surprising from Grau, who

usually attends to his tactical pro-
cedures with the utmost care, even
in unimportant games. After the
natural 26 g3, followed by the
exchange of bishops at g2 Black
would have to fight very hard to
obtain a draw.

| 26 | ... | Bxg2! |

A two-move combination (27 Bxg2
Rd1+ or 27 Rg4 Qf6) which not
only re-establishes the material
equilibrium but also irremediably
compromises the position of the
White king. From now on Eliskases
exploits his advantage in his usual
forceful style.

27	Rg4	Qf6
28	Rb1	Bf3
29	Rg3	Rd1

| 30 | Rxd1 | Rxd1 |

Threatening 31 . . . Qa6.

31	Qc4	Qc6
32	Qxc6	Bxc6
33	f4	

The only defence against 33 . . .
Bb5, but now in a few moves Black
forces a won pawn ending.

33	...	Ra1
34	f5	Kf8
35	f6	gxf6
36	Rh3	Bb5
37	Rf3	Ke7
38	e4	Ke6
39	White resigns	

GAME 54

Buenos Aires 1939
Queen's Gambit Declined

White: G. STAHLBERG (Sweden)
Black: L. PIAZZINI (Argentina)

1	d4	Nf6
2	c4	e6
3	Nc3	d5
4	Nf3	Be7
5	Bg5	0-0
6	e3	h6

This intermediary move, in connection with Lasker's . . . Ne4, is
the 'last cry' of this defence to the
Queen's Gambit.

7	Bh4	Ne4
8	Bxe7	Qxe7
9	cxd5	

The alternative 9 Qc2 gives Black a
satisfactory defence by simply playing 9 . . . Nxc3 10 bxc3 Nd7 (see
the game Lundin-Raud in the preliminary section).*

| 9 | ... | Nxc3 |

*See page 119

10	bxc3	exd5
11	Qb3	Rd8

This old move is, in my opinion, as good as Bernstein's 11 ... Qd6, successfully adopted later by Eliskases (in his games against Euwe at Noordwijk and against Grau at Buenos Aires). The present game, despite being lost by Black, confirms its value.

12	c4	dxc4!

Black shuns an exchange of queens (12 ... Nc6 13 cxd5 Qb4+ etc.) in order to be able to exploit better all the tactical chances that the position offers in the middle-game (White's uncastled king, the possibility of attacking with the knight at a5 etc.); all these chances are very clear.

13	Bxc4	Nc6
14	Qc3	Bg4

If now 14 ... Qb4 then 15 Rac1 and White obtains some pressure on the c-file.

15	0-0

Practically forced.

15	...	Bxf3
16	gxf3	Qf6
17	Be2	Rd6

Although Black obtains a satisfactory game with this last move it is not the most recommendable because it reduces the dynamism of the position with the temporary immobilization of the knight. A more logical procedure would be 17 ... Rd7 and if 18 Rab1 then 18 ... Nd8, followed by 19 ... c6, and Black

has neutralized White's threats on the queen's flank.

18	Kh1	Re8
19	Rae1	

A sufficient defence against 19 ... Nxd4 which would now be refuted by 20 exd4 Rde6 21 Bd1.

19	...	Qe6!

A fine positional move which gives Black a clear advantage, since White, in order to defend the attacked a-pawn, must lose a tempo.

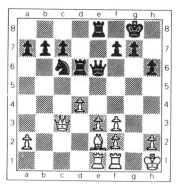

Position after 19 ... Qe6

20	Rg1!

A profound pawn sacrifice which shows that Ståhlberg had few illusions about the solidity of his position were he to continue with his passive defence. It is evident that if 20 a3 Qd5 21 Rg1 Rf6 22 Rg3 Qa5 virtually forces an exchange of queens, since if 23 Qa1 or 23 Qc1 Black would gain superiority with 23 ... Ne7.

20	...	Qxa2?

Having calculated the immediate consequences of this capture, Black is unable to resist the temptation, and is finally the victim of a positional attack executed in masterly style. He should have realized that his adversary was proposing an attack not on the king but on the queen, and that the sacrifice was not based on a particular combination but on a general appreciation of the position. Thus he should have persisted with his original idea 20 . . . Qd5! and if 21 Rg3 then 21 . . . Qa5.

21	d5	Ne5
22	e4	Rg6

One of the points of Black's scheme. If now 23 Qxc7 then 23 . . . Rxg1+ 24 Kxg1 Qb3! with counter-chances.

23 Rg3!

Making his king's position safe once and for all.

23	. . .	Rxg3

If 23 . . . Re7 then 24 Kg2.

24	hxg3	Re7
25	Kg2	

Threatening to hunt down the queen with 26 Bb5!, followed by 27 Ra1.

25	. . .	Qa4

In the case of 25 . . . a6 the attack 26 Qb4 would have been very good.

26	Ra1	Qd7
27	Rxa7	b6
28	f4	Ng6
29	Bf3	

After this Black has no good defence against the threat of 30 e5, followed by 31 e6 etc.

29	. . .	f6

Weakening the position of the knight, and causing immediate catastrophe.

30	Ra8+	Kh7
31	Qc2	Rf7

The last hope: 32 e5 fxe5 33 fxe5? Rxf3 34 Kxf3 Qxd5+.

32	e5	fxe5
33	Be4!	

With the threat (if 33 . . . Qg4) of 34 Bxg6+ Qxg6 35 Rh8+. **Black resigned.**

GAME 55

Cracow 1942
Queen's Gambit Declined

White: A. ALEKHINE
Black: KUNERTH

1	d4	d5		3	Nc3	Nf6
2	c4	e6		4	Nf3	c6

5	e3	Nbd7
6	Bd3	Bd6

The Meran Variation 6 . . . dxc4
7 Bxc4 b5 8 Bd3 a6 — so popular
in the past — is less frequently
played nowadays.

7	e4	dxe4
8	Nxe4	Nxe4
9	Bxe4	Nf6
10	Bc2	Bb4+
11	Kf1	

Sharper and much better than 11
Bd2 which is refuted by 11 . . . Qa5.

11	. . .	b6
12	h4	Bb7
13	Rh3	Bd6
14	Qe2	Qc7
15	b3	

More energetic would have been 15
Bd2 0-0-0 16 b4! and if 16 . . . c5
then 17 dxc5 bxc5 18 b5.

15	. . .	0-0-0
16	Bb2	h6

Instead of this passive move 16 . . .
c5 would be preferable.

17	Ne5	Rhe8?
18	a3!	Bxe5

After this exchange Black's situation
remains extremely precarious. But
now 18 . . . c5 would solve nothing
owing to 19 b4!

19	dxe5	Nd7
20	Rg3!	g5

A desperate move since 20 . . . g6
21 b4 could not offer Black worse

prospects.

21	hxg5	hxg5
22	Rxg5	Rh8
23	Qg4!	

Much superior to 23 Rh5 c5,
followed by 24 . . . Qc6 with an
effective threat.

23	. . .	c5
24	Ke2	Nb8
25	Rd1	Nc6

White to move

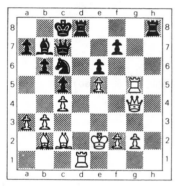

Position after 25 . . . Nc6

26	Rd6!	Rhf8
27	Rxd8+	Qxd8
28	Rg7	Kb8
29	Qf4	Qd7
30	Qd2	

Simpler than 30 g4 etc.

30	. . .	Qe7
31	Qd6+	Qxd6
32	exd6	e5!
33	Bf5!	Nd4+
34	Bxd4	exd4

35	g4	b5
36	Kd3!	

And not 36 cxb5 Bd5 37 Bc2 Rd8.

36	...	Ba6
37	g5	bxc4+
38	bxc4	Bb7
39	f4	Bg2
40	Kd2	

A shorter road to victory would have been 40 Ke2!

40	...	Bf1
41	Bd3	Bxd3
42	Kxd3	Kc8
43	Rh7!	Kd7
44	Rh6	f6
45	g6!	Re8

46	Rh5	Re3+

Or 46 . . . Kxd6 47 Rd5+ Kc6 48 Rf5.

47	Kd2	Rg3
48	Rxc5	Kxd6
49	Rd5+	Ke7

If 49 . . . Kc6 then 50 Rg5! fxg5 51 f5 etc.

50	f5	Rxa3
51	Rxd4	Rg3
52	Re4+	Kd6
53	Re6+	Kc5
54	Rxf6	Kxc4
55	Rf7	a5
56	g7	Kd4
57	f6	Black resigns

GAME 56

Buenos Aires 1939
Queen's Gambit Declined

White: V. MENCHIK (Great Britain)
Black: S. GRAF (Germany)

1	d4	d5
2	c4	e6
3	Nf3	Nf6
4	Nc3	Nbd7

A strong reply to this uncommon move is 5 cxd5 and after 5 . . . exd5 6 Bf4. White should not restrict the action of the bishop as she does in this game.

5	e3	Bb4

6	Bd3	c5
7	0-0	0-0
8	Bd2	

The fact is that White has no more effective move than this one, since there are none which would follow logically from the previous moves.

8	...	a6
9	cxd5	exd5

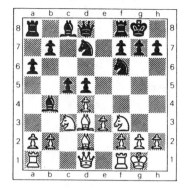

Position after 9 . . . exd5

10 Rc1

A grave strategic error from which White will find it difficult to recover. There were two possibilities of obtaining a combinative game: firstly the isolation of Black's d-pawn by means of 10 dxc5 with the continuation 10 . . . Nxc5 11 Be2 Ne6 (against the possible 12 a3) 12 Qb3, followed by 13 Rfd1 etc. Secondly, by allowing Black an extra pawn on the queen's side but at the cost of the exchange of her bishop at b4. For instance, 10 a3 Bxc3 11 Bxc3 c4 12 Bc2 b5 13 Ne5 Bb7 14 f3 a5 15 Qe1 with chances for both sides. From now on, White, on account of her passiveness, will be forced to face an increasingly restricted position.

10	. . .	c4
11	Bb1	Re8
12	Ne2	Bd6
13	Bc3	b5
14	Ng3	g6
15	Re1	

There are fewer moves available each time. The result of the text move is the necessity of placing the rook on a square that is scarcely pleasing and eventually vulnerable.

15	. . .	Bb7
16	Re2	b4
17	Be1	a5
18	Ng5	

The object of this complicated manoeuvre is finally to guarantee the square e5 for the knight. To achieve this White must try to threaten (or at least pretend to do so) e4 and thus provoke the Black f-pawn into advancing two squares.

18	. . .	Ng4
19	Nh3	f5?

Allowing White to complete her plan and obtain some chances of salvation. Much more in accordance with the position was 19 . . . Ndf6 when White would not be able to play 20 e4 immediately (because of 20 . . . dxe4 21 Rxc4 Ba6), nor prepare for it with 20 Bd2 (because of 20 . . . Ne4); after any other move Black would find it easy to strengthen her position by . . . a4-a3 or . . . Qc7, followed by . . . h5-h4.

20	Nf1	Qc7
21	f4	Ndf6

Since Black was not intending next move to play . . . Ne4, with which her plan would be completely in order, she could advance the a-pawn at once.

22	Bh4	a4
23	Ng5	Qe7
24	Re1	a3

25	b3	c3

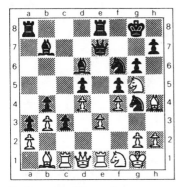

Position after 25 . . . c3

Black has obtained a won ending by advancing on the queen's wing. All that is necessary now is to open up a line on the opposite side of the board with the idea of penetrating the enemy position and compelling the required reduction of forces.

26	Nf3	Qg7
27	h3	Nh6
28	Bxf6	

It must be admitted that unfortunately this bishop had few prospects, whereas the Black knight at e4 would be a serious threat.

28	. . .	Qxf6
29	Ne5	Qe7

Here and on the following moves Black loses valuable time and directly provokes an attack on the king's flank. The logical plan was to bring the knight to e4 via f7 and d6 after playing 29 . . . Bf8.

30	Nh2	Rec8
31	Nhf3	Nf7

32	Bd3	Rc7
33	Qe2	Qd8
34	Rc2	Qc8

Both players are making a series of unusual and mysterious moves, probably under time pressure. Now White suddenly decides to exchange knights although there was no reason for doing so until the proper time. A more prudent plan would be first to obtain the formation h4, g3, Kg2, Rh1 and threaten an attack by h5. If White eventually provoked Black by means of such a threat into playing . . . h5 a definite draw would be assured.

35	Nxf7	Rxf7
36	Bb5	Rc7
37	Bd3	Bf8
38	Ne5	Bg7
39	Kh2	Bf6?
40	Rg1	Kf8?

The preoccupation with time is past and White now finds the following good move after careful consideration. In reality, the attack started by 41 g4! could have been successful had White not failed to appreciate her opponent's resources.

41	g4!	Bxe5
42	fxe5?	

This first move after the adjournment is the decisive mistake. 42 dxe5 is necessary in order to answer 42 . . . fxg4 with 43 Rxg4 (threatening f5) and 42 . . . Ba6 with 43 Rd1 Bxd3 44 Rxd3 Qa6 45 Qd1 etc. with sufficient counter-play. After the text move White's attacking chances quickly vanish and Black finally is able to force the entry of her queen into the enemy fortress.

42 ...	fxg4

43 Rf1+

The exchange of rooks is certainly well received by Black. Better and much more opportune would be 43 Rxg4 although Black, by playing 43 ... Ba6, would be in a position gradually to repel all the threats.

43 ...	Rf7
44 Rxf7+	Kxf7
45 hxg4	Qd8
46 Kg3	Kg7
47 Qf1	Qe7
48 Rf2	Rf8
49 Rf4	Bc8
50 Bc2	Be6

51 Rxf8?

This second exchange is as difficult to understand as the first one. The immediate 51 Qa6 would place Black in a complicated situation.

51 ...	Qxf8
52 Qa6	Qe7

53 Bd1

There was no defence against 53 ... h5 and Black could have played this move immediately; for instance, 53 ... h5 54 gxh5 gxh5 55 Bxh5 c2 56 Qc6 Qg5+ 57 Kf2 Qh4+ 58 Kg1 Qe1+, followed by 59 ... c1 (Q). But this slight carelessness does not spoil anything.

53 ...	Kf7
54 Kf4	

Preparing to reply to 54 ... h5 with 55 g5.

54 ...	h6
55 Qf1	Kg7
56 Kg3	h5

This should win quickly.

57 gxh5	Qg5+
58 Kf2	Qf5+

59 Bf3

After a king move there follows 59 ... Qxf1+ 60 Kxf1 Bf5 and White loses the bishop.

59 ...	Qc2+?

A simple winning move would be 59 ... g5.

60 Qe2?

Missing the opportunity to play 60 Kg3 Qxa2? 61 Be4 and the entry of the queen at f6 would force a draw. But 60 ... gxh5 61 Bxh5 Qf5, followed by 62 ... c2 would still permit Black to win.

Black to move

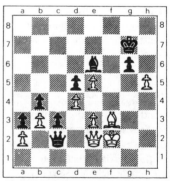

Position after 60 Qe2

60 ...	Qxe2+??

An incorrect move, the weakness of

which is not diminished by the fact that Black had obtained a won ending more or less accidentally. With 60 . . . Qb2 the second player would certainly achieve (speaking in general) a 'deserved' victory and at the same time an 'undeserved' world title. Undeserved because the present game demonstrates much more clearly than any argument that it is totally unfair to persuade a player of an acknowledged superclass like Miss Menchik to defend her title year after year in tournaments composed of very inferior players. It is not surprising that after so many tournaments she has lost much of her interest, and plays some games casually, much below her strength. But such accidental difficulties could not possibly be decisive in a championship, if it were settled, like any title of importance, in a match and not in a tournament. Miss Graf unquestionably has original talent but she lacks one of the present champion's finest qualities: interest in theoretical knowledge combined with the determination for self-perfection.

61	Kxe2	Bf5?

The last mistake, this time not through time pressure, and the last opportunity to win. Victory was still obtainable by 61 . . . g5! with the unanswerable threat of 62 . . . Kh6, followed by 63 . . . g4 and 64 . . . Kxh5. This time the execution is played less unhappily.

62	hxg6	Kxg6
63	Bxd5	Bb1
64	Kd1	

Had Black foreseen in her calculations this simple defence?

64	. . .	Bd3
65	Bc6	Kf7
66	d5	Ke7
67	e4	Kf7
68	e6+	Kf6
69	e5+	Ke7
70	Bb7	Bg6
71	Ba6	Be4
72	Bc4	Bg6
73	d6+	Kd8
74	Bd5	Black resigns

GAME 57

Consultation Game, Rio de Janeiro 1939
Queen's Gambit Declined

White: A. ALEKHINE and W. CRUZ
Black: A. SILVA ROCHA,
CHARLIER, and O. CRUZ

Game 57 Queen's Gambit Declined

1	d4	Nf6
2	c4	e6
3	Nc3	d5
4	Nf3	Be7

A good reply to the usual move 4 ... c5 is 5 cxd5 Nxd5 6 e3.

5	Bf4	0-0
6	e3	a6

This permits White to block the game in an effective way but the plausible alternative 6 ... c5 would have been equally favourable to the first player after 7 dxc5 Bxc5 8 cxd5 Nxd5 9 Nxd5 exd5 10 Bd3 Bb4+ 11 Kf1!

7 c5!

Practice has shown (and the present game confirms it) that after this move Black, if he wishes to defend his position and bring his queen's bishop into play, will be obliged to create positional weaknesses.

7	...	Nbd7
8	Bd3	Re8

With the idea of playing a combination similar to the one in the game Euwe-Spielmann, Mährisch-Ostrau 1923, 9 ... Bxc5 10 dxc5 e5 etc.

9	b4	c6
10	h3	

It is extremely important to conserve the queen's bishop, which would have had to be surrendered had White, instead of this, played 10 0-0 Nh5.

| 10 | ... | b6 |

The only possible attempt at emancipation. Now Black is again

threatening 11 ... bxc5 12 bxc5 Bxc5.

11	Bh2	bxc5
12	bxc5	

Position after 12 bxc5

| 12 | ... | e5 |

Although ingenious and correct from the tactical point of view, this move is revealed to be insufficient to equalize the battle, as would be any other try. Black's initial error was his sixth move.

13 Nxe5!

The continuation 13 dxe5 Nxc5 14 exf6 Bxf6 15 Rc1 d4! would have been dangerous and, finally, without advantage for White.

13	...	Nxe5
14	Bxe5	Bxc5
15	0-0!	

The result of the preparations of the last few moves is clearly in White's favour; Black's c-pawn is weak and the White bishop at e5 occupies a dominating position.

| 15 | ... | Bd6 |

16 f4

Equally strong is 16 Bxd6 Qxd6 17 Na4 since the sacrificial combination 17 . . . Bxh3 18 gxh3 Rxe3 would be refuted by 19 Kg2! However I consider it logical to maintain the bishop in its strong position.

16 . . .	Qe7

With the intention of playing 17 . . . Nd7.

17	Qc2	g6
18	Na4	Bb7
19	Rab1	Ra7

The only move. After 19 . . . Rab8 20 Nc5 would be decisive.

20 Rb3

White decides to defer the sacrifice of the exchange for one move. In effect the immediate 20 Rxb7 Rxb7 21 Qxc6 would allow the following counter-attack : 21 . . . Rd7! 22 Bxf6 Qxe3+ 23 Rf2 Rc7! 24 Qxd6 Rc1+ 25 Kh2 (if 25 Bf1 Rxf1+!) Qxf2 with advantage to Black.

20 . . .	Nd7

White to move

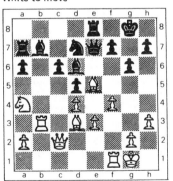

Position after 20 . . . Nd7

21 Rxb7!

Now the sacrifice is absolutely sound.

21	. . .	Rxb7
22	Qxc6	Bxe5

Relatively better was 22 . . . Nxe5 23 fxe5 Ba3 24 Qxd5 although this too would leave Black without hope.

23 Qxb7

The simplest, as 23 fxe5 would allow Black to save his d-pawn by 23 . . . Rb4!, after which he would be able to offer vigorous resistance.

23 . . .	Bg7

24 Kh2

Stronger than 24 Rf3 Nf6! 25 Qxe7 Rxe7 26 Bxa6 Ra7 27 Bb5 Ra5 with good drawing chances.

24	. . .	Rb8
25	Qxd5	Qxe3
26	Bc4	Qxd4

Black does not know how to evaluate his chances of equalizing the game in the ending that follows. It would have been preferable to try to combat his opponent's material superiority by playing, for example, 26 . . . Qe7 27 Bb3 Nb6 28 Nxb6 Rxb6 29 Re1! Qf8 although of course Black would have little hope in the long run.

27	Qxd4	Bxd4

28 Rd1

28 Bxa6 is impossible because of 28 . . . Rb4! with advantage to Black.

28	...	Nc5
29	Rxd4	Nxa4
30	Bxa6	

The rest does not present any serious difficulties since White will always be able to force an exchange of minor pieces at the opportune moment, thereby guaranteeing the triumphant march of his passed pawn. The final phase unfolded as follows:

30	...	Nc5
31	Bc4	Ne6
32	Re4	Rb4
33	Kg3	Kg7
34	Bd5	Rb6

35	Kf3	Rd6
36	Bxe6	fxe6
37	a4	Rc6
38	a5	h5
39	Ra4	Ra6
40	Ke4	h4
41	Kd4	Kf6
42	Kc5	g5
43	fxg5+	Kxg5
44	Kb5	Ra8
45	a6	Kf5
46	Rxh4	e5
47	Ra4	Black resigns

GAME 58

Buenos Aires 1939
Queen's Gambit Declined

White: E. LUNDIN (Sweden)
Black: A. SILVA ROCHA (Brazil)

1	Nf3	Nf6
2	c4	e6
3	Nc3	c5
4	d4	d5
5	Bg5	

The only advantage of this move over the usual 5 cxd5 is that it has been less practised and analysed.

5	...	cxd4
6	Qxd4	

After 6 Nxd4 e5 7 Nf3 d4 8 Nd5 Be7 White has achieved nothing.

6	...	Nc6

An old move that has been completely abandoned since the famous victory by Pillsbury (White) against Lasker at Cambridge Springs in 1904. If the present game does not manage to rehabilitate the move entirely, it does clearly demonstrate that its reputation has not been well judged, as has generally been thought for the last quarter of a century.

7	Bxf6	gxf6
8	Qh4	dxc4

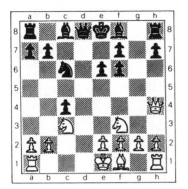

Position after 8 . . . dxc4

9 Qxc4?

As in his game against Michel, Lundin chooses here a move which shows an almost unbelievable ignorance of the most important variations in the opening. The game Pillsbury-Lasker mentioned above, and reproduced in nearly all chess books, continued 9 Rd1 Bd7 10 e3 Ne5 11 Nxe5 fxe5 12 Qxc4 with advantage to White. But even not knowing this, White could hardly expect to acquire any advantage by leaving development aside and moving only his queen. Of course Black, in the variation indicated, could, instead of 10 . . . Ne5, play 10 . . . Be7 11 Bxc4 Qa5 12 0-0 0-0 with opportunities for both sides but this alternative would be infinitely preferable to the line of play chosen which, in a few moves, leaves White in a desperate situation.

9 . . .   Qb6

10 0-0-0?

Beginning to play despairingly. A better defensive attempt for the already compromised situation would have been 10 Qb5.

10 . . .   Bd7

A safe and logical preparation for the following attack on the c-file. But Black could also, without any risk, have taken the pawn offered, since after 10 . . . Qxf2 neither 11 Nb5 Bh6+ 12 Kb1 0-0 nor 11 Ne4 Qe3+ 12 Kb1 Be7 would give White any serious chance. The embarrassing situation is the best proof of the anti-positional character of 10 0-0-0?

11 e3   Ne5

Avoiding 12 Qb5 as a possible answer to 11 . . . Rc8.

12 Nxe5   fxe5

13 Be2?

There is no time for quiet developing moves and this should have been understood. Adequate would be 13 Qb3 and if 13 . . . Bb4 then 14 Kb1 etc., trying to organize a defence.

13 . . .   Rc8

14 Qd3?

The fourth mistake, and this time decisive. The last defensive chance was offered by 14 Qb3 Bb4 15 Rd3.

14 . . .   Ba4

Winning at least the exchange.

15 Rd2

Game 59 Queen's Gambit Declined

Black to move

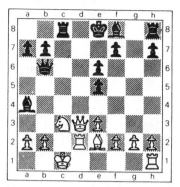

Position after 15 Rd2

15 ...   **Bb4!**

After this there is no remedy against the threat 16 ... Rxc3+ 17 bxc3

Ba3+. An astonishing result in a variation which for years has been considered 'mortally lost' for Black.

16 Kb1

Desperation.

16 ...   **Bxc3**

17 Rc1   **e4**

Also 17 ... 0-0 18 Rxc3 Rcd8 would have compelled resignation.

18 Qd4

Or 18 Qxe4 Bc6!

18 ...   **Bxd4**

19 Rxc8+   **Ke7**

20 White resigns

GAME 59

Buenos Aires 1939
Queen's Gambit Declined

White: V. KAHN (France)
Black: P. SCHMIDT (Estonia)

1	d4	Nf6
2	c4	e6
3	Nf3	d5
4	Bg5	Bb4+
5	Nc3	dxc4
6	e4	c5
7	Bxc4	

Together with the following two moves this is far more simple and profound than the romantic complications that arise from 7 e5 cxd4 8 Qa4+ Nc6 9 0-0-0.

7 ...   **cxd4**

8 Nxd4   **Qa5**

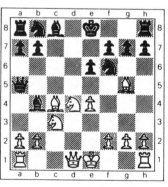

Position after 8 ... Qa5

9 Bxf6!

A Russian discovery that was tried for the first time in the game Kotov-Yudovich for the Soviet Championship in 1931. The key to this capture is to be found in the fact that after the plausible moves 9 . . . Bxc3+ 10 bxc3 Qxc3+ 11 Kf1 Qxc4+ 12 Kg1 White's remaining bishop would be untouchable because of the threat of 13 Rc1. Other possibilities, such as 12 . . . Bd7 13 Rc1 Qxa2 14 Nxe6!! or 12 . . . Nd7 13 Rc1 Qa6 14 Bxg7 Rg8 15 Bh6 etc. would immediately be disadvantageous to Black since he would have nothing better than to refuse the astute gift, thereby admitting that his opening tactics have failed by not producing the desired effect.

9 . . .   gxf6
10 0-0   Bd7

If Black were able to keep his pair of bishops he could hope to reach an endgame in which he might have fair compensation for his dislocated pawn structure and the denuded situation of his king. But, as the continuation shows, this is too difficult a task, especially because the bishop at b4 is exposed and held down by the necessity of protecting the weak Black squares in the centre.

11 Rc1   Nc6
12 Nb3

12 Ndb5 would be tempting but rather premature because of 12 . . . Ne5 13 Be2 Rd8 after which 14 Nd6+ Bxd6 15 Qxd6 Bc6 would lead only to an exchange of queens.

12 . . .   Qb6
13 Qe2

With the concealed plan of exploiting the insecure position of the Black king, a possibility that his opponent completely disregards.

13 . . .   Rc8?

A double error. First, Black loses the opportunity for profitable simplification by means of 13 . . . Bxc3 14 Rxc3 Ne5 15 Rd1 with only extremely slight advantage to White. Secondly, in the event of Black's not attempting to simplify, he could have protected the square b5 in one stroke by 13 . . . a6. From now onwards Kahn acquires the advantage in decisive fashion.

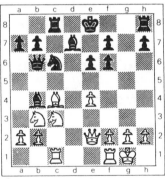

Position after 13 . . . Rc8

14 Bb5

By means of this powerful move White threatens to obtain a decisive positional advantage after 15 Bxc6 Rxc6 (if 15 . . . bxc6 then 16 Na4, followed by 17 Nc5) 16 Nd5! and Black's chances remain very limited.

14 . . .   Rd8

15 Rfd1

Renewing the same threat and intending 16 Rd3 if 15 . . . 0-0.

15 . . .   Be7

16 Na4

Now the occupation of c5 will quickly decide.

16 . . .   Qc7

17 Nac5   Bxc5

Or 17 . . . Bc8 18 Rxd8+ Bxd8 19 Nxb7 Bxb7 20 Bxc6+ Bxc6 21 Nd4 with advantage to White.

18 Nxc5   Bc8

White threatened 19 Nxb7 Qxb7 20 Rxd7 Rxd7 21 Bxc6 with sufficient advantage.

19 Rxd8+   Kxd8

20 Qc4!

With the unavoidable threat of 21 Nxb7.

20 . . .   Ke7

21 Nxb7   Bxb7

22 Bxc6   Rc8?

A grave mistake which loses at once. After 22 . . . Bxc6 23 Qxc6 Qxc6 24 Rxc6 Rd8 25 Rc7+ Kf8 26 g3 Rd2 27 Kg2 White would have to employ all his technical skill to win the rook ending.

23 Qb4+   Black resigns

This game, and of course the victory of Kotov, seems to signify it not the end of the whole Vienna Variation at least that of the move 6 . . . c5.

Queen's Gambit Declined, Slav Defence

GAME 60

Eleventh and last match game, New York 1942
Queen's Gambit Declined

White: S. RESHEVSKY
Black: I. KASHDAN

1	d4	d5
2	c4	c6
3	Nf3	Nf6
4	Nc3	dxc4
5	e3	

More in vogue is the variation 5 a4 (compare with the 1937 Alekhine-Euwe match). The present game certainly will not contribute towards bringing 5 e3 into fashion.

5 . . .   b5

6	a4	b4
7	Na2	e6
8	Bxc4	Nbd7
9	0-0	Bb7
10	Qe2	c5
11	Rd1	

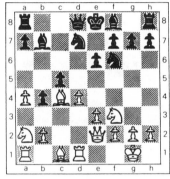

Position after 11 Rd1

11	...	cxd4

Against Fairhurst at Hastings in 1937 Reshevsky played 11 ... Qb6 but after 12 e4! he had a very difficult game to play. The question is whether Black by exchanging pawns and developing the bishop at c5 really avoids the pawn sacrifice! In all events after 11 ... cxd4 12 Nxd4 Bc5 13 e4!? Nxe4 14 Be3 Black finds himself gravely purturbed. A detailed analysis of the situation would cast clear light on the value of the whole variation.

12	Nxd4	Bc5
13	Nb3	

Reshevsky avoids the chief problem and Black will therefore find no difficulty in maintaining the equilibrium. The following attack on the

b-pawn can easily be parried.

13	...	Be7
14	a5	

The logical consequence of the preceding move.

14	...	0-0
15	Bd2	Qb8!
16	a6	

The exchange of the g-pawn for the b-pawn would clearly be advantageous to Black.

16	...	Bd5
17	Bxd5	exd5!

Much better than 17 ... Nxd5 18 e4 etc. The isolation of the pawn is fully compensated for by the free play of his pieces and the immobility of the White bishop.

18	Nd4	Qb6
19	Nc1	Nc5
20	Ncb3	Rfd8
21	Na5	

A demonstration without future.

21	...	Rdc8
22	Rdc1	Bf8

Now threatening to take the a-pawn and making the knight go back.

23	Nab3	Nfe4
24	Be1	Nxb3

24 ... g6, followed eventually by ... Bg7 deserved to be taken into consideration.

25	Nxb3	Nc5
26	Nd4	

After the exchange of knights White

would have found it impossible to avoid the liquidation of the isolated pawn by . . . d4.

26	...	Ne6
27	Nb3	Rc7

Playing for a win (instead of repeating moves) without great justification but at the same time without great risk.

28	Rxc7	Nxc7
29	Qd3	Rd8
30	Qd4	Qb8
31	h3	Ne6
32	Qd3	Qe5
33	Nd4	Nxd4?

It would be logical above all (in the sense of seeking complications) to play 33 . . . Rc8 because after the exchange of queens Black is left with no winning chances.

34	Qxd4	Qxd4
35	exd4	Rc8
36	Ra5!	

Black to move

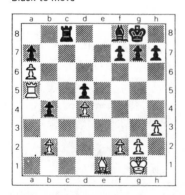

Position after 36 Ra5

36	...	Rc2?

Rather an elementary miscalculation. Sufficient to obtain a draw would be 36 . . . Rc6 37 Rxd5 (after any other move Black plays 37 . . . Bd6, followed by 38 . . . f6 and 39 . . . Kf7 etc.) Rxa6 38 Rd8 Ra1 39 Kf1 f6 40 d5 Kf7 41 Ke2 (if 41 d6 Rd1) Be7.

37	Rxd5	Rxb2
38	Rd7!	

This wins a pawn through the fact that the king is enclosed, which could easily have been avoided in the middle-game (see, for example, the note to Black's 24th move).

38	...	Rb1
39	Kf1	b3
40	Rxa7	g6

More natural seems 40 . . . f6 with the aim of bringing the king up to the centre as soon as possible. But it is pointless; in any case White must win.

41	Rb7	Ra1
42	Rxb3	Rxa6
43	Rb8	Kg7
44	Ke2	Ra2+
45	Kd3	Ra3+
46	Bc3	Bd6
47	Rb2	Be7

Or 47 . . . Kf6 48 Rb6 Ke7 (or Ke6) 49 f4. Technically the ending is easy.

48	Kc4	Ra4+
49	Kb5	Ra1
50	d5+	Kf8
51	Kc6	Ra8

52	Be5	Rc8+
53	Bc7	Bf6
54	Rb8	Rxb8

55	Bxb8	Bd4
56	Bd6+	Kg7
57	Bc5	**Black resigns**

GAME 61

Buenos Aires 1939
Queen's Gambit Declined

White: G. STAHLBERG (Sweden)
Black: T. VAN SCHELTINGA
(Holland)

1	d4	Nf6
2	e3	d5
3	Nf3	Bf5
4	c4	c6
5	Qb3	

Thus with a transposition of moves
one of the very well-known variations
of the Slav Defence is obtained.
Simplest for Black now is to offer an
exchange of queens with 5 . . . Qb6.

5	. . .	Qc7
6	cxd5	cxd5
7	Nc3	e6
8	Bd2	Nc6
9	Rc1	

White completes the mobilization
of his queen's side in the shortest
possible time and now hopes to take
advantage by exerting pressure on
the b-file.

| 9 | . . . | a6? |

A typical positional error. As the
continuation will show, Black not
only prevents nothing but dangerously weakens the diagonal a5–d8.
The simple 9 . . . Be7 would be
good because an eventual exchange
at c6 after 10 Bb5 would have
given Black sufficient play on the
open b-file. The prophylactic move
9 . . . Nd7 would also have been
better than the text.

10 Qa4!

Threatening 11 Bb5 and 11 Ne5.
If now 10 . . . Be7 then 11 Ne5
0-0 12 Nd1!

| 10 | . . . | Nd7 |

In adopting this defence Black
calculated well that he can avoid
immediate material loss. But his
positional error on the ninth move
will become more and more evident
in the following endgame.

| 11 | Bb5 | Rc8 |
| 12 | Bxc6 | Qxc6 |

White to move

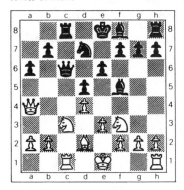

Position after 12 ... Qxc6

13 0-0!

This simple developing move assures White of an appreciable advantage in position. On the other hand the 'brilliant' move 13 Nxd5 would be a mistake because after 13 ... Qxc1+ 14 Bxc1 Rxc1+ 15 Ke2 Rc2+ 16 Nd2 exd5 etc., Black would remain with a rook and two minor pieces against the queen.

13	...	Qxa4
14	Nxa4	Rxc1

An extremely temerarious decision, since the devastating effect of the rook on the eighth rank is clear at first sight. But here there was no chance other than to abandon the open file as is shown by the following: (a) 14 ... Bc2 15 Nc5 Bxc5 (or ... Nxc5) 16 Rxc2, winning; (b) 14 ... Rc2 15 Ba5! b5 16 Rxc2 Bxc2 17 Rc1 Bxa4 18 Rc8+ Ke7 19 Bd8+ Kd6 20 Ng5 and wins.

15	Rxc1	Be7

The only move.

16	Rc8+	Bd8
17	Ba5	Ke7
18	Bb4+	Ke8
19	Ra8!	

With the aim of attacking the enemy pawns via a7.

19	...	Bd3
20	Ne5	Nxe5
21	dxe5	Bb1

If 21 ... Bb5 22 Nc5 Bc6 23 Rb8.

22	Nc5	b6
23	Nxa6	Bxa2

Black fights desperately to maintain the balance of forces. But his pieces are so badly distributed that White can easily choose various ways of execution.

24	Nc7+	Kd7
25	Nb5	Bc4
26	Ra7+	Kc8

If 26 ... Kc6 27 Nd4 mate.

27	Nd6+	Kb8
28	Rxf7	Rg8
29	Rb7+	Ka8
30	Rd7	Bd3
31	Nf7	Bh4
32	g3	Bb5
33	Rc7	Black resigns

Queen's Gambit Accepted

GAME 62

Buenos Aires 1939
Queen's Gambit Accepted

White: K. OPOCENSKY
(Czechoslovakia)
Black: E. LUNDIN (Sweden)

1	d4	d5
2	c4	dxc4
3	Nf3	Nf6
4	Qa4+	Nbd7
5	Nc3	e6
6	e4	

The present game shows that the development of the king's bishop on the diagonal f1—a6 should not be accompanied by the queen check on the fourth move. A good idea would be the adoption of the Catalan System beginning with 6 g3.

6	. . .	a6!

Here *Modern Chess Openings* gives admiringly 6 . . . c5 and produces a variation which leads to equality. Lundin's move is more convincing, because White now loses several tempi before finishing his development.

7 Bxc4

After 7 Qxc4 Black would have saved the following rook move and played the immediate 7 . . . b5 (if 8 Qc6 Ra7, threatening 9 . . . Bb7 and 9 . . . Bb4), followed by castling

and eventually, . . . Nb8.

7	. . .	Rb8

Compelling two consecutive retreats. Black's position is preferable.

8	Bd3	b5
9	Qc2	Bb7
10	0-0	

Since he is exposed to the possibility of an inferior position (the difficult situation of his pieces in the centre) he would have done better to select the dangerous line 10 e5 Nd5 11 Nxd5 (or 11 Bxh7 Nb4 12 Qb1 Bxf3, followed by 13 . . . c5) Bxd5 12 Bxh7, which would have obliged Black to show more tactical skill than was the case after the simple text move.

10	. . .	c5
11	Bf4	

At this stage 11 e5 would have been answered by 11 . . . c4.

11	. . .	Rc8
12	d5	

Since the alternative 12 dxc5 Nxc5 would leave Black with a technical problem that would be easy to

solve, Opocensky decides to
sacrifice a piece; but Black,
dominating the queen's flank,
permits himself the luxury of
ignoring the offer, and obtains
decisive supremacy simply by
occupying the squares of importance.

| 12 | ... | c4 |
| 13 | dxe6 | fxe6! |

There was no necessity to give
White two pawns and something of
an attack for the piece in the variation 13 . . . cxd3 14 exf7+ Kxf7 15
Qxd3.

| 14 | Be2 | Bb4 |
| 15 | e5 | |

If 15 Ng5 then 15 . . . e5, followed
by 16 . . . h6 or eventually . . . Qe7
etc.

15	...	Bxc3
16	bxc3	Nd5
17	Bg3	

If 17 Bd2 Black, before castling,
would have had in 17 . . . Qe7 an
easy way of stopping all the threats
(18 Ng5 Nxe5 19 Nxh7 Qh4).

| 17 | ... | 0-0 |
| 18 | Nd4 | |

Or 18 Bh4 Qb6 19 Ng5 g6. The
game is already decided strategically
in Black's favour.

| 18 | ... | Nc5 |
| 19 | a4 | Nf4! |

The beginning of a direct attack; if
20 Bxf4 Rxf4 21 axb5 axb5 22
Nxb5 he would have won the
exchange by 22 . . . Qd5 23 f3 (or
23 Bf3 Rxf3) Nb3.

20	Rfd1	Qg5
21	axb5	axb5
22	Bf1	

Black to move

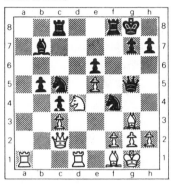

Position after 22 Bf1

| 22 | ... | Ncd3! |

More effective than 22 . . . Qxe5.
If 23 Nxb5 Black wins forcibly by
23 . . . Nxf2 24 Qxf2 Nh3+ 25 gxh3
Rxf2 26 Kxf2 Rf8+ 27 Ke1 Qe3+
28 Be2 Bg2 and 29 . . . Rf1 mate.

| 23 | Rxd3 | |

This act of desperation is more
justified than the attempt to
eliminate the intruder without a
sacrifice because this latter course
would lead him to a spectacular
catastrophe: 23 Bxd3 cxd3 24 Qb3
Bd5 25 Qxb5 Qxe5 26 Rxd3 Qe4 27
Rf3 Nh3+ 28 Kh1 Rxf3 29 Nxf3
Qxf3! and wins.

| 23 | ... | cxd3 |
| 24 | Bxd3 | Qxe5 |

The h-pawn now has no importance.

| 25 | Qb3 | |

Or 25 Bxf4 Qxf4 26 Nxe6 Qg4
winning.

25	...	Bd5
26	Qd1	

After 26 Qxb5 Rxc3 he would have lost even more material.

26	...	Rxc3
27	Bxb5	Bxg2

If now 28 Bxf4 Qxf4 29 Kxg2 Qxf2+ 30 Kh1 then simply 30 ... Rd8 31 Ra4 e5 winning.

28	Qd2	Rc5
29	Re1	

Now it appears that White can recover some of the material, but the following rejoinder destroys his last illusion.

29	...	Be4!
30	Qe3	Rxb5
31	Bxf4	

If 31 Nxb5 then 31 ... Nh3+, followed by 32 ... Qxb5+.

31	...	Rxf4
32	Nxb5	Rg4+
33	White resigns	

Queen's Pawn, Nimzowitsch Defence

GAME 63

Seventh match game, New York 1942
Queen's Pawn, Nimzowitsch Defence

White: S. RESHEVSKY
Black: I. KASHDAN

1	d4	Nf6
2	c4	e6
3	Nc3	Bb4
4	Qc2	

A variation very much in vogue up till 1933. It has been abandoned today because Black possesses various methods of attaining equal chances.

4	...	d5

5	cxd5	Qxd5

5 ... exd5 is also good enough for equality.

6	Nf3	c5
7	Bd2	Bxc3
8	Bxc3	Nc6
9	e3	0-0
10	Rd1	

This position occurred in the game

Capablanca-Fine in the AVRO Tournament and continued 10 . . . b6 11 a3, and Black obtained the inferior game. The present game shows that Black can equalize by taking the a-pawn.

10 . . .   Qxa2!

Erroneous would be 10 . . . cxd4 11 Nxd4 Nxd4 (or 11 . . . Qxa2 12 Nxc6 bxc6 13 Bb4! winning the exchange in view of the threat of 14 Bc4) 12 Rxd4 Qxa2 13 Bc4 etc.

11 dxc5   Nd5

12 Be2

Worth examining was 12 Ng5 provoking weaknesses in the enemy pawn position.

12 . . .   Ncb4

13 Qd2   Nxc3

14 Qxc3   Nd5

15 Qd2   b6!

He frees himself of the pawn which, otherwise, could have become uncomfortable. White is reduced to exchanging it because if 16 c6 the reply 16 . . . Ba6 would give Black the upper hand.

16 cxb6   axb6

17 0-0   Bb7

18 Rc1   Rfc8

Somewhat schematic play. Better would have been 18 . . . Rfd8 and if 19 Qd4 then 19 . . . Qa5 with an excellent game.

19 Ne5   Nf6?

Black does not seem to realize the possible danger. 19 . . . Qa5 would

be simple and good.

20 Nc4!

Now not only must the b-pawn be urgently defended but other Black squares of Kashdan's have lost strength owing to the remoteness of the queen. The most opportune move, although only relatively speaking, seems to be 20 . . . Rd8 21 Qc2! Be4 22 Qc3 Qa7 with a defensible position.

20 . . .   Qb3?

21 Qd4!

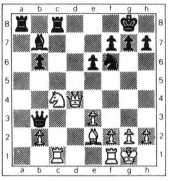

Position after 21 Qd4

21 . . .   Rc6

With this he loses a pawn, but there was already no satisfactory defence. If, for example, 21 . . . Nd5 then 22 Nd6 Rcb8 23 Qe5 with the formidable threat of 24 e4 and White wins easily. It should be noted that after 21 . . . Rc6 22 Bf3 would be a false step because of 22 . . . Nd5 23 Bxd5 exd5 24 Qxd5? Rc7, followed by 25 . . . Rac8.

22 Nd6   Rxc1

23 Rxc1   Qd5

24 Qxd5   Bxd5

25	Rc8+	Rxc8
26	Nxc8	

White now wins the b-pawn (if 26
... Nd7 27 Bb5) and the rest should
be no more than a question of
technique.

26	...	Kf8
27	Nxb6	Bb7

The following phase is very simple
and practically forced; both players
must quickly bring their kings to the
centre of the battleground.

28	f3	Ke7
29	Kf2	Ne8

And not 29 ... Kd6 because of 30
Nc4+ and 30 ... Kc5 is impossible
on account of 31 Ne5.

30	Nc4	f6
31	Ke1	e5
32	Kd2	Nc7
33	Bd3	h6
34	Na5	Bc8
35	Bc4	Kd6
36	Kc3	Nd5+

In the long run Black will not be
able to avoid the exchange of one
of the pieces. He prefers to con-
front the knight with the bishop
because generally a bishop is an
excellent weapon against a passed
pawn. But unfortunately the whole
of the right side of the board is
momentarily blocked and this fact
should sufficiently help Reshevsky's
task.

37	Bxd5	Kxd5
38	e4+	Ke6

38 ... Kc5 39 b4+ Kb5 40 Nc4
Kc6 etc. would have offered more
resistance.

39	Nc4	Ba6
40	Ne3?	

Incomprehensible! Immediately
decisive would have been 40 Kb4
f5 41 Kc5 fxe4 42 fxe4 Bb7 43
Nd6, followed by the advance of the
passed pawn. Or 42 ... Kf6 43 b4
Kg5 44 Nd6 Kf4 45 b5 Bxb5 46
Kxb5.

40	...	h5
41	Kb4	g6
42	Kc5	f5
43	b4?	

And even now, in spite of the time
lost, 43 Nc4! fxe4 44 fxe4 Bb7 45
Nd6 would win easily. The text
move loses a pawn and thereby
gives Black effective drawing
chances.

43	...	fxe4
44	fxe4	Bd3
45	b5	Bxe4
46	g3	Bf3
47	h3	Bh1
48	b6	Ba8
49	Nc4	Kf5
50	Kd6	

The only other possibility is 50 b7.
This does not win: 50 ... Bxb7 51
Nd6+ Kg5 52 Nxb7 h4 53 g4 Kf4
etc.

Black to move

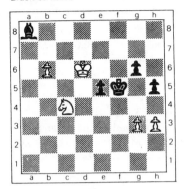

Position after 50 Kd6

50 ...   **h4?**

This sacrifice is premature and will be refuted by an exquisite manoeuvre by the White king. He should have played 50 . . . e4 with the following possible variations:

(a) 51 Ke7 g5 52 Kf7 (52 Kd6 e3) h4 53 g4+ Kf4 54 Kf6 Bd5 etc.

(b) 51 Ne3+ Kf6 52 Kc5 (if 52 h4 then evidently 52 . . . g5) h4 (now this move is correct) 53 gxh4 Ke5 54 Ng2 e3! 55 Nxe3 Kf4.

(c) 51 Ne3+ Kf6 52 Nd5+ (a hoax) Kf5! (and not 52 . . . Bxd5? 53 Kxd5 e3 54 b7 e2 55 b8 (Q) e1 (Q) 56 Qf8+ Kg5 57 Qf4 mate).

Other variations are simpler. This analysis shows that through his haste on the 43rd move White let the game slip away.

51 gxh4   **e4**

52 Ke7

White hereby makes sure of at least one passed pawn on the h-file. The main variation is 52 . . . Kf4 53 Kf6 Kg3 54 Kg5 Kxh3 55 Ne5 e3 56 Nxg6 and wins.

52 ...   **Bc6**

53 Kf7   **Bd5+**

54 Kg7   **Ba8**

55 Kh6!   **Bc6**

This accelerates the agony. If 55 . . . Kf6 White would have created himself a second passed pawn by 56 h5.

56 Na5   **Bd5**

If 56 . . . e3 White takes the bishop.

57 b7   **Bxb7**

58 Nxb7   **e3**

59 Nc5   **Ke5**

60 Nd3+   **Ke4**

61 Ne1   **Kf5**

62 Kg7   **e2**

63 Nc2   **Black resigns**

GAME 64

Buenos Aires 1939
Queen's Pawn, Nimzowitsch Defence

White: J. ENEVOLDSEN (Denmark)
Black: A. ALEKHINE (France)

1	d4	Nf6
2	c4	e6
3	Nc3	Bb4
4	Qc2	Nc6
5	Nf3	

If 5 e3 Black would not reply at once 5 . . . e5 because of 6 dxe5 Nxe5 7 Bd2, followed by 8 Nf3 with a pawn structure similar to that in some variations of the Budapest Defence, rightly considered advantageous for White (compare with the tenth game of the match Keres-Euwe in 1940), but would first play 5 . . . d6, followed by the advance of the e-pawn at the earliest opportunity.

5	. . .	d6
6	Bd2	

Not to be recommended, as Black on his next move will either save his king's bishop from the exchange or, as occurs in the game, induce his opponent to block the position, thereby gaining equal chances. Thus the usual 6 a3 is preferable.

6	. . .	e5
7	d5	Bxc3
8	Bxc3	Ne7
9	Nh4	

An artificial move which, however, it is hard to condemn, for White avoids the normal (and not always pleasant) development which, after 9 e4, would be 9 . . . Ng6 10 g3 0-0 11 Bg2 Nh5 (and not 11 . . . Ne8 because of 12 h4-h5), followed by 12 . . . f5 with the superior position for Black.

9	. . .	Qd7

The correct reply; Black not only forestalls 10 e4 (because of 10 . . . Qg4) but also forces control of f5 and prepares for . . . Ng6 without the possibility of being troubled by Nf5.

10	g3	Qg4

Although this manoeuvre is not as active as it appears at first sight, its immediate consequences are the moves 11 Qb3 and 16 Qc2 by White. It is dubious whether it is worthwhile expending so much energy merely in order to provoke White's f3. By continuing simply with 10 . . . Ng6 11 Nxg6 hxg6 Black would have been abundantly successful in his opening plan.

11	Qb3	

Virtually forced.

11	. . .	Ng6
12	f3	Qd7
13	Ng2	

After this White will manage to keep f5 under his control, obliging his opponent to seek compensation on the other side of the board. In prospect is an arduous struggle with many chances for both players.

13	. . .	0-0
14	e4	Qd8

Black needs to have d7 available for the following knight manoeuvre.

15	Ne3	Nd7
16	Qc2	a5
17	Bg2	

A very modest development, but

17 Bh3 would have been answered
by 17 . . . Nc5 or 17 . . . Ne7,
followed by 18 . . . Nc5, depriving
White of the hope of exploiting in
the more or less distant future the
advantage of the bishop pair.

17	...	Nc5
18	0-0	Bd7
19	b3	

If he had played the move 19 a4 to
block the position Black would
have replied 19 . . . Qb8 20 b3 Qa7
21 Rfe1 Ne7 with good prospects.

| 19 | ... | b5 |
| 20 | Rad1? | |

But here 20 cxb5 Bxb5 21 Rfe1 Ne7
would have been opportune. After
the text move Black's chances must
be considered better because of his
pressure down the a-file.

| 20 | ... | b4 |
| 21 | Bd2 | |

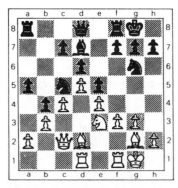

Position after 21 Bd2

| 21 | ... | Qb8 |

Black's tactics are characterized
by the fact that he will not spend

a single move on defence despite
the threatening advance of White's
king's side pawns. If White had
adopted another plan beginning
with f4, the Black fortress, after
. . . f6, would have been solid
enough to resist until the counter-
attack on the queen's wing had
once again reduced White to
passivity.

| 22 | Rb1 | |

Unsuccessfully trying to contain
the following advance.

| 22 | ... | a4! |
| 23 | h4 | |

If 23 bxa4 the conclusion would
be deadly, as the following variation
shows: 23 . . . Bxa4 24 Qb2 (24
Qc1 is even worse) Nd3 25 Qa1 Qb6
26 Kh1 Qc5 and then the doubling
of the rooks on the a-file.

| 23 | ... | Ne7 |

Threatening 24 . . . f5 and forcing
the following response which
weakens White's two squares h4 and
f4.

24	g4	axb3
25	axb3	Ra3
26	h5	Qb6
27	Kh2	Rfa8
28	Rb2	

With the object of preventing 28
. . . Ra2 29 Rb2 Rxb2, followed
by 30 . . . Ra3 with great advantage.

| 28 | ... | c6! |

As a number of White pieces are
tied down by the necessity of protecting vulnerable points, the
opening-up of the position is the

most appropriate plan. The text move (based on the consideration that after 29 dxc6 Nxc6 the control of d4 is much more important than the surrender of d5) opens up the way for the Black queen to the king's side via d8 and at the same time prepares for an eventual . . . f5 in case of dxc6 Nxc6.

29 f4

The danger of this advance which weakens all the Black squares is also clear, but White's chances were becoming more and more limited. Slightly better would be 29 g5 which I planned to answer with 29 . . . Rf8, eventually followed by . . . f5.

29 . . .	exf4
30 Rxf4	Ra1
31 dxc6?	

The decisive error which permits an even more effective co-operation of all the Black pieces. Also inadequate would have been the sacrificial combination 31 e5 dxe5 32 Rxf7? (planning 32 . . . Kxf7 33 Qxh7 with dangerous threats) because of the energetic answer 32 . . . e4 and if 33 Rxd7 then 33 . . . Qc7+ 34 Kh3 Nd3 winning. But after 31 Rf1! White's position, though inferior, would have held some defensive chances.

| 31 . . . | Nxc6 |
| 32 Nd5 | |

Black to move

Position after 32 Nd5

| 32 . . . | Qd8! |

A triumphant withdrawal, threatening both the king (with 33 . . . Qh4+) and the queen (with 33 . . . Nd4); White has no adequate defence.

33 Be3	Qh4+
34 Bh3	Ne5
35 Bxc5	dxc5
36 Qf2	

If 36 Qg2 Black could either win the exchange by 36 . . . Nd3 or double his rooks on the eighth rank with decisive effect, as Qg3 would be refuted by . . . Rh1+.

| 36 . . . | Rh1+ |
| 37 Kxh1 | Qxh3+ |

38 White resigns

If now 38 Qh2 then 38 . . . Ra1+ and mate in two; and if 38 Kg1 then 38 . . . Ra1+ 39 Qf1 Rxf1+ 40 Rxf1 Nf3+ etc. with an ending of queen against rook.

GAME 65

Buenos Aires 1939
Queen's Pawn, Nimzowitsch Defence

White: JACOBO BOLBOCHAN
(Argentina)
Black: C. POULSEN (Denmark)

1 d4	Nf6
2 c4	e6
3 Nc3	Bb4
4 Qc2	Nc6
5 Nf3	0-0
6 e3	Qe7

Black hereby allows the exchange of his king's bishop without any positional compensation. Some would have been obtained here by playing 6 . . . a5 and if 7 a3 then 7 . . . Bxc3+ 8 Qxc3 a4, eventually followed by . . . Na5.

7 a3	Bxc3+
8 Qxc3	d6
9 Be2	Ne4?

Since Black cannot hope to keep complete control over e4 in the long run and since, on the other hand, it is generally a doubtful strategy deliberately to place pawns on squares of the same colour as one's own bishop, the text manoeuvre should be replaced by the natural move 9 . . . e5, followed by the development of the bishop.

10 Qc2	f5
11 b4	Bd7
12 Bb2	Be8
13 0-0	Bg6?

The second reprehensible decision, since . . . f4 will never be a threat because of the reply Bd3. The natural and necessary move was 13 . . . Bh5, after which White would not find it so easy to displace or exchange the central knight.

14 Rae1

He could also have played 14 Nd2 immediately.

14 . . .	Rae8
15 Nd2	e5?

The third, and now decisive, mistake which surrenders to White complete control of the only open file. Necessary was 15 . . . Nf6 16 f4 etc. with a hard struggle in prospect. Now Bolbochán takes control in convincing style.

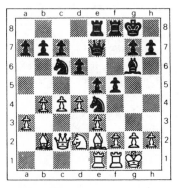

Position after 15 . . . e5

16	b5	Nxd2

The disagreeable alternative was 16 ... Nd8 17 Nxe4 fxe4 18 dxe5 dxe5 19 c5 with advantage to White.

17	Qxd2	Nd8
18	dxe5	dxe5
19	Bc3!	

Forcing a new and more important weakening of the enemy central position.

19	...	c5
20	Rd1	Bf7
21	Qd6!	

Simple but strong, as after the exchange of queens the eventual win is merely a question of time.

21	...	e4

Still Black should have played 21 ... Qxd6, since the advanced pawn gives White the opportunity to win in a few moves.

White to move

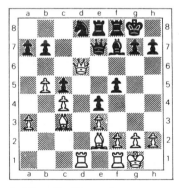

Position after 21 ... e4

22	Qg3!

Gaining an important tempo with

the aim of doubling rooks on the open file. Black is now forced to leave d5 without protection since 22 ... Be6 would be fatal because of 23 Bh5.

22	...	Bg6
23	Rd5	

This would also have been the reply to 22 ... Ne6.

23	...	b6

Or 23 ... Ne6 24 Be5 etc.

24	Rfd1	Ne6

The beginning of a despairing counter-combination.

25	Rd7	Nd4

If 25 ... f4 the answer would be simply 26 exf4 Nxf4 27 Bf1, winning.

26	R1xd4!	cxd4
27	Rxe7	dxc3
28	Rxe8!	

White does not have to fear 28 ... c2 because he can capture the pawn by means of 29 Rxf8+, 30 Qd6+, and 31 Qd2.

28	...	Rxe8
29	Qd6	f4

Black could have resigned here.

30	Qd4	c2
31	Qd2	f3
32	Bf1	fxg2
33	Kxg2	Bh5
34	Qxc2	Bf3+
35	Kg3	Re6
36	c5	**Black resigns**

GAME 66

Buenos Aires 1939
Queen's Pawn, Nimzowitsch Defence

White: V. PETROV (Latvia)
Black: V. MIKENAS (Lithuania)

1	d4	Nf6
2	c4	e6
3	Nc3	Bb4
4	Qc2	Nc6
5	Nf3	d5?

Mikenas's adoption of this inferior variation — the combination of the moves . . . Nc6 and . . . d5 — on a few occasions at Buenos Aires (see also his game with Capablanca) may be considered . . . one of Botwinnik's little sins. The Soviet champion made a point of adopting it in his decisive tournament game against Kotov in 1939 and won, but this result was independent of the opening. Still, since fashion is as tyrannical in chess as in other branches of human activity, another couple of years will probably pass before the ineffectiveness of this system is universally recognized.

6	a3	Bxc3+
7	Qxc3	a5
8	b3	

A necessary measure against 8 . . . a4, followed by 9 . . . Na5.

8	. . .	0-0
9	e3	

Although this restriction of the queen's bishop finally turns out happily, a more convincing way for White to reach an advantageous

position seems to be 9 Bg5, as played by Capablanca in the game mentioned above.

9	. . .	Re8
10	Bb2	Bd7

Still continuing with Botwinnik's plan. Black will eventually obtain the square b5 for his knight but the rest of his forces will be incapable of attack or defence.

11	Bd3	a4
12	b4	dxc4
13	Bxc4	Na7
14	0-0	Bb5

Position after 14 . . . Bb5

15 Rfe1!

The beginning of a calculated action in the centre. Comparatively speaking, Black's best chance of equalizing now consists of: 15 . . . Ne4 16 Qd3 Bxc4 17 Qxe4 (or 17

Qxc4 Qd5!) Bd5 18 Qc2 Nb5. After missing this opportunity he will never be able to re-establish the balance of the position, particularly since Petrov plays the following part of the game with great resolution and precision.

15 ...	Bxc4?
16 Qxc4	Qd5
17 Qc2	

Of course he does not take the c-pawn, as the entry of the Black rook to c2 after 17 ... Rfc8 would bring him serious difficulties. But after the text move 18 Qxa4 is a grave threat, which gives White the time he desires in order to play e4.

17 ...	Nb5

White's a3 will certainly be weak in an endgame of White bishop against Black knight, but unfortunately for the second player there arises a different type of offensive ending.

18 e4	Qh5
19 Ne5	Ng4

Otherwise his queen would have been uncomfortable after 20 Re3 etc.

20 Nxg4	Qxg4
21 Re3	

Owing to the potential strength of the bishop and the dynamic White pawn centre, the position of the Black king gradually begins to be dangerous. For the moment there is no time for the consolidation 21 ... c6 because of 22 Rg3, followed by 23 d5 etc.

21 ...	f6
22 Rae1!	

Quietly mobilizing all his reserves, since his opponent has no useful moves at his disposal. If, for example, 22 ... c6 then 23 d5! exd5 24 Bxf6! with advantage.

22 ...	Qh5
23 Rg3	

Again threatening 24 d5 and if 24 ... e5 then 25 Qc5!

23 ...	Qf7

White to move

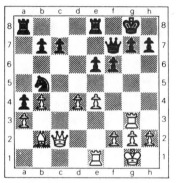

Position after 23 ... Qf7

24 e5!

This advance was calculated in several ways; firstly, the capture of the pawn, which could be answered either by the simple 25 dxe5 with the subsequent concentration of his four pieces (Re4, Bc1 etc.) against the king, or (probably more effective) by 25 Rxe5 Nd6 (if 25 ... c6 then 26 Reg5) 26 b5! with numerous possibilities on all parts of the board. Secondly, 24 ... f5 which would be refuted by 25 d5! exd5 26 e6. Thirdly, the text continuation, the purpose of which is the fine 26th move.

24	. . .	c6
25	exf6	Qxf6
26	h3!	

Of course 26 d5 would be a mistake on account of 26 . . . exd5. But now Black has no means of obstructing the d-pawn and must therefore take it, allowing the following disagreeable liquidation:

26	. . .	Nxd4
27	Qc4!	Rad8

The immediate 27 . . . Nf3+, as will be seen, would not have altered the consequences.

28	Re4	Nf3+

Now forced.

29	Rxf3	Qxb2
30	Rxe6	Rxe6
31	Qxe6+	Kh8
32	Qd7	Rg8

If this rook had been on a8 (compare with move 27) Black would have played exactly the same move.

33 Qxb7

With an extra pawn and the pawn in a better position, White must win. The method will consist of the logical exploitation of combined threats: (a) Against the weakness of the queen's flank; (b) to exchange of rooks, keeping only the queens; (c) finally, also against the king. Because of modern, highly developed technique, winning such positions is sometimes completely natural, but invariably about a dozen years

ago (compare, for instance, my last match game with Capablanca) it was considered a kind of achievement.

33	. . .	Qa1+
34	Kh2	Qe5+
35	g3	Qe4
36	Qf7	h6
37	Qf5	Qc4
38	Qd3	Qe6
39	Qc2	Qd5
40	Rd3	Qe6
41	Qc5	

Naturally not 41 Qxa4 because of 41 . . . Qe2. In the continuation, too, White will have to avoid such little tactical tricks.

41	. . .	Qf6
42	Rd6	Qf3
43	Qd4	Rf8
44	Kg1!	

After 44 Rxh6+ White would not have gained anything.

44	. . .	Kg8
45	Rd7	Rf7
46	Rd8+	Kh7
47	Qb2	

However at this moment he could exchange queens with advantage, (47 Qd3+) as the rejoinder 47 . . . Rf5 would not help because of 48 Qc2! But this opportunity cannot escape.

47	. . .	Qe4
48	Rd4	Qf3
49	Qc2+	g6

Now it is Black who avoids the practically hopeless rook endgame by not playing 49 . . . Qf5. But the subsequent weakness of the king's position is certainly not better.

50	Rd6	Rg7
51	Qd3	Qh5
52	Kg2	Qb5
53	Qf3	Qe5
54	Qxc6	

After this new loss Black could have trusted his opponent's ability to win with two extra pawns by gracefully resigning. The remainder offers little of interest.

54	. . .	Qb2
55	Qf3	h5
56	h4	Rc7
57	Qe4	Rg7
58	Rd5	Kh6

59	Qe3+	Kh7
60	Qd3	Kh6
61	b5	Rb7
62	b6!	

A little merriment (62 . . . Qxb6 63 Rd6 or 62 . . . Rxb6 63 Qe3+, followed by 64 Rd7+ etc.).

62	. . .	Qg7
63	Rd6	Rf7
64	Qd4	Qf8
65	Qd2+	Kh7
66	Rd7	Qe8
67	Rxf7+	Qxf7
68	Qd6	Qb7+
69	Kg1	Qe4
70	Qc7+	Kg8
71	b7	**Black resigns**

GAME 67

Buenos Aires 1939
Queen's Pawn, Nimzowitsch Defence

White: J.R. CAPABLANCA (Cuba)
Black: V. MIKENAS (Lithuania)

1	d4	Nf6
2	c4	e6
3	Nc3	Bb4
4	Qc2	Nc6
5	Nf3	d5?
6	a3	Bxc3+
7	Qxc3	a5

8	b3	0-0
9	Bg5!	

Instead of placing the bishop at b2 where it would be inactive for a long time, White uses it to eliminate the only well-developed Black piece, the king's knight.

9	. . .	h6

10 Bxf6	Qxf6
11 e3	

Position after 11 e3

11 . . .   Bd7

Clearly Black does not realize how difficult his position is. Otherwise, instead of making conventional moves which merely contribute to the formation of White's attack, he would have obtained a certain offensive in the centre by means of 11 . . . Re8 and if 12 Bd3 then 12 . . . a4 13 b4 dxc4 14 Bxc4 e5. White would easily have prevented this action by exchanging the pawn at d5 but the variation 12 cxd5 exd5 13 Bb5 would have been far more bearable than the development in the actual game.

12 Bd3   Rfc8

The poor king is alone and abandoned, but something had to be done to improve the situation on the queen's flank.

13 0-0   a4

The same manoeuvre as in the game Petrov-Mikenas, but with less effect if Black wishes to bring the knight to b5.

14 b4	dxc4
15 Bxc4	Na7
16 Ne5	

White's game plays itself. In effect his victory is due to one good move: 9 Bg5!

16 . . .   Be8

Mikenas is demoralized and does not offer resistance. Necessary was 16 . . . Bb5 17 f4 Bxc4 18 Qxc4 c6, after which it would be possible to prolong the fight.

17 f4	b6
18 Qd3	

Threatening 19 f5, and if Black prevents this with 18 . . . g6 then 19 g4 with the aim of 20 g5 hxg5 21 Ng4 etc.

Black to move

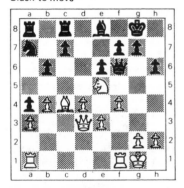

Position after 18 Qd3

18 . . .   Rd8

A desperate idea in a desperate situation. This move has the appearance of a trap but in reality it is a miscalculation. Another road to ruin was: 18 . . . Nc6 19 Qe4 Nxe5 (or 19 . . . Ne7 20 g4) 20 fxe5 Qe7 21

Bd3 g6 22 Rf6 and Black is irretrievably lost.

19	f5	b5

Black hopes that the bishop will not be able to move because of 20 ... Qxe5.

20	fxe6	bxc4
21	Rxf6	cxd3
22	exf7+	Bxf7

23 Rxf7

Since the pawn at d3 is fixed White can make his decisive material advantage tell.

23	...	Nb5
24	Rf2	Rd5
25	Nxd3	Re8
26	Rf3	Black resigns

José Raúl Capablanca

The first time I heard of Capablanca was in 1909, as indeed did all my contemporaries, when he won his match against Marshall in such astonishingly convincing fashion. Then he was twenty and I sixteen years of age. Neither his chess performance nor his style impressed me at the time. His play seemed 'new' but lacking in uniformity. And then when he won so fine a victory from the competitive point of view at San Sebastian, 1911, most of his games were won by surprising tactical resources. His real, incomparable gifts first began to make themselves apparent at the time of St. Petersburg, 1914, when too I came to know him personally. Neither before nor afterwards have I seen — and I cannot even imagine as well — such a flabbergasting quickness of chess comprehension as that possessed by the Capablanca of that epoch. Enough to say that he gave *all* the St. Petersburg masters the odds of 5-1 in quick games — and won! With all this he was always good-humoured, the darling of the ladies, and enjoyed wonderful good health — really a dazzling appearance. That he came second to Lasker must be entirely ascribed to his youthful levity — he was already playing as well as Lasker.

I met Capablanca for the second time in London in 1922. He was already World Champion, and had every intention of remaining so for the duration. In fact, at that moment his chess powers had reached their peak; a crystal-clear handling of the opening and middle-game, united with unsurpassed endgame technique. In character, however, he had become somewhat more nervous, and this nervousness manifested itself by his striving to put off as much as possible any match for the title, or else even to prevent it. For this reason he evolved the 'London Rules' which raised the stake for a match to 10 000 gold dollars. At that time it was difficult for him to imagine that any one of his rivals could get such a sum together. And in this he was right; since it was not for the sake of his rivals (in this case my insignificant self) but on account of Capablanca himself that the sum was raised in Buenos Aires in 1927 — in reality with the expectation of greeting him as world champion once again in a city which he had already visited twice and where he was extremely popular. People there were, of course, convinced that he would win the match against me. How did it happen that he lost to me? I must confess that even now I cannot answer this question with any certainty, since in 1927 I did not believe that I was superior to him. Perhaps the chief reason for his defeat was the over-estimation of his own powers arising out of his overwhelming victory at New York 1927, and his under-estimation of mine.

Be this as it may, with the loss of his title Capablanca also lost his form for some time, and began to pursue a policy that, given that he really wanted a return match, was calculated in no way to bring about such an eventuality, to put it mildly. Immediately after his defeat in fact he sought to bring about through F.I.D.E. (the chess counterpart of the League of Nations) new conditions for a title match, and this without consulting me. This was the sort of procedure I could not tolerate, and thus there arose a coolness and difference between us.

Some years later Capablanca came to a more correct decision, namely to attempt to show the chess world that he was the best candidate for the world championship by actual performance. And, indeed, he got so far in this respect as to win two very important tournaments in 1936 (Moscow and Nottingham). Then, however, his powers gave way, from the competitive rather than the pure chess point of view. His equal third (out of eight) at Semmering-Baden 1937, and his seventh (out of eight) in the AVRO Tournament showed the chess world that his hopes for the title were finally extinguished.

And even though until the end, for example in Buenos Aires, 1939, as I am about to demonstrate, he could still evolve true pearls of chess art, he had not sufficient stamina for obtaining practical success in a big tournament. All the same, Capablanca was snatched from the chess world much too soon. With his death we have lost a very great chess genius whose like we shall never see again.

GAME 68

Buenos Aires 1939
Queen's Pawn, Nimzowitsch Defence

White: J. ENEVOLDSEN (Denmark)
Black: J.R. CAPABLANCA (Cuba)

1	d4	Nf6	3	Nc3	Bb4
2	c4	e6	4	Qc2	0-0

5	a3	Bxc3+
6	Qxc3	d6
7	g3	Qe7
8	Bg2	

The same inexactitude as in the game van Scheltinga-Capablanca, Buenos Aires, 1939. Indicated was 8 Nf3 first.

8	...	e5
9	d5	a5
10	b3(?)	

A second inferior move instead of which he should have played 10 b4 as in the game mentioned. Black now obtains comfortable equality.

10	...	Nbd7
11	Nf3	Nc5
12	Nd2	

In order to prevent at this stage 12 ... Nfe4, followed by 13 ... f5.

12	...	Bf5
13	0-0	Nfe4
14	Nxe4	Bxe4
15	f3	Bg6
16	Be3	b6
17	b4	axb4
18	axb4	Nd7
19	Rfc1	

The last few moves of White, practically forced, were still good enough to keep the balance of the position. Now he threatens to simplify still more by playing 20 c5, and there is little for Black to do against this possibility.

19	...	f5

20	f4?	

Not only losing a most valuable tempo but also weakening the central squares without any compensation. White's best chance was still 20 c5, as the variation 20 ... bxc5 21 bxc5 Rxa1 22 Rxa1 Nf6 23 cxd6 cxd6 24 Qd2 etc., although slightly favourable to Black, did not actually represent any acute danger.

20	...	exf4
21	gxf4	Nf6

Already threatening to win a pawn by 22 ... Ng4.

22	h3	Rxa1
23	Rxa1	Re8
24	Ra3	Bh5
25	Qc2	Ne4

The only way to keep the initiative.

White to move

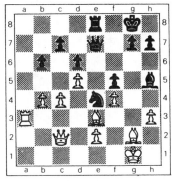

Position after 25 ... Ne4

26 Bd4?

The decisive mistake, instead of which he should *nolens volens* have taken the intruding knight. After 26 Bxe4 Qxe4 (or 26 ... fxe4 27

Qd2 Qh4 28 Kg2 with no tragedy to fear) 27 Qxe4 Rxe4 28 c5! (if 28 . . . Rxb4 29 c6) White, it is true, would have lost a pawn in some variations, but the reduced forces as well as the magic of opposite-coloured bishops would have secured him excellent drawing chances.

26 ...   Qh4!

After this it is already too late for White to take the knight, for after 27 . . . Rxe4 almost all his remaining pieces would be strongly threatened.

27 e3   Qe1+

28 Kh2   Bf3!

Elegant and effective, as 29 Bxf3 would lose immediately after 29 . . . Qg3+, followed by 30 . . . Nf2+.

29 Ra2   Re7

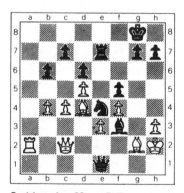

Position after 29 . . . Re7

White is now in a kind of positional stalemate, and Black can therefore quietly prepare everything for the decisive *coup*. In the event of entirely passive behaviour by White (Qb2-c2-b2 etc.) the next moves of Black would most likely have been . . . h6, . . . Kh7, followed by . . . g5!

30 Qa4   Kf7

Instead the win of the exchange by means of 30 . . . Qg3+ 31 Kg1 Nd2!? 32 Rxd2 Qe1+ 33 Bf1 Qxd2 would have been less convincing because of 34 Qa8+ Kf7 35 Qh8 Kg6 36 Qf8! and White is still fighting.

31 Qa8   Nd2!

Threatening 32 . . . Qf2.

32 Bxf3   Qf2+

33 Kh1

If 33 Bg2 then mate in two.

33 ...   Qf1+

34 Kh2   Nxf3+

35 Kg3   Nxd4

36 White resigns

GAME 69

Championship of the Balearic
Islands, 1944
Queen's Pawn, Nimzowitsch Defence

White: A. POMAR
Black: TICOULAT

1	d4	Nf6
2	c4	e6
3	Nc3	Bb4
4	e3	b6
5	Bd2	

An inoffensive but solid way of
combating Nimzowitsch's Defence.

5	...	Bb7
6	Nf3	0-0
7	Bd3	Bxc3

Black's first six moves were more or
less conventional but now it was
necessary to establish a plan with
the aim of completing the deploy-
ment of his forces in a satisfactory
way. To this end 7 ... d5, 7 ... c5
or 7 ... Be7, followed by ... d6
and ... Nbd7 would be plausible
ideas. The transaction in the text
is, however, inopportune, and
Pomar at once takes advantage of
the circumstance to seize the
initiative.

8	Bxc3	Ne4
9	Bxe4	Bxe4

White to move

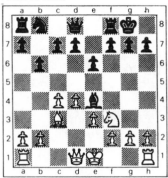

Position after 9 ... Bxe4

10 d5!

A very powerful move which presents Black with problems that are
difficult to solve. For instance, the
plausible rejoinder 10 ... f6 would
turn out to be inferior after 11 dxe6
dxe6 12 Nd4, followed by 13 Qg4
etc., and the line of defence chosen
by him is also inadequate. Relatively preferable would seem to be 10
... exd5 11 cxd5 (or 11 Qd4 f6)
Re8 with a hard, although defensible,
game.

10	...	c5
11	Nd2!	Bg6

After 11 ... exd5 12 Nxe4 dxe4 13
Qg4 f6 14 Qxe4 Nc6 15 0-0-0 White
would have had a crushing advantage.

12	h4	f5

There was no adequate defence left; 12 . . . f6 would have prolonged the game for a few moves but would not have changed the result.

13	Qf3	Na6
14	h5	Be8
15	Qg3	Qe7

16	d6	Qf7
17	h6	Qg6
18	hxg7	Rf7?

In his desperation Black leaves his queen to be taken. It is clear that 18 . . . Rf6 would not leave him any hope.

19	Qxg6	**Black resigns**

GAME 70

Fifth match game, New York 1942
Queen's Pawn, Nimzowitsch Defence

White: S. RESHEVSKY
Black: I. KASHDAN

1	d4	Nf6
2	c4	e6
3	Nc3	Bb4
4	a3	

With this move (Sämisch's) White imposes his will upon his opponent; as compensation for the slight structural pawn weakness he obtains the two bishops and many chances in the centre.

4	. . .	Bxc3+
5	bxc3	c5
6	e3	0-0
7	Bd3	Nc6
8	Nf3	d6
9	Qc2	e5

Allowing the blockade without White's being forced to play e4. More beneficial would seem 9 . . . Re8, threatening 10 . . . e5, followed

by 11 . . . e4. If White responds 10 e4 then 10 . . . h6 (avoiding the pinning of the knight), followed by 11 . . . e5.

10	d5	Ne7
11	0-0	Kh8

Preparing for 12 . . . Ne8, followed by 13 . . . f5. But White gets there first.

12	Ne1	Ne8
13	f4!	exf4
14	exf4	g6

With the purpose of exchanging the enemy king's bishop and directly reduce the possible action of the other bishop.

15	Nf3	

More prudent was 15 h3 in order to be able to answer 15 . . . Bf5 by 16 Bxf5 Nxf5 17 g4, followed by 18 f5 *without loss of material.*

15	...	Bf5
16	Bxf5	Nxf5
17	g4	Nh6!

Hoping (after 18 h3 for example) to play 18 . . . f5 with at least equal chances in view of the sad future of the bishop. But Reshevsky knows how to rise to the occasion.

White to move

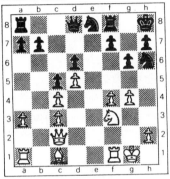

Position after 17 . . . Nh6

18 f5!

If this sacrifice is not sufficient to obtain a winning attack it is, nonetheless, the logical consequence of the previous manoeuvres and it gives his opponent multiple defensive problems, sometimes difficult to resolve over the board.

| 18 | ... | Nxg4 |
| 19 | h3! | Ne5! |

The best defence. If 19 . . . Ngf6 then 20 Bh6 Ng7 (or 20 . . . Rg8 21 Ng5) 21 Bg5! and 21 . . . Nxf5 is impossible because of 22 Nd2, followed by 23 Ne4.

| 20 | Nxe5 | dxe5 |

The White passed pawn is very displeasing, but Black has managed to obtain the magnificent blockading square d6 for the knight.

| 21 | Bh6 | Rg8 |
| 22 | f6 | g5 |

This move weakens the king's position; only the most simple move offers Black any benefit: 22 . . . Nd6 (and not 22 . . . Qd7 because of 23 Qh2!). The outcome of this move (22 . . . Nd6) might be: 23 Qe2! (23 Bg7+ Rxg7 24 fxg7+ Kxg7, followed eventually by . . . f5 is manifestly to Black's advantage) 23 . . . Nf5 (and not 23 . . . Re8 24 Bg7+ Kg8 25 Qe3, followed by 26 Qh6) 24 Rxf5 gxf5+ 25 Bg7+ Rxg7+ 26 fxg7+ Kxg7 27 Qxe5+ Qf6 28 Re1 Qxe5 29 Rxe5 Kf6 30 Re2 and White, thanks to his strong pawn at d5, should not lose the endgame.

| 23 | Qf5 | Rg6 |
| 24 | Bf8 | |

This ambitious move is based on the variation 24 . . . Nxf6 25 Bxc5 Qc8 26 Be7 and White recovers the material sacrificed with a clear advantage in the endgame. However the position achieved by means of 24 Bg7+ Nxg7 25 fxg7+ Rxg7 26 Qxe5, followed by Rae1 was not to be scorned. The occupation of the central squares and the weakening of the Black king's position would have offered more than adequate compensation for the pawn.

| 24 | ... | Nd6! |

The proper reply with which he could have drawn.

| 25 | Bg7+ | Kg8 |
| 26 | Qxe5 | |

Black to move

Position after 26 Qxe5

The position is extremely interesting. Black could obtain excellent drawing chances simply by playing 26 . . . Ne8, followed by 27 . . . Nxg7. But he had an even more effective method of guaranteeing this result. Kashdan could (and should) have taken the pawn with the knight. No doubt he allowed himself to be dissuaded by the fact that after 26 . . . Nxc4 27 Qe2! capturing the second pawn would be obvious: 27 . . . Qxd5 28 Rfe1 Nd6 29 Rad1, followed by 30 Rxd6 and wins. But after 27 . . . Qd6! White would have had nothing better than taking the knight, permitting perpetual check, since neither 28 Rf3 g4! nor 28 Rae1 Qg3+ 29 Qg2 Qxc3 would have given a satisfactory result.

26	. . .	Qd7?

An irreparable loss of time.

27	Rae1	h5

Of course not 27 . . . Re8 because of 28 Qxd6.

28	Qe7!	

The ending is easily won in view of the disastrous position of the Black king.

28	. . .	Qxe7
29	Rxe7	Rd8
30	Rfe1	Kh7
31	Kg2	g4

There is nothing to be done against the invasion plan of R1e5, followed after preparation by h4.

32	R1e5	gxh3+
33	Kxh3	Rg1
34	Rxh5+	Kg6
35	Ree5!	Rh1+
36	Kg4	Ne4
37	Rxh1	Nf2+
38	Kf4	**Black resigns**

If 38 . . . Nxh1 then it is mate in three moves.

GAME 71

Buenos Aires 1939
Queen's Pawn, Nimzowitsch Defence

White: S. TARTAKOWER (Poland)
Black: J. ENEVOLDSEN (Denmark)

1	d4	Nf6
2	c4	e6
3	Nc3	Bb4
4	Nf3	0-0

Fairly good. But this is no reason for Black not to accept the opportunity in this position of playing his queen's bishop to b7 after 4 . . . b6.

5 Bd2

A passive move after which Black will have no difficulty in equalizing. More enterprising is 5 Bg5.

5	. . .	d5
6	e3	a6

Simpler would be 6 . . . dxc4 7 Bxc4 c5 etc. but the text move cannot be considered deficient.

7	Qc2	dxc4
8	Bxc4	b5?

This is the decisive mistake, as will be convincingly demonstrated by Dr. Tartakower. Instead, 8 . . . c5 would still clearly be satisfactory for Black.

9 Bd3

Position after 9 Bd3

9	. . .	Nbd7

Black has a choice only between different inferior lines. For example, 9 . . . c5 10 dxc5 Bxc5 11 Ne4! winning a pawn, or 9 . . . Bb7 10 Ne4! Bxd2+ 11 Nfxd2 and Black remains with an incurable weakness on his queen's bishop's diagonal. The knight move, whose object is to prepare for . . . c5, allows the following devastating advance in the centre.

10	e4!	c5

11 e5

Very strong in spite of the following intermediary move by Black.

11	. . .	c4

Black hereby obtains a good support for his queen's side pawn majority, but the position of his king quickly becomes indefensible against the following attack. This short game is an attractive model for those enthusiasts who are inclined to pursue a particular advance on one sector of the board without worrying about all the details of the position.

12	Be2	Bxc3
13	bxc3	Nd5

White to move

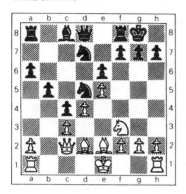

Position after 13 ... Nd5

14 Ng5!

Forcing either the win of a pawn and the exchange (after 14 ... f5) or a deadly weakness on the h-file (after 14 ... g6). In reality Black could have resigned at this moment.

14	...	g6
15	h4	N7b6

15 ... Qe7 was equally bad.

16	h5	f5
17	hxg6	hxg6
18	Rh6	Rf7

A desperate sacrifice that White could have refuted at once by 19 Rh8+, but the method chosen is also quite convincing.

19	0-0-0	Rg7
20	Rdh1	Kf8
21	Rh8+	Rg8
22	R1h7	Ne7
23	Nf7	Qc7
24	Bh6+	Ke8
25	Nd6+	**Black resigns**

GAME 72

Match: Spain v Portugal, 1945
Queen's Pawn, Nimzowitsch Defence

White: A. POMAR
Black: RIBEIRO

1	d4	Nf6
2	c4	e6
3	Nc3	Bb4
4	Bd2	

Pomar's preferred move.

4	...	d5
5	e3	0-0
6	Nf3	Nbd7
7	Bd3	a6

8 Qb3

This move is not bad, but strategically simpler would be 8 cxd5 exd5 9 0-0 with the purpose of beginning a minority attack on the queen's side.

8	...	c5
9	cxd5	cxd4

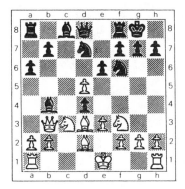

Position after 9 . . . cxd4

10 Nxd4?

White forgets that the Black knight can be placed at c5. After both 10 exd4 Bxc3 11 bxc3, followed by 12 0-0 and 10 Qxb4 dxc3 11 Qxc3 Nxd5 12 Qd4 he would maintain the better position thanks to his bishops.

10	...	Nc5
11	Qc2	exd5
12	0-0	Nxd3
13	Qxd3	Bd6
14	Nf5?	

This knight manoeuvre definitely does not improve his position. The logical plan was 14 Rad1, followed by 15 Bc1 and, eventually, b3 and Bb2.

| 14 | ... | Be5 |
| 15 | Ng3 | Bd7 |

It is clear that by playing 15 . . . d4 Black would eliminate all risk of losing, but in any case he does well to play for the advantage, since his position is perfectly solid.

16 Rfe1

Rather one would expect 16 Rfd1.

| 16 | ... | Bc6 |
| 17 | Rad1 | Ng4 |

Erroneous strategy because it allows the exchange of the precious king's bishop. The natural move 17 . . . Ne4 would leave Black with a much better game.

| 18 | h3 | Bxg3 |
| 19 | fxg3 | |

Notwithstanding the poor White pawn formation chances are now more or less equal since Black too has a weakness at d5.

| 19 | ... | Nf6 |
| 20 | Ne2 | Bb5 |

The elimination of the White knight is plausible but it does not break the equilibrium, as the bishop is in a position to counter the strong position of the knight at e4.

| 21 | Qf5 | Bxe2 |
| 22 | Rxe2 | Qc7 |

22 . . . Ne4 23 Bc1 leads to nothing.

| 23 | Bc3 | Ne4 |

This move, apparently a very powerful one, will be opposed by Pomar in a most effective way.

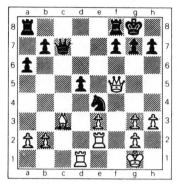

Position after 23 . . . Ne4

24 Be5!   **Qc4**

25 Qg4!

This wins the time necessary for 26 b3.

25 . . .   **f6**

26 b3   **Qc6**

27 Bb2   **h5?**

Too weak, because the queen at g6 will exert unpleasant pressure. The move 27 . . . Rad8 would have given a good game.

28 Qg6   **Rad8**

29 Rc1   **Qd6?**

Another mistake. There was no better resource than trying an exchange of queens with 29 . . . Qe8.

30 g4!

This wins at least a pawn and also gives an enviable position. Black's answer costs him the exchange, and his resistance therefore swiftly crumbles.

30 . . .   **h4**

31 Ba3!   **Qg3**

Of course he cannot permit 32 Rc7.

32 Bxf8   **Rxf8**

33 Qf5   **Ng5**

34 Kh1   **Ne4**

Clearly on account of time shortage, although the position was hopeless.

35 Qxd5+   **Black resigns**

Pomar knew how to exploit all his opportunities in the second part of this game.

GAME 73

Munich 1942
Queen's Pawn, Nimzowitsch Defence

White: K. JUNGE
Black: E. BOGOLJUBOV

1	d4	Nf6
2	c4	e6
3	Nc3	Bb4
4	f3	

Bogoljubov takes it upon himself to demonstrate in practice the deficiency of this treatment of the Nimzowitsch Defence by White, and herein lies the value of this game, although it was inadequately played by Junge.

4 ...	d5
5 a3	Bxc3+
6 bxc3	c5
7 cxd5	exd5!

After 7 . . . Nxd5 White could have played 8 dxc5 Qa5 9 e4 with an excellent game.

8 e3	Bf5!
9 Ne2	Nc6
10 Qb3?	

A loss of time which is all the more noticeable given White's retarded development. Necessary was the move 10 dxc5, followed eventually by Nd4.

Black to move

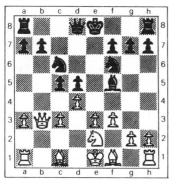

Position after 10 Qb3

10 ...	0-0
11 Ng3	

If 11 Qxb7 there would follow 11 . . . Na5 12 Qa6 Nb3 13 Ra2 Qe7, followed by . . . Rfe8 with clear advantage to Black.

11 ...	Bg6
12 dxc5	Qe7
13 c4?	

After this grave error the battle is practically resolved. But also after 13 Be2 h5! White's position would be mortally threatened.

13 ...	Nd4!
14 Qc3	Nc2+
15 Kf2	Nxa1
16 Qxa1	Qxc5
17 cxd5	Nxd5

The technical problem of forcing victory is undertaken by Black in irreproachable style: **18 Be2 Rfe8 19 Qd4 Qxd4 20 exd4 Rac8 21 Bd2 Rc2 22 Rd1 Nc3 23 Bxc3 Rxc3 24 f4 f6 25 Bb5 Rd8 26 a4 h6 27 Ne2 Rc2 28 Kf3 Bf7 29 g3 Bc4 30 Bxc4 Rxc4 31 Ra1 Rd5 32 Ke4 Ra5 33 f5 Raxa4 34 Rxa4 Rxa4 35 Kd5 Ra2 36 Nf4 Kf7 37 Kd6 b5 38 Kc5 a6 39 Nd5 Rxh2 40 Nc7 Rc2+ 41 White resigns**

King's Indian Defence

GAME 74

Buenos Aires 1939
King's Indian Defence

White: R. FLORES (Chile)
Black: M. NAJDORF (Poland)

1	d4	Nf6
2	c4	g6
3	Nc3	Bg7
4	Nf3	0-0
5	e4	d6
6	Be2	

This is more or less as playable as the usual 6 Be3 or 6 g3, followed by 7 Bg2.

6	...	Nbd7
7	0-0	e5
8	d5?	

The tension in the centre should be maintained as long as possible, and the blocking of the position would be justified only if it were related to some strategical plan. Preferable, therefore, is 8 Be3, and if 8 ... Re8 (8 ... Ng4 9 Bg5) then 9 Qc2, followed by 10 Rad1 etc. with advantage to White.

8	...	Nc5
9	Qc2	a5
10	b3?	

With the purpose of conserving the initiative. Bogoljubov's manoeuvre Nd2-b3 was indicated. The text move is not only an important loss of time; it also weakens the diagonal a1-h8, allowing Black to take advantage of this circumstance in forceful fashion.

| 10 | ... | Nh5! |

Already undertaking a direct attack which, in a few moves, will be irresistible.

11 g3

The remedy is almost worse than the disease. He should have gone forward with his mobilization by playing 11 Bg5 f6 12 Be3, followed by Ne1-d3 etc.

| 11 | ... | f5 |
| 12 | Nd2 | f4! |

Very strong, because an attempt to block the position with 13 g4 would not be successful owing to 13 ... f3! 14 Bxf3 Nf4 with a winning position.

13 Qd1

13 Bxh5 would also be perfectly hopeless as White's remaining minor pieces would be unable to take part in the defence of his king.

| 13 | ... | Bh3 |

14	Re1	fxg3
15	hxg3	

Black to move

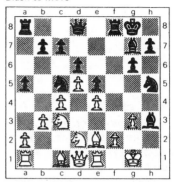

Position after 15 hxg3

15	...	Nf4!

Najdorf quite rightly resists the temptation of playing to the gallery by sacrificing the knight at g3 since, after 15 . . . Nxg3 16 fxg3 Qg5 17 Kh2 Rf2+ 18 Kxh3 Qh6+ 19 Bh5 White would not be lost. The text move is much faster.

16 Bf3

If 16 gxf4 of course 16 . . . exf4 threatening both 17 . . . Bxc3 and 17 . . . Qg5+.

16	...	Nfd3
17	Re2	Qf6

With the strong threat of 17 . . . Bh6.

18	Kh2	Bd7
19	Na4	

The weaknesses of the f-file cannot possibly be protected.

19	...	Nxa4
20	bxa4	Bh6
21	Ba3	Bxd2
22	Rxd2	Qxf3
23	Rxd3	Qxf2+
24	Kh1	Bh3
25	Rd2	

Or 25 Qg1 Qc2, followed by 26 . . . Rf2.

25	...	Qxg3
26	Qb3	Rf3

27 White resigns

A good example of the vigorous style of Poland's number two player.

Grünfeld Defence

GAME 75

Buenos Aires 1939
Grünfeld Defence

White: R. FLORES (Chile)
Black: M. CZERNIAK (Palestine)

1 d4	Nf6
2 c4	g6
3 Nc3	d5
4 cxd5	Nxd5
5 e4	Nxc3
6 bxc3	c5
7 Bb5+	Bd7
8 Bxd7+	Qxd7
9 Nf3	Bg7
10 Be3	Nc6
11 0-0	cxd4
12 cxd4	0-0

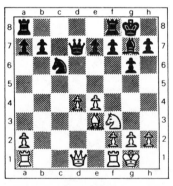

Position after 12 . . . 0-0

Thus the 'classical' position of this defence has been attained. Its characteristics are: on the White side, an insecure pawn centre and the possibility of eventual attacks on the king's flank, and on the Black side, a pawn majority on the queen's wing which, however, cannot be utilized until the endgame. The result will largely depend on the battle that is undertaken for the vital squares on the open c-file. The position is very similar to that of a favourable line of the Semi-Tarrasch Defence, although perhaps slightly more advantageous to Black.

13 d5

The alternative is 13 Qd2, preventing the Black move 13 . . . Na5 and inducing him to reply 13 . . . b6, which would weaken his c6.

13 . . .   Ne5?

An instructive strategic error whereby Black directly provokes the following attack on his king. Indicated was 13 . . . Na5 14 Bd4 Bxd4 15 Qxd4 Rfe8, after which 16 Ne5 Qc7 17 Ng4 would be parried by 17 . . . Qf4. It is clear that Black cannot play 13 . . . Bxa1 here because of 14 dxc6! Qxd1 15 Rxd1 Bc3 16 cxb7 Rab8 17 Rb1, followed by 18 Ba7 etc.

14	Nxe5	Bxe5
15	Rb1	b5

Hoping that his rapid advance on this wing will make White abandon his plans in the centre. The first player could, and probably should, prevent the placing of the Black bishop at c3 by firstly playing 16 Qd3. But it seems that it did not occur to him and he thought that this manoeuvre, obstructing the c-file, would make it more difficult for Black to develop a counter-attack.

16	f4!?	Bc3
17	Qd3	b4
18	f5	

Not threatening anything for the moment but forcing Black to take into account possible pressure (after fxg6 hxg6) on f7 or the formation Rf3-h3, followed by Bd4.

18	...	Rfc8

Also after 18 ... Rab8 19 Rf3 Qb5 20 Qc2, followed by 21 Qf2, the assault would develop according to White's wishes.

19	Rf3	

At this particular moment the doubling of the rooks is out of place, since the intended opening of the f-file would not produce dangerous threats. Preferable first is 19 h4 with the object of exerting pressure on the enemy king side after 20 fxg6 fxg6 21 h5, depriving it of its pawn protection.

19	...	Qd6

Principally with the aim of 20 ...

Be5, followed by 21 ... Rc3.

20	fxg6	hxg6

Preparing for the following bishop retreat and, of course, not considering the strength of his opponent's exchange sacrifice. 20 ... fxg6 21 Rbf1 Be5 (or 21 Bd4 a5) would offer an adequate defence.

21	Rbf1	Bf6

If 21 ... f6 the attempt 22 e5 fxe5 23 Rf6 would be refuted by 23 ... e4 24 Rxd6 exd3 25 Rxg6+ Kh7. But 22 Rg3 threatening 23 Rxg6+ would have decided the game in White's favour. Of less danger than the provocative text move is 21 ... Rf8.

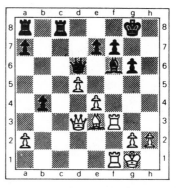

Position after 21 ... Bf6

22	Rxf6!	

A bold sacrifice, the consequences of which cannot be calculated precisely and can only be the subject of a general appreciation of the position. In any case, the young Chilean master deserves praise for his courage and determination.

22	...	exf6

23 Bd4   a5!

The only possible defence and in no way without hope since 24 Bxf6 could be answered by 24 . . . Rc1! 25 Rxc1 Qxf6 and 24 Rxf6 by 24 . . . Rc1+ 25 Kf2 Qxh2. White must therefore seek means of attacking.

24 Qe3

Now threatening 25 Bxf6 with deadly effect.

24 . . .   Rc4

If now 25 Rxf6 then 25 . . . Qc7 26 d6 Rc1+ 27 Kf2 Qc2+ 28 Kg3 Rd1 with salvation.

25 Bxf6!

White's skill in offering an exchange of queens is truly surprising. Because of the enormous activity of the bishop (with its mating threats and support of the passed pawn) the ending is won for White.

25 . . .	**Qc5**
26 Qxc5	**Rxc5**
27 d6	**Rc6**

Unhappily for Black he cannot play 27 . . . Ra7 because of 28 Bd4 winning a clear rook. 27 . . . Rcc8 would also be fatal owing to 28 d7 Rd8 29 Rf3 Rxd7 30 Rh3.

28 e5   a4

After the plausible 28 . . . Ra7 White would force victory by 29 Rd1 Rd7 30 Rd5! Rc1+ 31 Kf2 Rc2+ 32 Ke3 Rxa2 33 Rb5 and wins.

29 Rf4!

The double threat of 30 Rxb4 and 30 Rh4 decides the game. The counter-attack that follows is completely hopeless.

29 . . .	**Rc1+**
30 Kf2	**Rc2+**
31 Ke3	**Rac8**
32 Rxb4	**R2c3+**
33 Ke4	**Rc2**
34 Bg5	**Rxa2**
35 d7	**Ra8**
36 Rc4	**Black resigns**

GAME 76

Cracow/Warsaw 1942
Grünfeld Defence

White: RUSSHER
Black: WALCICER

1	d4	Nf6	5 cxd5	
2	Nf3	g6		
3	c4	Bg7		
4	Nc3	d5		

After the experience of recent years, this move is justified only when a player desires a draw.

5	...	Nxd5
6	e4	Nxc3
7	bxc3	c5
8	Bc4	

The series of moves sanctioned by theory is 8 Be2 0-0 9 0-0 cxd4 10 cxd4 Nc6 11 Be3 Bg4 12 d5 and after 12 . . . Bxa1 13 Qxa1 and White recovers the exchange by means of Bh6. However this game seems to prove that the method selected by White is practicable.

8	...	0-0
9	h3	cxd4
10	cxd4	Nc6
11	Be3	Qa5+
12	Bd2	Qa3

The queen has no more effective rejoinder, since if 12 . . . Qb6 there would follow 13 Rb1 and if 12 . . . Qc7 then 13 Rc1.

13	**Rb1!**	**Nxd4!**

An excellent idea but not too recommendable from the practical point of view as it can only lead to a draw.

14	Bb4	Nxf3+
15	Kf1?	

Just what Black wanted. After 15 Ke2! (and not 15 gxf3 Bc3+) Black would have to submit himself to a draw by repetition of moves by means of 15 . . . Nd4+ 16 Ke1 — not 16 Kf1 Be6! 17 Bxa3 Bxc4+ 18 Ke1 Nb5 with advantage.

Black to move

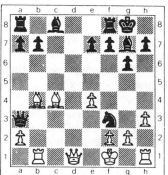

Position after 15 Kf1

15	**...**	**Be6!**

A beautiful move which decides the game.

16 Be2 Qxa2 17 Bxf3 Rfd8 18 Qe1 Rac8 19 g4 b6 20 Bxe7 Bc3 21 Qc1 Rd2 22 Bh4 Bd4 23 Qe1 Rcc2 24 Rh2 Bc4+ 25 Kg1 Rxf2 26 Rxf2 Rxf2 27 Bxf2 Bxf2+ 28 Qxf2 Qxb1+ 29 Kh2 Qa2 30 Qxa2 Bxa2 31 White resigns. A game not without theoretical interest.

GAME 77

Buenos Aires 1939
Grünfeld Defence

White: R. GRAU (Argentina)
Black: V. MIKENAS (Lithuania)

1	d4	Nf6
2	c4	g6
3	Nc3	d5
4	Bf4	Bg7
5	e3	0-0

Probably this move will be completely abandoned because of having achieved little success after the following moves: 6 cxd5 Nxd5 7 Nxd5 Qxd5 8 Bxc7 Nc6 (the attack initiated by 8 . . . Na6 is not sufficient, as is proved by the game Lilienthal-Keres, Moscow, 1939; 9 Bxa6 Qxg2 10 Qf3 Qxf3 11 Nxf3 bxa6 12 0-0!, which is clearly in White's favour). Since 5 . . . c5 (experimented with at Buenos Aires) does not satisfy either on account of 6 dxc5 0-0 7 cxd5 Qa5 8 Qd2, what will be the next reply to 4 Bf4?

6	Qb3	c5

The well known Botwinnik variation.

7	cxd5	cxd4
8	exd4	e6!?

New and hazardous, instead of the solid and adequate . . . Nbd7-b6. In this game, sadly, White does not try to refute the pawn sacrifice.

Position after 8 . . . e6

9 Nf3?

This would be partially justified if White was certain to obtain comfortable equality with a solid game. In the text continuation, however, he is left with an unpleasant isolated pawn. If he decided to play 9 dxe6 on the other hand he would have to surrender the advantage to his opponent. In that case Black would have at his disposal various attacking moves, but none of them appears good enough to arrive at a convincing result. For example, 9 . . . Bxe6 10 Qxb7 Qxd4 11 Nge2, or 9 . . . fxe6 10 Nf3, or 9 . . . Re8 10 d5! fxe6 11 0-0-0 etc. Relatively more promising would be 9 . . . Qxd4 10 Nge2 Qc5 11 exf7+ Rxf7. But here too White would have ample defensive possibilities, beginning with 12 Be3. This little opening problem was not solved at Buenos Aires, and it may be necessary to await another international tournament, if there are any.

9	. . .	Nxd5
10	Be5	Nc6
11	Bxg7	Kxg7

12 Bb5

This was the last moment for attaining a symmetrical position by 12 Nxd5, but after 12 . . . exd5 he would not have time to castle on the king's side, and 13 0-0-0 would be almost suicidal on account of the open c-file. On the other hand, after the text move Black will gain a splendid diagonal for his bishop.

12 . . .   Na5

13 Qc2   b6

14 0-0   Bb7

15 Qd2?

The possibility of 15 . . . Nf4 was certainly not pleasant, and it is not surprising that White should try to prevent it. But the loss of a pawn or a bad pawn structure on the king's side (as occurs in the game) is the most that would have resulted from this knight move. After 15 Rfd1 Nf4 16 Ne1 Qg5 17 Bf1 White, though not completely happy, would have gained some relief.

15 . . .   Nxc3

16 Qxc3

It really is a task to decide which variation is worse, the text or 16 bxc3 Bxf3 17 gxf3 Qd5.

16 . . .   Rc8

17 Qd3   Bxf3

18 gxf3

After 18 Qxf3 Qxd4 Black with his extra pawn would also have had the better position.

18 . . .   Qg5+

19 Kh1   Rfd8

20 Ba6   Rc7

21 Qe3   Qf6

22 Rfd1   Rcd7

23 Rac1

Hoping to obtain some chances of saving himself after 23 . . . Rxd4 24 Rxd4 Rxd4 25 Qc3. Black could deal with this by 25 . . . e5! 26 b4 Nc6 and in this case he would have adequate means of parrying the attack (27 Qxc6 Rd1+). But he prefers, and rightly, to centralize his knight first.

23 . . .   Nb7

24 b4

The queen and rook struggle after 24 Bxb7 would be as hopeless for White as it will be in a couple of moves.

24 . . .   Nd6

25 Bd3   Nf5

26 Bxf5

Forced.

26 . . .   Qxf5

27 Rd2   Qf6

28 Rcd1   Rd5

29 Qe4   Rf5

It becomes all too clear that White will not be capable of defending his d-pawn and his king-side weakness at the same time.

30 Rd3   Rdd5

31 Kg2   Rf4

32 Qe3   Qh4

33 Ra3   a5

34 bxa5   bxa5

35 Qc3   e5!

The *coup de grâce* !

36 Rxa5   exd4

Attacking the queen and threatening to win a rook by 37 . . . Qg5+.

White resigned.

Samuel Reshevsky, an American of Polish origin, was the child prodigy who — a strange thing in the game of chess — has succeeded in becoming an exceptional player in his maturity.

Can Reshevsky be considered to have sufficient abilities to seek the world title? In view of his successes the opinion of his colleagues (I am amongst them) and the pre-war chess press is that there can be no doubt about it. But in order to be able to form a definite opinion on this matter it would be necessary to know the view of the person concerned: what does Reshevsky think of his chances? Does he truly desire to play a match for the world title? This is of importance, because without being able to count on the firm decision of the candidate nobody would be interested at the present time in organizing an encounter. Before 1940 I was quite certain that two masters, Botwinnik and Flohr, wished to fight for this title. Neither of the two matches could be brought about, and the above-mentioned challengers know very well that I had decided to face them.

As regards Keres, his position in 1938—9 was less resolved; he gave the impression of preferring to let a few years pass. But in 1943, perhaps influenced by the disastrous results he obtained against me in recent meetings (+3 =3 —0 in my favour) he resolutely declared that he had not the slightest intention of challenging me to a match. Fine too, in 1940, made an analogous declaration.

For my part, being of course disposed to accept all challenges that come to me from qualified opponents — such is my duty as a sportsman — I consider the most difficult problem (and therefore the most interesting both for the chess world and for myself) to be a match against Botwinnik and against Reshevsky. Both are players of stature, each with his own well pronounced individuality and both are seasoned fighters. Both have continued their sporting activity in their respective countries and have demonstrated their ability to maintain their strength. From the clash of our styles there would surely arise battles that would excite interest in the chess world.

Eight years have passed without a world championship match taking place. This should not happen; it does not delight me to be Champion without having the chance of putting my title in play, especially when there is no shortage of opponents worthy of aspiring to it. I am not ignorant of the fact that the present circumstances place obstacles before the realization of such encounters; nor am I unaware that those difficulties are not insuperable. In any case there will be no obstacles from myself. Once more I insist on repeating that which I have published on several occasions: that is, that the articles which were stupid and untrue from a chess point of view and which were printed signed with my name in a Paris newspaper in 1941, are a falsification.* It is not the first time that unscrupulous newspapers have abused my name in order to publish inanities of that kind but in the present case what was published in *Pariser Zeitung* is what has caused me the most grief, not only because of its content but also precisely because it is impossible for me to rectify it.

This explanation is necessary. Without it all discussion about the possibility of organizing matches for the world title would be pointless. Colleagues know my sentiments and they know perfectly well how great is the esteem in which I hold their art and that I have too elevated a concept of chess to become entangled in the absurd statements poured out by the above-mentioned Parisian newspaper.

On the other hand, I bow to and rely on the sane judgement of the chess world. Let it appoint the challenger for the title and the place in which the battle is to be fought. I am ready and I await its orders.

GAME 78

First match game, New York 1942
Grünfeld Defence

White: S. RESHEVSKY
Black: I. KASHDAN

1	d4	Nf6
2	c4	g6
3	Nc3	d5
4	Bf4	

A variation that was very much in fashion before the war (particularly during the AVRO tournament of 1938). This fashion would lead to very complicated positions should Black try to take the initiative in the centre by sacrificing one or two pawns.

4	...	Bg7

5	e3	0-0!?

Position after 5 ... 0-0

*They were virulently anti-Semitic. E.W.

Creating for White this problem: should he accept the c-pawn? After 6 cxd5 Nxd5 7 Nxd5 Qxd5 8 Bxc7 White would certainly obtain an advantage in the endgame in case of 8 . . . Na6 9 Bxa6! Qxg2 10 Qf3 Qxf3 11 Nxf3 bxa6 12 0-0 etc. (Flohr-Botwinnik AVRO, 1938). But after 8 . . . Nc6! 9 Ne2 Bg4, followed by 10 . . . Rac8 Black reaches an attacking position full of promise. The game Keres-Lilienthal (Moscow, 1940) continued in this way and ended in a draw. Reshevsky prefers to shun these complications but he becomes entangled in other greater ones in the following moves.

6 Qb3

If 6 Rc1 Black can also play 6 . . . c5, as did Reshevsky himself against Capablanca in the AVRO tournament.

6 . . .   c5

The pawn sacrifice variation inaugurated by this move was considered absolutely correct after the game Capablanca-Flohr in the AVRO tournament. The new move 10 Qd1! played by Reshevsky in this game produces fresh doubts regarding its value.

7	dxc5	Ne4!
8	cxd5	Qa5
9	Ne2	Nxc5

The developing move 9 . . . Na6 is not more effective because White can reply with 10 Nd4 Naxc5 11 Qb5.

10 Qd1!

This withdrawal offers more security than 10 Qc4 as played by Capablanca against Flohr. In fact after 10 . . . Na6 11 Nd4 Black, with 11 . . . e5! (instead of 11 . . . Bd7) 12 dxe6 Bxe6 13 Nxe6 Nxe6 would have obtained an advantage in development that would have been lucrative compensation for the lost pawn.

10 . . .   e5

The principal object of this move is to take the square d4 from the White knight. After the plausible reply 11 Bg3 Black could continue his attack with 11 . . . Bf5 (12 Nc1) or, better still, with 11 . . . b5 (12 a3 b4 13 axb4 Qxb4 with a promising game).

11 Bg5!

A profound and very well calculated manoeuvre; on 11 . . . Ne4 White with 12 Be7 Re8 13 Ba3 would have assured himself of a game without danger (because 13 . . . b5 would in this case be refuted by 14 Qb3!) and would not have great development difficulties to overcome. In reply to Black's next move Reshevsky has a surprising stroke which justifies the defensive plan initiated with 10 Qd1!

11 . . .   f6

Apparently very effective because after 12 Bh4 Black recovers the pawn by 12 . . . Qb4, keeping the initiative.

White to move

Position after 11 ... f6

12 a3!

With this move he imposes his will
on his opponent. Kashdan may
certainly recuperate his sacrificed
pawn but after 12 ... fxg5 13 b4
Qb6 14 bxc5 Qxc5 15 Ne4 Qa5+
16 Qd2 Qxd2+ 17 Kxd2 g4 18
N2c3 White would attain a superior
ending thanks to his passed pawn
and the solid position of his knight
at e4. Consequently Black must
continue the attack by advancing
his centre pawns. But this attack,
which in other circumstances might
have been dangerous, will be very
ineffective in view of the back-
wardness of his queen's side development.

12	...	Ne4
13	Bh4	g5
14	Bg3	f5
15	f3	Nxc3

15 ... Nxg3 16 hxg3 offered still
fewer chances.

| 16 | Nxc3 | f4 |
| 17 | Bf2 | e4 |

18 Rc1

The impetuous advance of the
Black pawns has reached its
maximum intensity, and one realizes
that he has not really achieved anything. If, for example, he plays 18
... fxe3 19 Bxe3 exf3 20 gxf3 Re8
21 Qd2 it is evident that White has
nothing to fear.

| 18 | ... | Bf5 |

He tries to complete his mobilization
but is too late.

| 19 | Be2 | exf3 |
| 20 | gxf3! | |

Simpler than 20 Bxf3 which would
have created pointless complications
after 20 ... Re8 21 Qd2 fxe3 22
Bxe3 Qb6 etc. (If 23 Kf2? then 23
... Rxe3!).

| 20 | ... | fxe3 |
| 21 | Bxe3 | Nd7 |

Hoping after 22 Bxg5 Qb6 to be
able to fish in troubled waters.
Reshevsky rightly prefers to place
his king in safety as the pawn presented
to him can guarantee victory.

22	0-0	Rae8
23	Bd4	Ne5
24	Kh1	

A good precautionary move before
beginning the decisive action in the
centre. In fact Black cannot take
advantage of the moment of respite,
as his adversary is free from vulnerable points.

| 24 | ... | a6 |

With this he prevents 25 Nb5. But
White now has an open field in

which to deal forceful blows.

25 d6!

With, amongst others, the threat of 26 Qb3+.

25 ...   Kh8

26 b4!   Qd8

A forced move because if 26 ... Qxa3 27 Nd5! and wins.

27 Nd5   g4

The variations 27 ... Qxd6 28 Bc5 and 27...Re6 28 Bb6 leave no hope and Black tries one last skirmish.

28 Nc7

Reshevsky does not let himself be frightened by ghosts.

Black to move

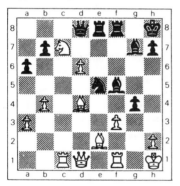

Position after 28 Nc7

28 ...   gxf3

He rejects 28 ... Qh4. In fact this move would have been victoriously refuted by 29 Nxe8 g3 30 Rf2! (but not 30 Bg1 Qh3 31 Rf2 gxf2 32 Nxg7 fxg1(Q)+ 33 Qxg1 Rg8 etc.) gxf2 31 Nxg7 and wins.

29 Bxf3   Nxf3

30 Bxg7+   Kxg7

31 Nxe8+   Qxe8

32 Rc7+   Kg8

Or 32 ... Kh6 33 Rxf3 Be4 34 Qd2+ Kh5 35 Rc5+.

33 Re7

33 Rxf3 Be4 34 Qb3+ also wins at once.

33 ...   Qg6

34 Qd5+   Kh8

35 Rxf3   Black resigns

GAME 79

Third match game, New York 1942
Grünfeld Defence

White: S. RESHEVSKY
Black: I. KASHDAN

1	d4	Nf6
2	c4	g6
3	Nc3	d5
4	Qb3	dxc4

With this capture Black abandons the centre to his opponent but he trusts that he will be able to resolve in his favour the important problem of the development of his queen's bishop. The difficulty for White — who will have more freedom of movement available during the first phase of the game — will consist of finding vulnerable points in the enemy position. In the end he manages this, but not without weakening his own position on the queen's side. The game is instructive, particularly as regards strategy.

5	Qxc4	Be6
6	Qd3	

Simpler than, and at least as good as, 6 Qb5+ Nc6 7 Nf3 Nd5! (played by Flohr in the tournament at Kemeri in 1937), which after 8 e4 a6 9 Qa4 Nb6 10 Qd1 Bg4 11 Be3 Bg7 does not lead to any tangible result.

6	...	Bg7
7	e4	c6
8	Nf3	0-0
9	Be2	Ne8!

Seeking an exchange of the queen's bishop for a bishop before White has finished his development. It is evident that exchanges contribute to the unfolding of Black's game.

10	0-0	Nd6
11	Qc2	

If 11 b3 Black can play 11 . . . c5 12 dxc5 Nxe4! or 12 d5 Bxc3 13 Qxc3 Nxe4 14 Qb2 Bxd5 15 Bh6 Nf6 16 Bxf8 Qxf8 with two pawns for the exchange and a solid position.

11	...	Bc4
12	Bf4	Bxe2
13	Qxe2	Qb6

A well known manoeuvre in this type of position because of my matches against Bogoljubov and Dr. Euwe. As White clearly has no interest in exchanging queens, the Black queen will occupy a strong position at a6 and at the same time will exert a certain pressure against the enemy queen's wing.

14	Rad1	Qa6
15	Rd3	Nd7
16	e5	

A move with a double intention whereby White virtually binds himself to forcing a decision by an attack against the king. As Black does not have any threat at his disposal 16 Rfd1, liberating the queen from the defence of the rook and reserving for himself a wider field of action, was most logical.

16	...	Nb5!
17	Ng5	

17 e6 would not lead to anything practical after 17 . . . Nxc3 18 bxc3 fxe6 etc.

17	...	Nxc3
18	bxc3	h6
19	Ne4	c5!

Now Black achieves a truly favourable situation: the c-file and the pawn majority on the queen's side.

20	Rfd1	cxd4
21	cxd4	Rac8
22	Qd2	Rfd8!

This indirectly defends the h-pawn. If 23 Bxh6 then 23 . . . Nxe5! 24 Rh3 Rxd4 25 Qxd4 Nf3+ 26 Rxf3 Bxd4 27 Rxd4 Qxa2 28 Rfd3 f5 with advantage thanks to the dislocation of the White pieces.

23	h4	Kh7
24	h5	

White must obviously try to attack at all costs, but Black has adequate defensive resources.

24	. . .	g5
25	Bg3	

Sacrificing the bishop would be incorrect play: 25 Bxg5 hxg5 26 Nxg5+ Kg8 27 Qf4 f6! 28 Rg3 Nxe5.

25	. . .	Rc4

Rather a complicated move which in the long run does not achieve its object. Sufficient to maintain the balance would be 25 . . . f5. For instance, 26 Nc3 Rc4 27 Bh2 Kh8 or 26 exf6 Nxf6. The sacrifice 26 Nxg5+ hxg5 27 Qxg5 would be refuted by 27 . . . Qe6! 28 d5 Qf7 29 e6 Qf6 30 Qg6+ Qxg6 31 hxg6+ Kxg6 32 exd7 Rxd7 and Black appears to have a good game.

26	f4	f5
27	Nc3	

The only plausible move. 27 exf6 Nxf6 28 Nc5 Qc6 would certainly be scarcely recommendable.

27	. . .	gxf4
28	Bxf4	

Black to move

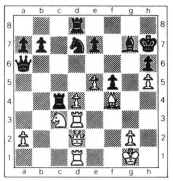

Position after 28 Bxf4

Without doubt Kashdan examined with this move the simplifying variation 28 . . . Nc5 29 dxc5 Rxd3 30 Qxd3 Rxf4 31 Qxa6 bxa6. The final position obtained hereby would certainly be favourable to White but it would however offer some prospects of resistance because the two White pawns would be threatened (the c-pawn by 32 . . . Rc4). But thanks to some finesses worthy of mention White can reach his goal in a few moves: 32 Rd7! and now:

(a) 32 . . . Bxe5 33 Rxe7+ Bg7 34 Nd5 Rd4! 35 Nf6+ Kh8 36 Re8+ Bf8 37 c6! Rc4 38 Rxf8+ Kg7 39 Nd7 Rxc6 40 Rf7+ and wins.

(b) 32 . . . Rc4 33 Nd5 Rxc5 34 e6! Bf8 (if 34 . . . Ra5 35 Nxe7Rxa2 36 Nxf5 and wins) 35 Nxe7 Bxe7 36 Rxe7+ Kg8 37 Rxa7 Kf8 38 Rxa6 and wins.

(c) 32 . . . e6 33 c6! Rc4 34 Nd5! exd5 35 c7 d4 36 e6 d3 37 e7, winning.

But in this position Black does not need to simplify the game, as White's threats can easily be parried, and the most propitious way of doing this is to *revert to the counter-attack*.

28 ...   e6

Black appears to have forgotten for the moment that his king may be exposed to a direct attack. The text move not only cuts the communication of the queen with the king's side but also weakens the surrounding squares, a factor that Reshevsky exploits in masterly style. A good stroke would be 28 ... Qe6!, threatening an eventual ... Nc5. The variations 29 Rg3 Qf7 30 Rg6 Nf8 and 29 d5 Qb6+ 30 Be3 Qa5 would be to Black's advantage; so in all likelihood White would be left with no better resource than 29 Ne2, and then Black, by responding with 29 ... Qf7 maintains his game with at least equal fighting chances.

29 Rg3!   Nf8

This provokes the sacrifice. With 29 ... Qb6! he could still have stopped the direct threats. For example, 30 Rg6 Nf8 31 Rxg7+ (if 31 Bxh6 then 31 ... Nxg6 32 hxg6+ Kg8) Kxg7 32 Bxh6+ Kf7 33 Qg5 Rcxd4 34 Qf6+ Ke8 35 Qxf8+ Kd7 36

Qf7+ Kc8. But with 30 Kh1 White would have kept up the pressure.

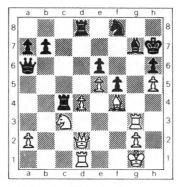

Position after 29 ... Nf8

30 Rxg7+!   Kxg7

31 Bxh6+   Kh7

Or 31 ... Kf7 32 Qg5 Qb6 33 Qf6+ Ke8 34 Bxf8 and wins.

32 Qg5   Rd7

33 Bxf8   Rxc3

34 Qg6+   Kh8

35 Qe8!   Rcc7

36 Be7+   Kg7

37 Qf8+   Kh7

38 Qf7+ and mates next move.

Up until move 28 Kashdan played very well. Reshevsky seized his chance to profit from his tactical opportunity.

GAME 80

Ninth match game, New York 1942
Grünfeld Defence

White: S. RESHEVSKY
Black: I. KASHDAN

1	d4	Nf6
2	c4	g6
3	Nc3	d5
4	Qb3	c6
5	Nf3	Bg7
6	Bf4	

This is a safe developing move which secures White a tranquil game. But as the game shows, Black obtains in the continuation the necessary time to develop his own forces. The move 6 e3, in appearance more modest, seems to give White more chances of security and initiative.

6	...	0-0
7	e3	dxc4
8	Bxc4	Nbd7
9	0-0	Nb6
10	Be2	Be6
11	Qc2	Nbd5
12	Be5	Bf5
13	Qd2	

White can allow himself this loss of time with impunity owing to the solid structure of his pawn position. But it is not hard to foresee that Black will have no great difficulty in solving the problems in his position once and for all.

13	...	Nxc3
14	Qxc3	Ne4
15	Qb4	

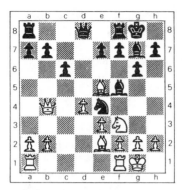

Position after 15 Qb4

15	...	f6!

Now Black is going to exchange his knight for the bishop and thereby obtains the advantage of the two bishops. It is clear that this advantage is of a relative nature on account of the weakening of his king-side pawn position, but it is quite adequate to equalize the chances.

16	Bg3	Qd7
17	Rfd1	Kh8
18	Nd2	Nxg3
19	hxg3	Rfd8
20	Rac1	Bf8
21	Qc3	

Slightly preferable would have been 21 Qc4. In any event, the loss of a tempo in this quiet position is not of great importance.

21	...	Bg4

After 21 ... Be6 White, with 22 Nb3, would have been capable of practically compelling the exchange of this bishop, leaving opposite-coloured bishops.

| 22 | Qc4 | |

22 f3, followed by 23 Kf2 would, without any risk, have made it a more lively contest. But Reshevsky, with his two-point lead, is immovably unwilling to take on the slightest indication of a risk.

22	...	Bxe2
23	Qxe2	e6
24	Ne4	Qf7
25	Nc5	

It would have been more natural to play 25 Qf3 first. Now Black succeeds in freeing himself completely.

25	...	e5!
26	dxe5	fxe5
27	b3	Rd5
28	Rxd5	cxd5
29	Nd3	Bg7
30	e4!	Rd8

The game is moving rapidly towards a draw, the reciprocal advances being balanced.

31	exd5	Qxd5
32	Nb2	e4
33	Nc4	Bd4
34	Ne3	Qe5
35	Ng4	Qe7
36	Re1	Re8
37	Qc4	Qg7
38	Qd5	h5!
39	Ne3	Bb6
40	Nc4	

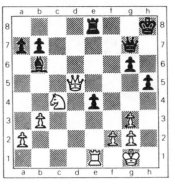

Position after 40 Nc4

40	...	Qc3!

As was to be anticipated, at the moment when White's pressure against the isolated pawn has reached its maximum intensity Black has available a counter-attack which will quickly force his opponent to accept the draw. If now 41 Re2 then simply 41 ... e3.

41	Rxe4	Rxe4
42	Qxe4	Qa1+
43	Kh2	Bxf2
44	Qe8+	Kg7
45	Qd7+	Kg8
46	Qc8+	Kh7
47	Qd7+	

Evidently not 47 Qxb7+ Kh6. But if now 47 ... Kh6? then 48 Qd2+.

47	...	Qg7
48	Qe6	Bd4
49	Nd6	b6
50	Ne4	Kh6
51	Nd6	Kh7
52	Ne4	Kh6

Drawn

GAME 81

Tenth match game, New York 1942
Grünfeld Defence

White: I. KASHDAN
Black: S. RESHEVSKY

1 d4

For the first time in this match Kashdan chooses to begin with the queen's pawn, the last two Ruy López games not having given satisfactory results. Reshevsky decides to combat him with the same procedure and uses his opponent's weapon, the Grünfeld Defence, a resolution all the more justified psychologically for the fact that his lead allows him quietly to await the conclusion.

1 ...	Nf6
2 c4	g6
3 Nc3	d5
4 Bf4	

The same quiet variation as was played in the ninth game. The present game is a repetition up to the thirteenth move with an unimportant inversion.

4 ...	Bg7
5 e3	c6
6 Nf3	0-0
7 Qb3	dxc4
8 Bxc4	Nbd7
9 0-0	Nb6
10 Be2	Be6
11 Qc2	Nbd5
12 Be5	Bf5

13 Qb3

Played by Capablanca against Flohr at Semmering-Baden, 1937. Black's next move is enough to equalize; White's victory in the game mentioned was due merely to subsequent errors.

13 ...	Qb6
14 Bc4	Nxc3
15 bxc3	Ne4
16 Qa3	Bxe5
17 Nxe5	Qc7

Evidently not 17 ... Nd2 18 Qxe7.

18 Rad1	Nd6
19 Bb3	

Since after the following advance of the a-pawn this bishop cannot be maintained it would be more opportune to retreat it at once to d3.

19 ...	a5!

Threatening to win a piece with 20 ... a4.

20 Qc1	a4
21 Bc2	c5

Creating an unfavourable situation in the centre.

22 Bxf5	Nxf5

White to move

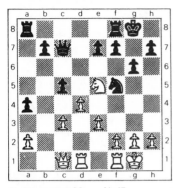

Position after 22 . . . Nxf5

The games are in an almost identical position and the battle should only just be beginning. Everything makes one anticipate a long, rigorous, positional battle which could be started by, for example, 23 Qa3 b6 24 Rb1 etc. Instead of playing thus, Kashdan commits a grave tactical error.

23 e4?   **cxd4!**

24 Ng4?

A second mistake, undoubtedly due to the commotion produced by the first one. His best resource would be to sacrifice the pawn by 24 Nxf7! Rxf7 25 exf5 dxc3 (25 . . . Rxf5 26 cxd4 is no better) 26 fxg6 hxg6 27 Qc2, threatening the g-pawn and at the same time 28 Rd3, followed by 29 Rc1. The text move does not lose material for the moment but it produces a deadly weakness at c3 which Reshevsky will have no difficulty in exploiting.

24 ...   **Nd6**

25 Rxd4   **Rac8**

Very good! White cannot easily

take the pawn because of 26 Rxa4 Qc6 (stronger than 26 . . . Qd7 27 Nh6+) 27 Rb4 (or 27 Rd4 Nxe4 28 c4 Nd6 29 Ne5 Qa4 and the pawn will not escape from its destiny) Nxe4 28 c4 Nd6 29 Ne3 Qc5 30 Nd5 Rfe8 with the threats 31 . . . Nxc4 and 31 . . . b5.

26 Ne3

Position after 26 Ne3

26 ...   **Nb5!**

A mistake would be 26 . . . Qxc3 27 Qxc3 Rxc3 28 Nd5. But now White cannot play 27 Nd5 because of 27 . . . Nxd4, nor 27 Rxa4 owing to 27 . . . Nxc3 winning.

27 Rc4   **Qe5**

28 f4

A desperate advance which does nothing but precipitate the inevitable defeat.

28	...	Qe6
29	f5	Qb6
30	Rxc8	Rxc8
31	c4	Nd6
32	Kh1	Nxe4

The beginning of the harvest.

33	Nd5	Qd6
34	fxg6	hxg6
35	Qb1	Rxc4
36	Qxb7	Nf2+

37	Kg1	Ng4!
38	Nxe7+	Kg7
39	Qb2+	f6
40	White resigns	

Queen's Indian Defence

GAME 82

Buenos Aires 1939
Queen's Indian Defence

White: K. OPOCENSKY
(Czechoslovakia)
Black: J.R. CAPABLANCA (Cuba)

1	d4	Nf6
2	c4	e6
3	Nf3	b6
4	g3	Bb7
5	Bg2	Bb4+
6	Nbd2	c5

Less usual and less elastic than 6 . . . 0-0 because White could now obtain the advantage of the two bishops by 7 a3 Bxd2+ (or 7 . . . Ba5 8 0-0, followed by 9 Nb3) 8 Qxd2.

7	0-0	cxd4
8	Qa4	

Trying to complicate matters without any practical benefit. Simpler would be 8 Nb3, recovering the pawn with a good game.

8	. . .	Nc6
9	Nb3	Bc5

Obliging his opponent to make an effort in order to recapture the pawn, which would have been so easy before.

10 Bg5

10 Rd1 would have sufficed to equalize, but the text move which develops a piece is not to be condemned.

10 . . .   Qc7?

10 . . . Qc8, threatening to protect the queen's pawn with 11 . . . e5 would have been consistent with the previous move.

11 Bxf6?

Instead of gaining an important

tempo by 11 Bf4 (and if 11 . . . e5 12 Nxe5 or 11 . . . d6 12 Nfxd4), White prefers to transpose the game into a regular gambit, an undertaking which is certainly not justified by the exigencies of the position.

11 ...	gxf6
12 Rad1	e5
13 Nxc5	

Hoping that Black's consolidation in the centre will only be illusory on account of e3.

13 ...	bxc5
14 Nh4	Ne7
15 e3	Bxg2
16 Nxg2	Rb8

With an extra pawn and a reasonably agreeable game, Black should content himself with simply completing the development of his forces. After 16 . . . 0-0 17 f4 e4, the d-pawn would be immune from capture (18 exd4 cxd4 19 Rxd4? Qc5, followed by 20 . . . Nf5) and 18 f5 would be answered by the simple 18 . . . Nc6 and eventually . . . Qa5 with advantage. The manoeuvre initiated by the rook move merely makes the White queen go to a more effective square.

17 Qa3	Qb6
18 b3	Qb4
19 Qc1!	

And not 19 Qxa7 Nc6 20 Qc7 Ke7 21 Nh4 Ke6 etc., winning.

| 19 ... | d5 |

At first sight this appears promising, but in reality the pawn advanced in the centre is a burden for the rooks and will soon demonstrate its weakness. 19 . . . Nc6 would have been better.

| 20 f4 | |

Justified by the circumstances.

20 ...	e4
21 exd4	cxd4
22 f5!	

Opening up new possibilities for the queen, king's rook and knight at the proper time.

| 22 ... | d3 |
| 23 Rf4 | |

Forestalling 23 . . . 0-0 (because of 24 Rg4+, followed by 25 Qh6) and strongly threatening 24 cxd5.

| 23 ... | Qb6+(?) |

A better defence would be offered by 23 . . . Rc8 and if 24 Qe3 then 24 . . . Kf8. The queen manoeuvre is not favourable for Black.

| 24 Kh1 | Qd4 |

White to move

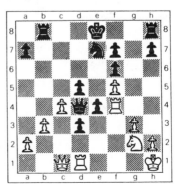

Position after 24 . . . Qd4

25 Qe3?

Having secured a promising position, White, under time pressure, makes several disadvantageous moves, and as a consequence loses rapidly. By playing the simple 25 cxd5 he would have confronted Black with an unpleasant choice; either to exchange the queen for two rooks in the variation 25 . . . Nxd5 26 Rxe4+ Qxe4 27 Re1 Qxe1+ 28 Qxe1+ Kf8 29 Qd2, followed by 30 Qxd3, or to lose both centre pawns after 25 . . . Qxd5 26 Qe3 (also strong is 26 Qc3).

25 . . .   Qe5

26 Qxa7?

This capture is suicidal. The only reasonable move was 26 Qe1! after which he would have had many chances.

26 . . .   0-0

27 Ne3   Ra8

28 Qc5

Absolutely hopeless because of the following development. The last practical opportunity consisted of 28 Qb7. The following 'sacrifice' of the knight is forced; after 28 . . . d4 29 Nd5 Nxd5 30 cxd5 e3 White would have lost at once.

28 . . .   d4

29 Qxe5   fxe5

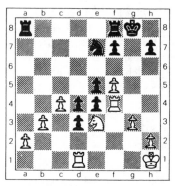

Position after 29 . . . fxe5

Such an agglomeration of pawns in the centre has rarely been seen in a game.

30 Rxe4   dxe3

31 Rxe3   f6

32 g4   Rxa2

33 Rexd3   Nc6

34 h4

Sometimes a player is so short of time that he does not have enough even to resign.

34 . . .   Nd4

35 R1d2   Rxd2

36 Rxd2   Nxb3

37 Rd6   Nd4

38 Kg2   h5

39 g5   Nxf5

40 Re6   Nxh4+

41 White resigns

GAME 83

Munich 1942*
Queen's Indian Defence

White: A. ALEKHINE
Black: P. KERES

1	d4	Nf6
2	Nf3	b6
3	c4	Bb7
4	g3	e6
5	Bg2	Be7
6	0-0	0-0
7	b3	

Avoiding the inevitable simplification that would occur after 7 Nc3 Ne4!

7	...	d5

Recommendable too is 7 ... c5 since 8 d5 would be answered by 8 ... Nxd5!, followed by 9 ... Bf6.

8	Ne5	c6

8 ... c5 is of course more enterprising.

9	Bb2	Nbd7
10	Nd2	c5
11	e3	

Sustaining the central tension and at the same time gaining a certain advantage in space.

11	...	Rc8
12	Rc1	Rc7
13	Qe2	Qa8?

The rook at c7 is not secure, and this move helps White to undertake a favourable mobilization.

*The decisive game for the Championship of Europe. E.W.

Much better was 13 ... Qb8, followed by 14 ... Rfc8.

14	cxd5!	Nxd5
15	e4	N5f6
16	b4!	

Taking the greatest possible advantage of the deficient position of the Black rook at c7.

16	...	Rfc8
17	dxc5	bxc5
18	b5	a6?

Also after 18 ... Nxe5 19 Bxe5 Rd7 20 Nb3 Black's game would be inferior but allowing the opening of the a-file is practically suicidal.

19	a4	axb5
20	axb5	Qa2

Keres must have overlooked the rejoinder. In any case his position is already hopeless.

White to move

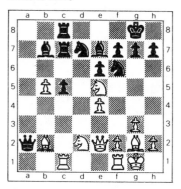

Position after 20 ... Qa2

| 21 | Nec4! | Qa8 |
| 22 | Bxf6! | |

Winning the exchange anyway.

| 22 | ... | gxf6 |

If 22 ... Bxf6 23 b6 or 22 ... Nxf6 23 Nb6 etc.

23	b6	Rc6
24	e5	Rxb6
25	Nxb6	Nxb6
26	Bxb7	Qxb7
27	exf6	Bxf6
28	Ne4	Be7
29	Qg4+	Kh8
30	Qf4!	

Threatening not only 31 Qxf7 but also 31 Nxc5!

| 30 | ... | Bf8 |
| 31 | Nxc5 | Qc7 |

After 32 ... Rxc5 White would recover the piece either at d4 or at e5.

| 32 | Nxe6 | Qxf4 |
| 33 | Nxf4 | Black resigns |

GAME 84

Buenos Aires 1939
Queen's Indian Defence

White: K. OPOCENSKY
(Czechoslovakia)
Black: P. KERES (Estonia)

1	d4	Nf6
2	c4	e6
3	Nf3	b6
4	g3	Bb7
5	Bg2	Be7
6	Nc3	

More usual first is 6 0-0 and only after 6 ... 0-0 does he proceed

with 7 Nc3.

| 6 | ... | Ne4 |
| 7 | Bd2 | |

Playing with the preconceived idea that the exchange of this bishop by ... Nxd2 (as happened, for example, in an analogous position in the 21st match game Alekhine-Euwe 1937) would not be advantageous to Black.

The present game, however, has only one innovation: the development of the White bishop at c3, which gives White better chances than the old 7 Qc2 and if 7 . . . Nxc3 then 8 Qxc3 or bxc3.

7 . . .   d6

The basis of White's strategical threat is d5, a move that would now be answered by the exchange of the White queen's bishop, followed by 9 . . . e5.

8	0-0	Nd7
9	Qc2	Nxc3
10	Bxc3	Nf6
11	d5	

If 11 Rfe1 Black, by answering 11 . . . Be4, would have forced his opponent to use another tempo, wasting his energy with the aim of obtaining control of e4. The text move initiates a transaction leading to a simplified position with equal prospects for both sides.

11 . . .   e5

12 Nxe5

A typical pseudo-sacrifice in this particular variation of the Queen's Indian.

12	. . .	dxe5
13	d6	Bxg2
14	dxe7	Qxe7
15	Kxg2	0-0
16	Rfd1	Rfe8

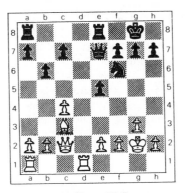

Position after 16 . . . Rfe8

The over-protection of e5 will be necessary sooner or later, with the object of giving the queen a role; her next manoeuvre (via e6 or c5) may now become distressing for White. The simplest way for Opocensky would be to protect his most vulnerable point: 17 Qf5 Qc5 18 Qf3 and if 18 . . . Qxc4 19 Bxe5 or 18 . . . e4 19 Qf4. The 'radical' means (17 b4?), in order to prevent 17 . . . Qc5, actually chosen by him instead of that line, compromises his pawn structure on the queen's side and later induces Black to force exchanges to try his luck in the subsequent promising endgame.

| 17 | b4? | Qe6 |
| 18 | Bb2 | h5 |

Virtually forcing the reply. After the blockading of the pawn configuration on the vital sector of the board, the knight's chances of action are increased.

| 19 | h4 | a5 |

On making this advance Keres has already clearly decided to accept the weakness of his b6 though this is from a purely theoretical point of view. He anticipates that, owing to the closed nature of the position, White will not be able to exploit the weak sector, at least, with the aid of his bishop. A bold strategical plan which, as the continuation proves, is fully justified by the circumstances.

| 20 | b5 | Rad8 |
| 21 | a4 | c6 |

Threatening to establish a new attacking operation on the c-file after 22 ... cxb5, and thereby inducing his opponent into temporarily surrendering the d-file in order to avoid disagreeable eventualities.

| 22 | Rxd8 | Rxd8 |
| 23 | Rc1 | c5 |

Completing the blockade of the queen's side, which leaves White with two vulnerable points (a4 and c4) against Black's one (b6). The desire behind White's next moves is to give his bishop the chance to attack b6.

24	Qc3	e4
25	Rc2	Ne8
26	Bc1	Rd1

Playing 26 ... Nd6 would have no effect because of 27 Rd2.

| 27 | Bf4 | Nd6 |

Once the open file is occupied Black has no trouble in accepting the exchange of the minor pieces, especially as the alternative 27 ... f6 would have given White certain chances after 28 Rd2 Rxd2 29 Qxd2 Qxc4 30 Qd8 Qe6 31 Bc7 etc.

28	Qe5	Qxe5
29	Bxe5	f6
30	Bxd6	Rxd6
31	f3	Rd4

Keres's play, at least in this part of the game, is not of the same standard as in the preceding phase, with the result that he nearly lets the deserved victory slip away. Here, for instance, there was no reason to waste time with the rook since the White move 32 fxe4 cannot possibly be considered a threat. Simpler, then, would be 31 ... Kf7, followed by 32 ... Rd1 and 33 ... Ra1, with the simple win of White's a-pawn without surrendering the square b6 to White (if 34 Rd2 then 34 ... Ke7). We shall also find some similar inexactitudes in the following moves.

32	fxe4	Rxe4
33	Kf3	Rd4
34	e3	Rd6
35	Ke4	

An important detail in this ending is that, as matters stand, White cannot propose an exchange of rooks since the pawn endgame would be hopeless for him. For instance, 35 Ke2 Kf7 36 Rd2 Rxd2+ 37 Kxd2 Ke6 38 Ke2 Kf5 39 Kf3 g5, winning easily.

35	...	Kf7
36	Rc1	Ke6
37	Rc2	Rd1
38	Ra2	

Black to move

Position after 38 Ra2

38 ...	Rg1?

Black attacks the enemy weaknesses in the wrong order. First 38 ... Rc1, forcing the reply 39 Kd3, and only then 39 ... Rg1 (or 39 ... Kf5), followed by 40 ... Rxg3 and 41 ... g5 would have left White virtually without any chance of resisting.

39 Kf3	Rc1
40 Rd2	

The only hope, although weak.

40 ...	Ke7

Another indifferent move which finally gives White some defensive opportunities. An easy way of winning would be 40 ... Rxc4 41 Rd8 Rxa4 42 Rb8 Rb4 43 Rxb6+ Kd5 44 Rb8 Kc4, after which the a-pawn could be stopped only at the cost of the White rook.

41 Ke4	Ke6
42 Rd8!	Rxc4+
43 Kd3	Rxa4
44 Rb8	

The difference between the present position and the variation mentioned above is clear: the situation of the White king at d3 prevents the invasion of its rival to c4 via d5.

44 ...	Kd5
45 e4+	

Naturally this pawn is immune owing to the possibility of 46 Rd8+.

45 ...	Ke5
46 Rxb6	Rxe4
47 Rb7	Rg4
48 b6	Kd6
49 Rf7	Rxg3+
50 Kc2	

Or 50 Kc4 Kc6 51 b7 Rg4+, followed by 52 ... Rb4 winning.

50 ...	Rg4?

Keres's play is decidedly negligent. After 50 ... a4 51 b7 Rb3 52 Rxg7 f5 53 Rh7 Ke5 White would surely have had to resign.

51 b7	Rb4
52 Rxg7	a4?

And now 52 ... f5 followed by 53 ... Ke5 was indicated. The text move leaves an extremely delicate endgame in which Keres has to make a considerable effort in order to grasp the elusive half-point.

53 Rf7	Kc6
54 b8(Q)!	Rxb8
55 Rxf6+	Kb5
56 Rh6	Rg8
57 Rxh5	

Who would have thought that White

was going to free his h-pawn and use it as a counter-attacking weapon in this ending! Opocensky's endgame resistance deserved a better fate.

57	...	Rg2+
58	Kc3	Rg3+
59	Kc2	Kb4
60	Rh8	Rg2+
61	Kb1	Rh2
62	h5	c4
63	Rb8+	Kc3
64	Rh8	Rh1+
65	Ka2	Kd2
66	h6	c3
67	h7	Kc2

The position attained after a series of more or less forced moves is won for Black, although it is curious to note that victory can be achieved only in a way reminiscent of a composed study. This particular rook endgame (rook's pawn on one side of the board against bishop's pawn on the other) does not seem to have been analysed in complete detail, as at Buenos Aires, during the game and after it, several masters remained convinced that the legitimate result from the position should have been a draw.

68	Ka3	Rh4
69	Ka2	Rh3

Black begins the winning manoeuvre.

70	Ka3	Kc1

White to move

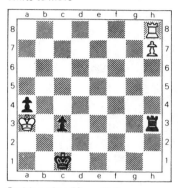

Position after 70 ... Kc1

71 Kxa4

At this moment White surprised those present at this interesting fight by embarking upon one of the two roads which represent suicide. The other was 71 Ka2, the refutation of which consists of 71 ... Rh2+ and then, firstly: 72 Ka1 c2 73 Rg8 Kd2 74 Rd8+ Kc3 75 Rc8+ Kb3 76 h8(Q) Rxh8 77 Rb8+ Kc4 and wins. A derivation from this line is: 73 Ka2 a3! 74 Kxa3 (if 74 Rg8 Kd2 75 Rd8+ Ke1 winning) Kb1 75 Rb8+ Ka1 76 Rc8 Rh3+ 77 Ka4 Kb2 78 Rb8+ Ka2 79 Rc8 Rh4+ 80 Ka5 Kb3 81 Rb8+ Ka3 82 Rc8 Rh5+ 83 Ka6 Kb3 84 Rb8+ Ka4 85 Rc8 Rh6+, followed by 86 ... Rxh7+ and wins. Secondly, the following might have been played: 72 Ka3 c2 73 Rg8 Kb1 74 Rb8+ Ka1 75 Rc8 Rh3+ 76 Kxa4 Kb2 etc., entering the previous line.

71 ... c2

72 Rg8

Desperation! The maximum resistance would have been achieved by 72 Ka5 Rh4 73 Ka6 Rh5 74 Ka7 Kb2 75 Rb8+ Ka1 76 Rc8 Rxh7+ winning.

72	...	Rxh7
73	Kb3	Kb1
74	White resigns	

GAME 85

Cracow 1940
Queen's Indian Defence

White: E. BOGOLJUBOV
Black: L. RELLSTAB

1	d4	Nf6
2	Nf3	b5

It is certainly not possible to recommend this move since Black unnecessarily binds himself to a risky policy. White can easily expand at once.

3	Bg5	Bb7
4	e3	a6
5	Nbd2	e6
6	a4	b4
7	Bd3	c5
8	0-0	Be7

Another loss of time. More advisable seems 8 . . . Nc6 or 8 . . . d5.

9	dxc5	Bxc5
10	e4	Be7?

It was absolutely essential to play 10 . . . d6 although White would have obtained the advantage in any case by 11 e5 dxe5 12 Nxe5 Qd4 13 Nef3 Qd7 14 Re1 0-0 15 c4 bxc3 16 bxc3, followed by 17 Qc2 and 18 Rad1.

11	e5	Nd5
12	Bxe7	Nxe7
13	Nc4	

Black's d6 could not be more weak.

13	...	Nc8
14	Re1	

Positionally sound and at the same time a cleverly laid trap!

14	...	d5

This is just the reply for which White was hoping. But anyway, nor would the continuation 14 . . . 0-0 15 Be4! Nc6 16 Qd3 offer Black anything other than an indefensible position.

15	exd6	Nxd6

White to move

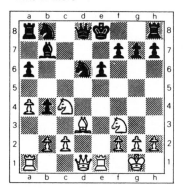

Position after 15 . . . Nxd6

16 Bg6!!

A wonderful move which decides the game brilliantly.

16 ...   **hxg6**

Or 16 . . . Ke7 17 Nxd6 Qxd6 18 Qxd6+ Kxd6 19 Bxf7 Bd5 20 Rad1 winning immediately.

17 Nxd6+	**Ke7**
18 Nxb7	**Qc7**
19 Qd5	

Saving the piece and ensuring victory. Nonetheless a finish more worthy of the pretty combination would be 19 Qd4! with the deadly double threat of 20 Rxe6+ and 20 Qxb4+.

19 ...	**Rh5**
20 Qe4	**Nc6**
21 g4!	**Black resigns**

The White knight is liberated.

Queen's Pawn, Benoni Defence

GAME 86

Buenos Aires 1939
Queen's Pawn, Benoni Defence

White: T. VAN SCHELTINGA (Holland)
Black: K. OPOCENSKY (Czechoslovakia)

1 d4	**Nf6**		**4 d5**	**d6**
2 c4	**g6**		**5 e4**	
3 Nc3	**c5**			

Unusual and clearly decided upon within the plan of sacrificing a pawn on the fifth move.

In accordance with Black's desires. A safe alternative would be to play 5 g3, followed by 6 Bg2 and only then advance the e-pawn.

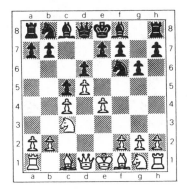

Position after 5 e4

5 ...   b5!?

A bold and interesting positional sacrifice. As compensation for the pawn Black will obtain, in the course of the game: firstly, two open files; secondly, combined pressure (both vertically and diagonally) on White's b2. The effectiveness of such pressure is demonstrated, amongst other cases, by the sensational game Nimzowitsch-Capablanca in the St. Petersburg Tournament of 1914.

6 cxb5   Bg7

7 Nf3

Both sides must first of all finish their development and White does this in a simple and rational way. Speaking in general terms, van Scheltinga plays only good moves in the continuation, yet nevertheless his advantage is being reduced little by little. This is the reason why I have occupied myself with this game, in the belief that the Opocensky Gambit needs further examination.

7 ...   0-0

8 Be2   a6

9 0-0   axb5

10 Bxb5   Qb6

Threatening 11 . . . Nxe4.

11 Nd2

Tempting, although the simple 11 Qc2 would be more in accordance with the position. In that case Black's reply would still be 11 . . . Ba6.

11 ...   Ba6

12 Nc4   Qb7

13 Bxa6   Qxa6

14 Qe2

If White did not wish to obstruct his bishop's diagonal by retreating the knight, then there was no other choice.

14 ...   Nbd7

15 Be3

Other bishop moves, such as 15 Bd2 and 15 Bg5, were also to be considered, but none of them would radically alter the situation in White's favour.

15 ...   Rfb8

16 Rab1

Instead of this move, 16 a3 Ne8 17 Rac1 would have kept the extra pawn, although only for a short time, as Black would simply have played 17 . . . Ne5 18 Nxe5 Qxe2 19 Nxe2 Bxe5.

16 ...   Ne8

White to move

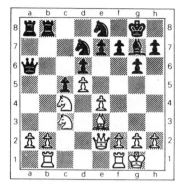

Position after 16 . . . Ne8

17 Rfe1?

This brings the game to a pre-mature end, but also after the practically forced move 17 Rfc1 Black would have maintained the equilibrium with 17 . . . Bxc3 18 Rxc3 Qxa2, conserving his positional advantage.

17 . . .   Bxc3!

Forcing the win of a piece after 18 bxc3 Rxb1 19 Rxb1 Ne5.

18 White resigns

Dutch Defence

GAME 87

Buenos Aires 1939
Dutch Defence

White: V. PETROV (Latvia)
Black: S. TARTAKOWER (Poland)

1	d4	f5
2	g3	Nf6
3	Bg2	e6
4	Nh3	

Less frequent, but for that not less promising, than 4 Nf3.

4	. . .	Be7
5	c4	0-0
6	Nc3	d6
7	0-0	Qe8

8 Qb3

Thus far the moves are the same as in the game Levenfish-Riumin, 1934 but then White played 8 Nf4 Bd8 9 e4 e5! and Black easily equalized.

8 . . .   Nc6?

In this type of position it is generally unfavourable to allow White to play d5 without the possibility of replying with . . . e5. At this precise moment the develop-

ment of this piece will be even
more troublesome for Black who,
because of the insufficient protection of his b7, will be obliged
to exchange at d5, after which his
e6 will remain lamentably weak.
Instead of the indifferent text,
8 . . . c6 is the proper move.

9 d5!   **exd5**

Naturally not 9 . . . Nd4 10 Qd1 e5
11 e3.

10 cxd5   **Ne5**

11 Nb5!

Immediately concentrating all his
forces on the weakness at e6.

11 . . .   **Bd8**

12 Nd4   **Kh8**

13 Nf4   **c5**

This eliminates the weakness on
the c-file but creates another one,
at d6, which will be particularly
vulnerable after the inevitable
exchange of his king's bishop.

14 Nde6   **Rg8**

15 Nxd8   **Qxd8**

16 Ne6

With apparently simple moves
White has obtained two new bene-
fits: the pair of bishops and occupation of e6. His next problem will be
to assure himself of permanent
control of this square.

16 . . .   **Qe7**

17 f4   **Nf7**

Hoping to dislodge the intruder by
18 . . . Nd8.

18 e4!

The spectacular beginning of an
interesting attack.

18 . . .   **Nxe4**

As the acceptance of the pawn
sacrifice is evidently forced, Black
rightly decides at least to eliminate
one of the enemy bishops.

19 Bxe4   **fxe4**

White to move

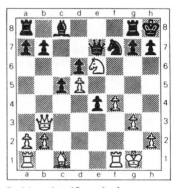

Position after 19 . . . fxe4

20 f5

Completely in accordance with the
daring plan initiated, and, of course,
sufficient to maintain superiority.
A simple and no less convincing
line would be 20 Re1, followed by
21 Rxe4 and Bd2-c3.

20 . . .   **Ne5**

The only chance.

21 Bg5(?)

But this new combination, based
on a temporary sacrifice of the
exchange, should lead only to a
draw. Indicated was 21 Qe3 Bxe6
22 fxe6 Raf8 23 Rxf8 Rxf8 24
Qxe4 Nf3+ 25 Kg2 with overwhelming positional advantage.

21	...	Qf7
22	**f6**	

Instead of 22 Qe3, which would have been not only unwise but also immediately disadvantageous, owing to 22 ... Nf3+ 23 Kg2 Qh5 etc.

22	...	Nf3+
23	**Rxf3**	**exf3**
24	**Rf1**	**gxf6**

This is a relatively safe line; if 24 ... Bxe6 25 dxe6 Qg6 26 f7 Qxg5 27 fxg8(Q)+ Kxg8 28 Qxf3 Qe5 29 Qf7 and White's passed pawn would be a danger.

25 Rxf3

If 25 Qxf3 Black could have played 25 ... Rg6 26 Bxf6+ Kg8.

25	...	Rg6?

The likeliest move, apparently guarding against the rejoinder. If he had played 25 ... Rxg5 26 Nxg5 Qg6 27 Ne6 Bxe6 28 dxe6 Re8 he would have removed any risk of losing.

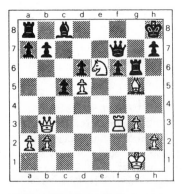

Position after 25 ... Rg6

26 Bxf6+!

This forces the exchange of queen for rook and minor pieces (in this position very advantageous), as the alternative 26 ... Rxf6 would quickly be fatal for Black: 27 Qc3 Bxe6 28 Rxf6 Qg7 29 dxe6 Re8 30 e7 Kg8 31 Qc4+ Kh8 32 Rf7 Qh6 33 Kh1, followed by g4-5 and wins.

26	...	Kg8
27	**Be5!**	**Qe7**
28	**Rf8+**	**Qxf8**
29	**Nxf8**	**Kxf8**
30	**Bf4**	

Material is almost equal, but that is the only satisfaction that Black can derive from the position. His king is exposed, his queen's side is undeveloped and d6 is permanently weak.

30	...	b6

The queen's long journey of infiltration cannot in any way be prevented. If, for example, 30 ... Rb8 then 31 Qa4 a6 32 Qa5 b6 33 Qa4 b5 34 Qa5 etc.

31	Qb5	Bh3
32	**Qc6**	**Rd8**
33	**Qc7**	**Rd7**
34	**Qc8+**	**Kg7**

Or 34 ... Kf7 35 Qh8.

35 Bd2

Forcing victory, or at least the gain of the exchange.

35	...	Rf6
36	**Bc3**	**Kf7**
37	**Bxf6**	**Kxf6**

38	Qh8+	Kf5
39	Kf2	Ke4
40	Qe8+!	Kxd5

If 40 . . . Kd4 the move 41 Qh5 would have won the bishop anyway.

41	Qh5+	Kc6
42	Qxh3	d5
43	Qe6+	Kc7

44	Ke3	a5
45	a4	d4+
46	Kd3	Rd6
47	Qf7+	Rd7
48	Qf4+	Kc6
49	h4	Rd6
50	Qe4+	**Black resigns**

Budapest Gambit

GAME 88

Buenos Aires 1939
Budapest Gambit

White: T. VAN SCHELTINGA
(Holland)
Black: S. TARTAKOWER (Poland)

1	d4	Nf6
2	c4	e5
3	dxe5	Ne4
4	Nd2	Nc5
5	Ngf3	Nc6
6	g3	Qe7
7	Bg2	Nxe5
8	0-0	d6

Against me in London in 1932, Dr. Tartakower played 8 . . . g6 here, but after 9 Nb1! Nxf3+ 10 exf3 Bg7 11 Re1 Ne6 12 Nc3 etc. he was quickly at a disadvantage.

And as the alternative of the text will demonstrate itself to be hardly satisfactory either, 8 . . . Nc6, preventing 9 b4 would have offered Black better chances for his development.

9	b4!	Ncd7
10	Bb2	g6
11	Nxe5	dxe5
12	c5	

Threatening to create a weakness on Black's queen's side, a threat that cannot be avoided owing to White's superior development.

12	...	Bg7
13	Nc4	0-0
14	c6?	

After his strong development, White begins to play without precision. The logical continuation to the previous play would be 14 Na5!, threatening not only 15 Nxb7 but above all 15 c6 bxc6 16 Nxc6, winning the exchange. Black would have to play 14 . . . c6 and after 15 Nc4 Rd8 16 Qc2 Nf8 17 Nd6 Ne6 18 e3 his position would remain critical. But it must be admitted that van Scheltinga's move does not preserve all the advantage achieved in the opening.

14	...	bxc6
15	Bxc6	

Not 15 Na5 because of 15 . . . Nb8.

15	...	Rb8
16	b5	Rd8
17	Ba3	

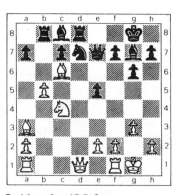

Position after 17 Ba3

17	...	Qe6!

A fine defensive move. At first sight it would seem that 17 . . . Qf6

would be more natural, keeping the rook protected and intending 18 . . . Nb6, but in this case White would attack the a-pawn by 18 Qa4 and Black would not have (as he does after the text move) the only adequate defence 18 . . . Bb7, because of the possibility of 19 Bxd7 Rxd7 20 b6. It should also be noticed on the other hand that after 18 Qa4, 18 . . . Nb6 would not be sufficient either because of 19 Qxa7! Nxc4 20 Qxb8 Nxa3 (or 20 . . . Bh3 21 Qxc7 Bxf1? 22 Be7 winning) 21 Qxc7 etc.

18	Na5!	Qf6

Because now he does not have to reckon with the possibility of 19 Qa4.

19	Qc2	

19 Bg2 is rather better here but the text move is also good enough.

19	....	Nf8
20	Rfd1?	

This does not threaten anything and gives his opponent an important tempo to complete his development. The correct way of maintaining the positional advantage consisted of the modest withdrawal 20 Bg2! with two no less modest threats: 21 Nc6 and 21 Qxc7. If 20 . . . Ne6 then 21 Nc6 Nd4 22 Nxd4 exd4 23 Qxc7, threatening 24 Be7. In neither case would Black find any compensation for the material surrendered.

20	...	Bf5
21	Qc5	Ne6!

This well conceived counter-attack could have saved the game.

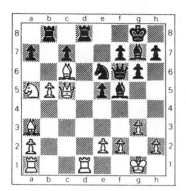

Position after 21 . . . Ne6

22 Qe7

A wise decision, because after 22 Qxa7 White would have been in real danger without any legitimate hope of winning. For instance, 22 Qxa7 Nd4 23 Qxc7 Nxe2+ 24 Kg2 e4 (this would also be the reply to 24 Kf1) 25 Be7 and Black can force perpetual check by 25 . . . Bh3+! 26 Kxh3 Qf5+ 27 Kg2 Qf3+ 28 Kf1 Qh1+ 29 Kxe2 Qf3+ etc. Or 24 Kh1 e4!! 25 Be7 Bg4!! 26 Rxd8+ Bf8! winning.

22 . . .   e4!

The active co-operation of all Black's pieces will counter-balance his weakness on the queen's wing in the endgame.

23 Nb3   e3

Planning to answer 24 fxe3 with 24 . . . Qe5.

24	Qxf6	Bxf6
25	Rac1	Rxd1+

Insufficient would be 25 . . . Nd4 26 Nxd4 Bxd4 because of 27 Be7! exf2+ 28 Kg2. After the following exchange a drawn position will be attained.

26	Rxd1	Bc2
27	Rd7	Bxb3
28	axb3	exf2+
29	Kxf2	Rd8
30	Rxd8+	Nxd8
31	Bd5	

If 31 Bc5 then simply 31 . . . a6.

31	. . .	Bd4+
32	Kf3	Ne6
33	Ke4	Bb6

Since the White king's intrusion into Black's queen's side can be prevented a draw is almost assured.

34	Be7	Nd4
35	Bc4	Nf5
36	Bg5	Bg1

The beginning of a suicidal manoeuvre. The simple way to obtain a draw was 36 . . . Kg7 37 g4 f6! etc.

37 Bf4   Bxh2?

After 37 . . . Bb6 Black would have nothing to fear. After this capture on the other side of the board the bishop will become imprisoned, and its liberation will cost too much material. This adventure was the consequence of time pressure.

38	Kf3	Bg1
39	e3	h6
40	Bd3!	g5
41	Bxc7	Ne7

Or 41 . . . Nxe3 42 b6 axb6 43 Bxb6 g4+ 44 Ke2 and wins.

42	Bb8	g4+
43	Ke2	h5

44	Bxa7	Bh2
45	Kf2	h4
46	gxh4	Bd6

The bishop has freed itself but the game is definitely lost. This is the consequence of Black's imaginary and sterile defence in the middle-game.

47	Bd4	f5
48	b6	f4
49	exf4	Bxf4

50	Be4	Kf7
51	b7	Bb8
52	h5	Ng8
53	Bd5+	Kf8
54	Bxg8	Kxg8
55	Kg2	Kh7
56	Bf2	Black resigns

In spite of certain inexactitudes, this is an excellent game by van Scheltinga.

Albin Counter Gambit

GAME 89

Madrid 1943
Albin Counter Gambit

White: F. SAMISCH
Black: A. MEDINA

In this game Sämisch was the victim of routine. Singularly he believed that in the variation selected by his opponent Black would have to castle on the king's side. When he castled on the queen's side, Sämisch lost his head and almost immediately committed the decisive error.

1	d4	d5
2	c4	e5
3	dxe5	d4
4	Nf3	Nc6

5	Nbd2	Be6
6	g3	Qd7
7	Bg2	Nge7
8	0-0	Ng6
9	a3	Be7
10	b4	0-0-0

In reality castling here marks the beginning of a combination and is based on the consideration that White could not capture on the thirteenth move.

11	Bb2	Bh3

12 b5

At all events 12 Qa4 would be better.

12 ...	Ncxe5
13 Qa4	**Bxg2!**
14 Kxg2	**Nxf3**
15 exf3	

And here 15 Nxf3 is preferable.

15 ...	Bc5
16 Rad1	**Qf5**
17 Nb3	**Rd6!**

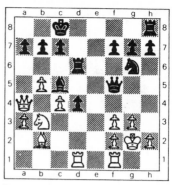

Position after 17 . . . Rd6

18 Nd2

White sees disaster coming, but it is too late. If, for instance, 18 Nxd4 then 18 . . . Nh4+! 19 gxh4 Rg6+ 20 Kh1 Bxd4 winning a piece. A short and instructive game.

18 ...	Nf4+!
19 gxf4	**Rh6**
20 White resigns	

Queen's Pawn Game

GAME 90

Buenos Aires 1939
Queen's Pawn Game

White: V. PETROV (Latvia)
Black: R. GRAU (Argentina)

1 d4	d5
2 Nf3	**Bf5**

This uncommon defence has been the object of a special study by the current champion of Argentina. The present game in no way speaks in its favour.

3	c4	e6
4	Qb3	Nc6
5	Bd2	

If 5 Qxb7 then 5 . . . Nb4, followed by 6 . . . Rb8 forcing a draw.

5	. . .	Rb8
6	e3	a6!

All this is part of the system; at this moment it was necessary to prevent the manoeuvre 7 cxd5 exd5 8 Bb5.

7	Bd3	

Since Black is taking his time to mobilize the rest of his forces, White could do the same thing and prevent the following simplification by playing first 7 a3. After the text move Black will have little problem in equalizing.

7	. . .	Bxd3
8	Qxd3	Nb4
9	Bxb4	

Or 9 Qb3 dxc4 10 Qxc4 Qd5.

9	. . .	Bxb4+
10	Nbd2	Nf6
11	0-0	

If 11 c5 then 11 . . . Ne4 and after the exchange of all the minor pieces White's slight advantage would be virtually impossible to exploit.

11	. . .	0-0

Permitting the following blocking of the game, after which Black's position becomes very difficult, if not definitely lost. Necessary was 11 . . . c5 with comfortable equality.

12	c5!	

Threatening to win the bishop by 13 Nb3, followed by 14 a3.

12	. . .	Bxd2
13	Nxd2	c6
14	f4	Nd7
15	b4	f5

Black has no satisfactory alternative. If, for example, 15 . . . b5, White would not need to take *en passant*, because of 16 . . . Qxb6 with a counter-attack, but could force control of the a-file by playing 16 a4, followed by Ra3, Rfa1 and, if necessary, R1a2 and Qc3-a1.

16	a4	Qc7
17	Rfc1	

With this move and his next White prevents for good the advance of the Black b-pawn.

17	. . .	Ra8
18	b5	Rfb8
19	Nf3	

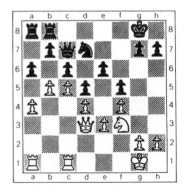

Position after 19 Nf3

White's pressure has been rapidly accomplished and he now has the possibility of restricting the mobility of the enemy pieces by an eventual pawn advance on the king's side (h3, g4 etc.). Black's reply renders unnecessary this extra effort and allows a decisive intrusion down the a-file.

| **19 . . .** | **axb5?** |

The decisive strategic mistake, instead of which 19 . . . Qd8 should have been played, with the object of continuing 20 . . . axb5 21 axb5 Ra5! The transposition of moves gives White time to establish an advanced post at a7.

| **20** | **axb5** | **Qd8** |
| **21** | **b6!** | **Rxa1** |

If Black omits this exchange White will in time become master of the open file by playing Qc3, followed by Rxa8 and Ra1.

| **22** | **Rxa1** | **h6** |

After 22 . . . Ra8 23 Qc3 Rxa1+ 24 Qxa1 Qb8 25 Qa7 Black would lose because the defensive square d8 would be accessible to his knight only in five moves (Nf8-g6-h8-f7-d8) whereas the offensive square a5 would be reached by the White knight in three.

23	**Ra7**	**Kf7**
24	**Qe2**	**g6**
25	**Nd2**	

From now on it becomes clear that the game will be decided by an eventual sacrifice at b7, but White's plan for realizing this is pretty and instructive.

25	**. . .**	**Nf6**
26	**Nb3**	**Ke8**
27	**Na5**	**Qc8**

| **28** | **Qa2** | |

28 Nxb7 Rxb7 29 Qa6 Rb8 would not be adequate for White. But now he threatens to win by 29 Nxb7 Rxb7 30 Rxb7 Qxb7 31 Qa7.

| **28** | **. . .** | **Nd7** |

White to move

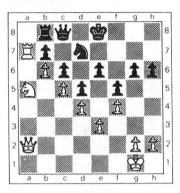

Position after 28 . . . Nd7

This is the ideal defensive position to stop any breakthrough on the queen's wing. Had Black been able to maintain it he would have saved the game, but unfortunately the next excursion by the White queen will make the Black knight move (with the aim of protecting the king's side) to a square from which it will not be able to return to d7.

| **29** | **Qf2!** | **Nf6** |

The alternative would be 29 . . . Kf7 30 Qh4 h5 31 Qg5 Nf6 32 Qh6!

30	**Qh4**	**Ng8**
31	**g4!**	**Kf7**
32	**g5!**	

Now the Black knight has no way of defending the queen's side.

32 . . .   h5

33 Qf2!

After the return of the queen the sacrifice will win immediately.

33 . . .   Ke8

34 Qa2   Ne7

35 Nxb7!   Rxb7

36 Rxb7   Qxb7

37 Qa7!

With the knight at d7 Black would have had the defence 37 . . . Qb8 but now it is all over.

37 . . .   **Black resigns**

A game of undoubted didactic value.

GAME 91

Buenos Aires 1939
Queen's Pawn Game

White: V. MIKENAS (Lithuania)
Black: M. CZERNIAK (Palestine)

1 d4   e6

2 Nd2

Mikenas's speciality, against which the simple 2 . . . d5 is a solid reply.

2 . . .   c5

3 dxc5   Bxc5

This move entails the exchange of the Black bishop for the White knight. Against Mikenas at Warsaw in 1935 I played 3 . . . Qa5 4 c3 Qxc5, equalizing without difficulty.

4 Ne4   d5

5 Nxc5   Qa5+

6 c3   Qxc5

7 e4

As White possesses the bishop pair it is useful and completely correct to open up the position.

7 . . .   dxe4

8 Be3

An important tempo. White can always recover the pawn with 9 Qa4+ or 9 Qg4.

8 . . .   Qa5

This idea is not a happy one. Preferable would be 8 . . . Qc7 9 Qa4+ (if 9 Qg4 then 9 . . . f5) Nc6 10 Qxe4 Nf6 11 Qh4 with level chances.

9 Qg4   Ne7

10 Qxg7   Ng6

11 h4

Black's position is opaque and requires much caution. If 11 . . . h5 then 12 Bg5, after which 13 0-0-0 or the equally good 13 g4 hxg4 14 h5. But Black's actual continuation (11 . . . Qe5), exchanging queens in an inferior middle-game, is open to criticism.

11 ...	Qe5

12 Qxe5

If 12 Qh6 Black could play 12 . . . Nc6 13 h5 Nge7 with a possible defence.

12 ...	Nxe5
13 Bd4	Nbd7

The only defence. If 13 . . . Nbc6 Black loses ground after 14 Bb5 0-0 15 Bxc6 Nxc6 16 Bf6.

14 Bb5	0-0
15 Rh3	f6

Forced. If 15 . . . f5? 16 Bxd7, followed by 17 Rg3+. White now wins a pawn but at the cost of losing the pair of bishops and allowing his opponent to counter-react. After his dubious opening Czerniak has defended his position excellently, thereby obtaining chances.

16 Re3	a6!
17 Bxd7	Nxd7
18 Rxe4	e5
19 Be3	f5
20 Rc4	f4
21 Bd2	b6

Preparing for 22 . . . Nc5. This gives White the opportunity to make a combinative reply; and it would have been relatively better to mobilize the sedentary pieces by 21 . . . Nf6.

22 Nf3

An exactly calculated counter-attack. If now 22 . . . Re8 then 23 Ng5

Nc5 24 b4 Nd3+ 25 Ke2 Bf5 26 Rc7.

22 ...	Nc5

23 Nxe5!

If now 23 . . . Re8 then simply 24 Rxc5 bxc5 25 Bxf4 with three pawns for the exchange.

23 ...	Bb7
24 0-0-0	Rae8
25 Bxf4	

Another of the points of the combination initiated by 22 Nf3.

25 ...	Rxf4
26 Rxf4	Rxe5

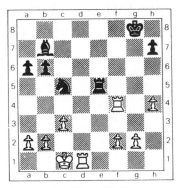

Position after 29 . . . Rxe5

At first sight it seems that White will encounter difficulties in making the endgame go in his favour. But in reality a peculiar circumstance (which was calculated several moves beforehand) allows the gain of a piece through the threat of mate.

27 Rd8+	Kg7
28 b4!	Ne6
29 Rd7+	Kg6
30 Rg4+	Kf5

31 f3

This is the circumstance mentioned above. The move of the f-pawn (which would have had the same effect if the Black king had gone to h5) not only protects the rook but also prepares for the stroke 32 Rf7 mate. Thus Black has no time to

save the bishop.

31	**...**	**Re1+**
32	**Kd2**	**Bxf3**
33	**gxf3**	**Black resigns**

This is one of the best games that the Lithuanian champion played at the Buenos Aires Olympiad.

GAME 92

Buenos Aires 1939
Queen's Pawn Game

White: V. MIKENAS (Lithuania)
Black: A. ALEKHINE (France)

| **1** | **d4** | **e6** |
| **2** | **Nd2** | |

One of the ideas behind this uncommon move is to enter into the regular Colle System after having induced Black to play . . . d5. White thereby avoids all the variations related to the fianchetto of Black's queen's bishop; for instance possibly 2 Nf3 Nf6 3 e3 b6.

| **2** | **...** | **d5** |

Played deliberately in accordance with White's desires, with the object of verifying Black's chances in this conventional line of defence. I have indicated a more promising line in the notes to the game between Mikenas and Czerniak.

| **3** | **e3** | **c5** |
| **4** | **c3** | **Qc7** |

With the purpose of answering 5 f4 with 5 . . . cxd4, thus forcing 6 cxd4

and also making use of the advantage of the open c-file.

| **5** | **Bd3** | **Nc6** |
| **6** | **Ngf3** | **cxd4** |

Several times I have had occasion to criticize this exchange in similar positions (although generally speaking after the development of the king's knight) since the pawn structure, which is characteristic of the Exchange Variation of the Caro-Kann, gives White a definite advantage in space when, as is the case here, the Black queen's bishop is behind the pawn chain. Nevertheless in the present game I decided to play the exchange with the object of proving once again whether it is worthwhile modifying the usual development of the Black pieces, placing the king's knight at e7 instead of at f6. However a later analysis showed me that such a

modification would augment my
opponent's advantage and I finally
decided to adopt in its totality the
line that I had previously criticized
with such surety, with the result
that throughout the whole game I
had to endure strong pressure and
survived only at the cost of considerable effort.

| 7 | exd4 | Bd6 |
| 8 | 0-0 | Nf6 |

If instead of this 8 . . . Nge7 then
9 Re1 Ng6 (if 9 . . . 0-0 10 Ng5 with
advantage to White) 10 g3, followed
eventually by Ng5 with a promising
initiative. On the other hand 8 . . .
g5!? 9 Nxg5 Bxh2+ 10 Kh1 would
have been decidedly too wild for a
tournament encounter.

| 9 | Re1 | Bd7 |
| 10 | Qe2 | |

Thus White has obtained genuine
control of e5 and now threatens to
occupy this square with the knight.
The principal object of Black's next
manoeuvre (which was calculated
with great exactitude, since it
creates a transitory weakness on the
king's flank) is to make possible the
move . . . Nxe5 as an immediate
answer to Ne5.

| 10 | . . . | Nh5! |
| 11 | g3 | g6 |

Still with the same purpose.

12	Ne5	Nxe5
13	dxe5	Be7
14	Nb3	

With the disagreeable threat of 15
Bh6.

14	. . .	Ng7
15	Bh6	Nf5
16	Bxf5	gxf5
17	Qh5	Rg8

Black is able to protect his
vulnerable points efficiently.

| 18 | Bf4 | Rg7 |
| 19 | Nd4 | 0-0-0! |

Possible only because of the un-
protected position of the White
bishop in the variation 20 Nxf5?
exf5 21 e6 Qxf4.

| 20 | Rad1 | Qb6 |

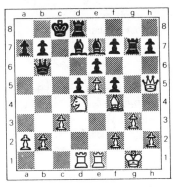

Position after 20 . . . Qb6

Black is out of danger, and gradually
begins to utilize his threats. White
therefore hopes for the first
opportunity to simplify, trusting
that this will assure him of a comfortable endgame.

| 21 | Qe2 | Bc5 |
| 22 | Be3 | Kb8 |

An easy draw was to be obtained
by forcing bishops of opposite
colours (22 . . . Bxd4 23 Bxd4
Qa5); but, without fearing them, I

was attracted by the possibilities offered by the resulting rook ending.

23	Nb3	Bxe3
24	Qxe3	Qxe3
25	Rxe3	Ba4!
26	Rd4	Bxb3
27	axb3	

Very often such doubled pawns are not only not defective but even serve to improve the chances of the player who has them. But here, as the instructive continuation will demonstrate, their existence will permit Black to unleash a propitious counter-attack at the most critical moment.

27	...	Rg4
28	f4	

Nor would the alternative 28 Rxg4 fxg4 29 Rd3 have given White any convincing advantage after 29 . . . Rg8 30 Rd4 h5 31 Rf4 Rg7, threatening Kc7-d7-e7, followed by Rg5 etc.

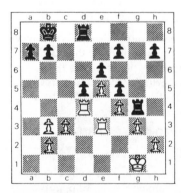

Position after 28 f4

28	...	h5

Black, undoubtedly, is trying to complicate matters. For example, there was no necessity at this time to exchange the h-pawn, since the White rook, after the previous move, will not have access to that weakness. The text move should therefore have been replaced by 28 . . . Rgg8 29 Red3 Kc7, eliminating any danger related to the possibility of c4. Now the endgame enters a dramatic phase.

29	c4	h4
30	cxd5	Rxd5

In place of this 30 . . . exd5 31 Kf2 hxg3+ 32 hxg3 Rg6 33 Red3 would have led virtually to the same position.

31	Rxd5	exd5
32	Kf2	hxg3+
33	hxg3	Rg6!

In the present difficult circumstances this is Black's only chance of saving himself, since the alternative 33 . . . Kc7 34 e6! fxe6 35 Rxe6 would have been hopeless sooner or later.

34	Rd3	Rb6

Or 34 . . . Kc7 35 Rxd5 Rb6 36 Rd3 Rh6, reaching the same position.

35	Rxd5	Kc7!

After the apparently natural 35 . . . Rxb3 White would have secured a winning position by playing 36 Rd7! For instance, 36 . . . Rxb2+ 37 Ke3 a5 38 Rxf7 a4 39 Rxf5 a3 40 e6, practically forcing the exchange of this pawn for Black's a-pawn, after which the rest would be easy.

36	Rd3	Rh6
37	g4!	

The most promising continuation, in which the majority of variations guarantee White a winning advantage. If White played a passive move, 37 Kg2 for instance, my intention was to proceed with 37 ... a5, threatening 38 ... Rc6 39 Rc3 Rxc3 40 bxc3 b5 with advantage to Black.

37	...	fxg4
38	Rc3+	

Of course if 38 Kg3 Rh3+.

38	...	Kd7
39	Kg3	f5!

At first sight a surprising decision, as White now obtains a dangerous passed pawn; but otherwise, after Kxg4 and Kf5, the co-operation of the White king and rook with the two king's side pawns would quickly have become crushing.

40	exf6	Rxf6
41	Kxg4	Rg6+
42	Kf5!	

White is unable to keep both his queen's side pawns, solely because they are doubled. If, for example, 42 Kf3 then simply 42 ... Rh6.

42	...	Rg2
43	Kf6	Rxb2
44	f5	b5

Played in conjunction with the following king march to b4. Otherwise the alternative 44 ... a5, avoiding the White move b4 in a number of variations, would have

been more flexible.

45	Rg3!	Kd6!

Insufficient would have been 45 ... a5 because of 46 Kg7 a4 47 bxa4 bxa4 48 f6 Kc6 49 f7 Rf2 50 Rg5!, winning.

46	Kg7	Kc5
47	f6	Kb4
48	f7	Rf2
49	Rg6!	

After 49 f8(Q)+ Rxf8 50 Kxf8 a5 a clearly drawn game would have resulted. But after the text move Black has to avoid an ending which is not at all clear and which is full of traps.

Black to move

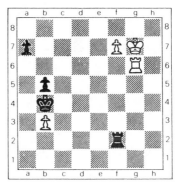

Position after 49 Rg6

49	...	Kxb3!

Very simple in appearance but even more simple and natural at first sight would be 49 ... a5, firstly since the continuation 50 f8(Q)+ Rxf8, followed by 51 ... a4 would give Black an extra tempo compared with the line indicated above; secondly, 50 Rf6 would be a move to be feared exactly as much as in the actual game. And yet 49 . . . a5? would have lost after the subtle reply 50 Rb6! Then either:

(a) 50 . . . a4 51 bxa4 Kxa4 52 Rf6 Rg2+ 53 Kh7 Rh2+ 54 Kg6 Rh8 55 f8(Q) Rxf8 56 Rxf8 b4 57 Kf5 b3 58 Rb8 Ka3 59 Ke4 b2 60 Kd3 and wins. Or:

(b) 50 . . . Kxb3 51 Rxb5+ Ka4 52 Rb6 Ka3 53 f8(Q)+ Rxf8 54 Kxf8 a4 55 Ke7 Ka2 56 Kd6 a3 57 Kc5 Ka1 58 Kc4 a2 59 Kb3 Kb1 60 Ka3+ Ka1 61 Rh6 and wins.

50 Rf6

Now, however, this is the only possible attempt at winning.

50 . . .   **Rg2+**

51 Rg6

Or 51 Kh7 Rh2+ 52 Kg6 Rh8 with an easy draw.

51 . . .   **Rf2**

52 Rf6   **Rg2+**

53 Kh7

He could have made one last try with 53 Kf8, threatening to win with 54 Ke8! However this would probably have been abortive because of 53 . . . Rc2! 54 Ke7 Rc8 55 f8(Q) Rxf8 56 Rxf8 b4 57 Kd6 Ka2!, followed by 58 . . . b3.

53 . . .   **Rh2+**

54 Kg7   **Rg2+**

Drawn

The last phase is of some importance for the theory of rook endings.

GAME 93

Buenos Aires 1939
Queen's Pawn Game

White: M. CZERNIAK (Palestine)
Black: S. TARTAKOWER (Poland)

1 d4   **d5**

2 Nd2

This move could have a meaning as a reply to 1 . . . e6 (Mikenas' idea) with the aim of inducing Black to play . . . d5. But in the present position its effect is merely to restrict White's own chances, leaving his opponent with a free choice.

2 . . .   **Bf5**

3 c4   **e6**

4 e3

If immediately 4 Qb3 then 4 . . . Nc6.

4 . . .   **c6**

5 Qb3

Purely psychological chess. White hopes that his opponent, 'playing to win' will avoid an exchange of queens. Objectively, more in the spirit of his eccentric second move would be development by, for instance, Ne2-g3, followed by Nf3 and Bd3.

| 5 | ... | Qc8 |

After 5 . . . Qb6 Black's position with the free bishop would have been preferable. Now, however, White manages to complete rapidly the mobilization of his forces and, at the appropriate moment, to open the position by means of e4, finally obtaining the initiative.

6	Ngf3	Nf6
7	Bd3	Bxd3
8	Qxd3	Nbd7
9	0-0	

All is now prepared for the advance in the centre and Black cannot prevent it.

| 9 | ... | Bb4? |

There was no reason to leave the Black squares without protection by exchanging this bishop. Natural and good, in order to maintain the positional balance, would be 9 . . . Be7 10 e4 dxe4 11 Nxe4 Nxe4 12 Qxe4 0-0.

10	e4	Bxd2
11	Nxd2	dxe4
12	Nxe4	Nxe4
13	Qxe4	Nf6?

Another superficial move, as though the knight could not possibly be taken on this square. Given that 14 d5 is not a threat because of 14 . . . cxd5, followed by 15 . . . Nf6, immediate castling was indicated.

| 14 | Qh4 | 0-0 |
| 15 | Bg5 | Nd7 |

Owing to the absence of an influential square in the centre, the knight is now much weaker than the bishop, and this circumstance in the present state of the middle-game is enough to decide the game in White's favour. In fact up to a certain point the champion of Palestine utilizes his positional advantage in convincing fashion.

| 16 | Rfe1 | f6 |

Creating a weakness at e6 but temporarily defending his king's position.

17	Bf4	Re8
18	Re3	Nf8
19	Bd6	Qd7
20	c5	Ng6
21	Qh3	

This will soon cause another weakness in Black's position by . . . f5. 21 Qh5 would not have been so strong on account of the defence 21 . . . Qf7 22 Rh3 Nf8.

| 21 | ... | Rad8 |
| 22 | Rae1 | f5 |

If 22 . . . Nf8 then 23 f4, threatening f5, fxe6, e7 etc.

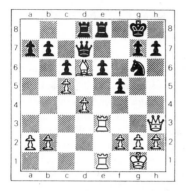

Position after 22 ... f5

23 g4?

One of the strengths of White's position is the complete absence of vulnerable points (because of the unmovable bishop at d6, d4 cannot be considered a weakness) and for this reason his advantage in space should be exploited without creating weaknesses. A rational way of achieving pressure against Black's e6 would be 23 R3e2!, threatening 24 Qb3. If then, for instance, 23 ... b6 24 Qb3 Kf7, then 25 g3, followed by h4-h5 etc., gradually paralysing all Black's pieces. On the other hand the text move, which threatens nothing (24 gxf5 exf5 25 Rxe8+ Rxe8 26 Rxe8+ Qxe8 27 Qxf5? Qe1+, followed by 28 ... Nh4+ winning) merely opens up new possibilities for Black.

23	...	Qf7
24	f4	

In some variations the Black move ... f4 had to be reckoned with.

24	...	b6
25	Qh5	

Better first would be 25 b4 in accordance with the previous blockading strategy.

25	...	Nh8?

White now obtains a clearly superior game. The alternative 25 ... fxg4 26 Qxg4 Nf8, eventually followed by ... Qg6 offered better practical chances.

26	Qxf7+	Nxf7

If 26 ... Kxf7 then 27 gxf5 and 28 Re7+.

27 Bc7 !

Much better than 27 Rxe6 Nxd6 28 cxd6 Rxe6 29 Rxe6 fxg4 or 27 gxf5 Nxd6 28 cxd6 Rxd6 29 Rxe6 Rexe6 30 fxe6 Kf8.

27	...	Rxd4
28	Rxe6	Rxe6
29	Rxe6	Nh6

At last the poor knight enters the game and now develops a monkey-like agility.

30	g5	Rd1+

And not 30 ... Ng4 31 Re2, threatening 32 h3.

31 Kf2

After 31 Kg2 Rd2+ 32 Kf3 Ng4 Black would threaten perpetual check on the squares h2 and f1. And if 32 Kf1 then 32 ... Ng4 with perpetual check on h2 and f3. Quite a few resources!

31	...	Ng4+
32	Ke2	Rh1
33	b4!	Rxh2+
34	Kd3	Rxa2?

Both sides have played this difficult ending with strength and imagination, but now Black lapses and neglects one detail in this position, the natural exchange of pawns. After 34 . . . bxc5 35 bxc5 Rxa2 36 Rxc6 Ra4! White's chances, based on the strong passed pawn, would have been rather better despite his material disadvantage, but the game would probably have been drawn.

White to move

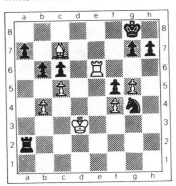

Position after 34 . . . Rxa2

35 Bxb6!

A surprising tactical stroke, typical of Czerniak's inventive play. If 35 . . . axb6 the winning variation would be 36 cxb6 Ra8 37 Rxc6 Rb8 38 Kc4 Ne3+ 39 Kc5. Or 38 . . . Nf2 39 Kb5 Nd3 40 Rc4, followed by 41 Ka6.

35 . . .   Nf2+

Neither this check nor 35 . . . Ra3+ 36 Kd4 (the only move) can bring salvation. In fact Black has ruined his plans for good by taking the a-pawn.

36 Kc4   Nd1

There was no defence against 37 Rxc6.

37 Rxc6   Rc2+

38 Kb3?

A lamentable error, evidently caused by time shortage. By playing 38 Kd3! Rc3+ 39 Kd2 axb6 40 Rxb6 White would reach an ending that would be easy to win. Now Black recommences the battle.

38 . . .   Rc3+

39 Ka4

If Black now captured the bishop (how natural!) White would be content to obtain a draw; for example, 39 . . . axb6 40 Rxb6 Ne3 41 c6 Nd5 42 Rb8+ Kf7 43 b5 h5! Instead of this Black, under time pressure, played:

39 . . .   a6?

After this there is practically no fight left.

40 Rc8+   Kf7

41 Bc7!

The most effective way of parrying the mate threat.

41 . . .   Nb2+

42 Ka5   Ra3+

43 Kb6   Nd3

44 c6!   Nxb4

45 Bd6   Rb3

45 . . . Nd5+ would be better.

46 c7   Nd5+

47 Kc6   Nxc7

48 Rxc7+   Kg8

49 Be5   Black resigns

GAME 94

Consultation Game, Rio de Janeiro
1939
Queen's Pawn Game

White: O. TROMPOWSKY,
A. SILVA ROCHA, and CHARLIER.
Black: A. ALEKHINE and O. CRUZ

1	d4	Nf6
2	Bg5	

This move, by which White *a priori*
foregoes the possibility of the combined play of the two bishops, is
rightly considered less energetic
than 2 c4 or 2 Nf3. On occasions
with the White pieces it is per-
missible to play a certain number
of eccentricities without the risk
of disturbing the balance of the
position.

2	...	d5

The simplest. An interesting alternative would be 2 . . . Ne4 3 Bh4
d5 4 f3 Nd6 5 Nc3 Nf5 6 Bf2 e5!?

3	Bxf6	exf6
4	e3	Be6

With the idea of preventing the
formation 5 c4, followed by 6 Nc3.
Black's chief objective is to keep
control of d5 and, eventually, e4.

5	Nd2	c6
6	c4	Bb4
7	cxd5	Bxd5

Another plausible idea was 7 . . .
cxd5 with the continuation 8 Qa4+
Nc6 9 Bb5 Bxd2+ 10 Kxd2 0-0,
after which Black would certainly
have nothing to fear. In this case
the chances would have had to be

considered roughly equal on account
of the better structure of the White
pawns on the one hand but the
harmonious position of the Black
pieces on the other.

8	a3	Ba5
9	Nf3	f5

Ensuring once and for all the
balance of the centre, although at
the cost of a slight delay in development.

10	Bd3	g6
11	0-0	0-0

As will be seen, this move, so
natural in appearance, will give
Black some difficulties in the
development of his queen's side.
This could easily have been avoided
by means of 11 . . . Nd7 and if 12
e4? then 12 . . . fxe4 13 Bxe4 Nf6
14 Bxd5 Nxd5 15 Re1+ Kf8 and
White has no real compensation for
his isolated pawn.

12 Bc4!

A good reply which not only
deprives Black of his principal
weapon but also prevents, from the
positional point of view, the
developing move 12 . . . Nd7.

12	...	Na6

A decision inspired by the possibility

of compensating for the weaknesses resulting from 13 Bxa6 bxa6 by the possession of the strong bishop pair. If then 14 Qe2, Black could choose either 14 . . . Bxd2 15 Nxd2 Qb6 or simply 14 . . . Qc8.

13 Qb3

Black to move

Position after 13 Qb3

13 . . .   Nc7!

By means of this move Black succeeds in protecting d5, thereby maintaining the equilibrium. Thus

13 . . . Bxc4 would be unsatisfactory: 14 Nxc4 Rb8 15 Nxa5 Qxa5 16 Ne5 with the threat of 17 Nd7.

14 Qxb7

Forcing equality. White could also have played without risk, but also without great chances of success, 14 Bxd5 Qxd5 15 Nc4, against which manoeuvre the right reply would be 15 . . . Bb6 16 Qb4 Na6 with an even game.

14	**. . .**	**Rb8**
15	**Qxa7**	**Ra8**
16	**Qb7**	

Clearly 16 Qc5 is not playable, owing to 16 . . . Ne6. The repetition of moves is therefore virtually forced for both sides.

16	**. . .**	**Rb8**
17	**Qa7**	**Ra8**

Drawn

This short game is of a certain theoretical interest.

GAME 95

Buenos Aires 1939
Queen's Pawn Game

White: O. TROMPOWSKY (Brazil)
Black: P. VAITONIS (Lithuania)

1	**d4**	**Nf6**
2	**Bg5**	

With this move (his favourite) the present Brazilian champion has obtained very good results, for

instance a draw against me at Rio de Janeiro and against Alexander (after having had an absolutely won position) at Buenos Aires. This game demonstrates that Black, without any effort and by making the most natural developing moves, can obtain a good position.

| 2 | ... | d5 |
| 3 | Bxf6 | |

This exchange is a necessary part of White's 'system'.

| 3 | ... | exf6 |
| 4 | e3 | Bd6 |

As the continuation shows, this is as good as trying to prevent the advance of the c-pawn directly with 4 ... Be6 (as in the Rio de Janeiro game mentioned above) or indirectly with 4 ... Bf5 (as Alexander played). In this latter case, if 5 c4 then 5 ... Bxb1, followed by 6 ... Bb4+.

5	c4	dxc4
6	Bxc4	0-0
7	Qh5	

This, after a few moves, will be shown to be a waste of time. It is more than doubtful how the immediate 7 Nc3 would have improved White's middle-game chances.

| 7 | ... | Nd7 |
| 8 | Nc3 | f5! |

An important practical detail; clearly White cannot take this pawn on account of 9 ... Ne5.

| 9 | Nge2 | Nf6 |
| 10 | Qf3 | Re8 |

Quite good but probably more exact would be 10 ... c6 and if 11 0-0-0 then 11 ... Qa5.

11	0-0-0	c6
12	Ng3	Qa5
13	Nh5	

As White's pieces have fewer possibilities than Black's, an exchange of one of them can only be in White's favour.

| 13 | ... | Nxh5 |
| 14 | Qxh5 | Be6 |

White to move

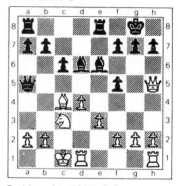

Position after 14 ... Be6

15 d5?

An instructive error but one almost unbelievable in a player of Trompowsky's strength; instead of the manoeuvre 15 Bxe6 fxe6 16 Kb1, followed by 16 Rc1, whereby a drawn game would have been assured, White deliberately opens up the c-file for a direct attack by his opponent, and this at the moment when his forces are dislocated and absolutely unprepared for protecting his threatened king. In the continuation the Lithuanian master has an easy task, and does what is necessary to bring the battle to a rapid conclusion.

15	...	cxd5
16	Bxd5	Rac8!

White probably did not see this good intermediate move. In any case the simple 16 . . . Bb4 would have been favourable to Black.

17	Bxe6	Rxc3+!

The obligatory consequence of the previous move.

18	Kb1

18 bxc3 Qxc3+ 19 Kb1 Rxe6 would merely be a transposition of moves.

18	...	Rxe6
19	bxc3	Qxc3

20	Qe2

This loses the queen perforce. If 20 Rc1 then 20 . . . Qd3+ 21 Rc2 Re5, winning.

20	...	Bc7
21	Qc2	Rb6+
22	Kc1	Qa3+
23	Kd2	Rb2
24	Rc1	Rxc2+
25	Rxc2	Ba5+
26	Ke2	g6
27	Rhc1	Qd6
28	g3	Kg7
29	Kf1	

The inevitable end.

29	...	Bd2
30	White resigns	

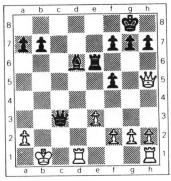

Position after 19 . . . Qxc3

GAME 96

Salzburg 1943
Queen's Pawn Game

White: E. BOGOLJUBOV
Black: A. ALEKHINE

1	d4	Nf6
2	Bg5	

A completely inoffensive move that offers Black the chance of rapidly equalizing the game.

2 ...   d5

3 c3

The Brazilian champion Trompowsky, and also Richter, generally played 3 Bxf6. After the text move Black will effectively avoid the doubling of his pawns.

3 ...   Ne4

4 Bh4   Qd6

Artificial, especially since nothing could be said against 4 . . . g5 5 Bg3, followed by 5 . . . g4; this would undoubtedly be beneficial to Black because White would have to deal with strong threats. The opening is treated deficiently by both players.

5 Nd2   Bf5

But more energetic would have been 5 . . . Qh6 6 Nxe4 Qxh4 7 Ng3 e6 8 Nf3 Qd8, remaining in possession of the pair of bishops. The text move quickly compensates for White's weaknesses.

6 Ngf3   Nd7

7 Qb3   0-0-0

Herewith he assumes too many obligations without any advantage. Very playable was 7 . . . f6 — and also 7 . . . Qb6, since in the latter case White could not happily play 8 Qxd5 owing to 8 . . . Nxd2 9 Qxf5 Qxb2 10 Rd1 Nc4 11 Qd3 Qxa2.

8 Nxe4   Bxe4

9 Bg3   Qc6?

Until now Black's play has not presented any danger but the pro-

vocative text move offers White advantageous possibilities. After the essential move 9 . . . Qb6 10 Nd2 Bg6 nothing would have happened for Black to bewail.

10 Nd2   Bg6

11 e3   e6

12 c4   Qb6

A rather sad necessity since if 12 . . . dxc4 there would follow 13 Nxc4 and 14 Rc1 with an irresistible attack.

13 c5   Qa5

Or 13 . . . Qxb3 14 axb3 Kb8 15 b4, followed by Be2 and 0-0, afterwards doubling the rooks on the open a-file.

14 a3!

Exact and mortifying. White is threatening Qd1 and then b4.

14 ...   e5!

The proper defence, as if 14 . . . c6 the reply by White 15 Qb4! would be very grave.

15 Qd1   c6

16 dxe5?

A mistake, based on an erroneous conception of the general situation on the board, by virtue of which Black suddenly secures the initiative and moves over to counter-attack. White's prospects of a victorious expansion later on require control of the centre, maintaining the tension. After 16 b4 Qc7 17 Be2 Black would not be able to try for counter-play by means of 17 . . . Be7 owing to 18 0-0, when White's threats on the queen's flank would be decisive.

16 ...   Qxc5

17 Rc1

Another imprecise move. Better would have been immediately 17 Be2, as the exchange of queens 17 ... Qc2 18 Qxc2 Bxc2 would be punished by 19 e6! with the threat of 20 Rc1, 21 Rxc6+ and 22 Ba6 mate.

17 ...   Qb6

18 Be2

18 b4 f6! would also have had its disadvantages.

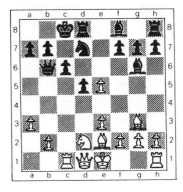

Position after 18 Be2

18 ...   Nc5

The move of the enemy king's bishop gives Black the opportunity to secure an estimable advantage. But it would have been much more effective to punish White's negligence by 18 ... Qxb2, whereby he would threaten both 19 ... Nxe5 and 19 ... Bxa3. Neither the reaction 19 Rxc6+ bxc6 20 Ba6+ Kc7 21 e6+ Kb6! nor 19 e6 Nc5 20 exf7 Nd3+ 21 Bxd3 Bxd3 22 Nb3 Bc4 23 Rxc4 dxc4 24 Qg4+

Rd7 25 Qxc4 Qb1+ 26 Nc1 Qb5 would have ended satisfactorily for White. In any case the text move will also make White consider the need to adopt heroic measures in order to save himself.

19 b4

After 19 0-0 Black would have had at his disposal 19 ... Nd3 and also 19 ... Qxb2, both moves of great strength.

19 ...   Nd3+

20 Bxd3   Bxd3

21 Nf3   Bc4

22 Nd4   a5!

By means of 22 ... Qa6 23 Rc3 c5 24 bxc5 Bxc5 Black could fix the White king in the centre of the board indefinitely. But the move chosen presents White with the 'obligation' of sacrificing the exchange, in the hope of thereby reducing Black's threats.

23 Qg4+   Rd7

24 Rxc4   dxc4

25 0-0   c5!

An important detail in Black's counter-offensive. The queen's power now lets itself be felt effectively over the centre.

26 bxa5   Qg6!

To compel an exchange of queens, thus annulling White's aggressive chances. Bogoljubov, however, manages to find a momentary solution to the conflict which is truly astonishing.

Game 96 Queen's Pawn Game

White to move

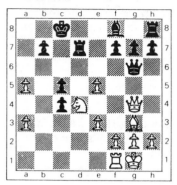

Position after 26 . . . Qg6

How can White avoid the exchange of queens that would clearly be fatal for him?

27 a6!!

A wonderful idea that deserved a better fate. If Black now plays 27 . . . Qxg4 White continues 28 a7, followed by 29 a8(Q)+; and if he plays 27 . . . bxa6 then 28 Qf3!, with a strong attack in both cases. But after the simple counter-measure that follows White sees his illusions destroyed.

27 . . .   **Qxa6**

28 Ne2   **Qe6**

Nor would the attack on the queen by 28 . . . h5 have been bad. If 29 Qe4 there would follow 29 . . . Be7, threatening to win a piece. If 29 Qf4, best would be 29 . . . Qe6.

29 Qe4   **f5**

With the aim of frustrating White's idea of developing his knight via c3.

30 Qc2   **g5**

31 f4   **g4**

A weak move in time pressure. The control at the thirty-second move prevents Black from considering the move 31 . . . Be7, the derivations from which would have been the following: (a) 32 fxg5 Bxg5 33 Nf4 Qxe5! 34 Ng6 Bxe3+ 35 Kh1 Qxg3! (b) 32 e4 Rf8 33 fxg5 Bxg5 34 exf5 Be3+ 35 Kh1 Rd2 36 Qe4 Qxf5!, winning in either case. The text move makes the position difficult again.

32 e4!   **Rf7**

33 exf5   **Rxf5**

34 Bh4

This apparently very commendable move allows the Black army renewed activity by means of an astute stroke. On the other hand Black would have had very complicated problems to resolve if White had played at once 34 Qe4, with the idea of continuing with Bf2-e3 and Ng3 or Nc3-b5 (or -d5).

34 . . .   **Bh6!**

Through this bishop move various speedy sacrificial paths are created. For example, 35 Be7 Qxe5! 36 fxe5 Be3+ 37 Rf2 Rxf2. Also 35 g3 Rxe5! 36 fxe5 Be3+ 37 Rf2 Rf8 38 Nf4 Qxe5 etc. But the most interesting fight results from the move that White selects, whereby he believes he will gain some advantage.

35 Qe4   **Rhf8**

Clearly this move is necessary to parry the threat of 36 Ng3.

36 g3

How can Black, faced with the threat of Rd1-d6, now defend his pawn at c4? The two unexpected moves that follow provide the answer.

Black to move

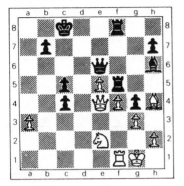

Position after 36 g3

36 ...   **Qd7!!**

The protection of the threatened pawn is abandoned! But the truth is that this pawn is protected 'secretly'. If White plays 37 Qxc4 he would receive as a punishment 37 ... Rxe5! and if 38 fxe5? then 38 ... Be3+, followed by 39 ... Qc6+.

37 Rc1

What else?

37 ...   **Re8!!**

The complement to the combination. If White eventually takes the pawn the reply ... Rexe5 would have a decisive effect.

38 Kg2

Clearly disconcerted by Black's strong threat, White assists the enemy attack. If 38 Rb1 Black would make his position safe after 38 ... Rf7 but the game would have been prolonged, although

White's king position would be very vulnerable.

38 ...   **Rexe5**

39 fxe5   **Bxc1**

40 Nxc1   **Qe6!**

Now, of course, the e-pawn has no defence, and White is therefore forced to investigate heroic possibilities of obtaining compensation.

41 h3   **gxh3+!**

Even more energetic than 41 ... h5.

42 Kh2   **Rf2+**

43 Kg1   **Rg2+**

44 Kh1

If 44 Kf1 there follows 44 ... Qf7+! 45 Bf6 Qd7 46 Qf3 Qd2 winning. Or 45 Qf4 Qxf4+ 46 gxf4 Rc2 47 Ne2 Rxe2 with the same result.

44 ...   **Qd7!**

45 Qf3   **Qd4!**

46 Qf8+

If 46 Qf1 there follows 46 ... Rf2.

46 ...   **Kc7**

47 Qe7+   **Kb6**

48 Qd6+

The last hope. If 48 ... Kb5 49 a4+ Kb4? then 50 Qxd4 cxd4 51 e6 Rc2 52 Bg5 and White wins.

48 ...   **Qxd6**

49 exd6   **Kc6**

50 Be7   **Rc2**

51 Bg5   **Kxd6**

52 a4   **h5**

In order to launch forth immediately on White's a-pawn.

53 White resigns

A struggle carried out by both sides with great aspirations for victory and therefore occasioning considerable difficulties and not a few mistakes. This was the first game since 1934 that I succeeded in winning from Bogoljubov with the Black pieces.

English Opening

GAME 97

Buenos Aires 1939
English Opening

White: M. CZERNIAK (Palestine)
Black: A. ALEKHINE (France)

1	c4	Nf6
2	Nc3	e5
3	g3	d5
4	cxd5	Nxd5
5	Bg2	Nb6

Entering the Dragon Variation of the Sicilian Defence (with one tempo less and colours reversed) in the conviction that one tempo less is not sufficient to transform a very favourable line into a bad one. In fact this game, like any other played in recent years, seems to demonstrate that by playing in this way Black need have no fears about obtaining equality.

6	Nf3	Nc6
7	0-0	Be7
8	d3	0-0

9	Be3	f5

The idea of this move is to induce White to begin the fight for c5 before he would have wished. The usual 9 . . . Bg4 or 9 . . . Be6 would have left the opponent with greater prospects of a choice.

10	Na4	f4
11	Bc5	Bg4
12	Rc1	Bd6

This is an important part of the mobilization plan. Otherwise the pressure on b7 after 13 Bxe7 Qxe7 14 Nc5 would have been somewhat disagreeable.

13 Re1

This move will lead sooner or later to the loss of control of d4, after which a Black knight at this square

will be able to cause serious discomfort.

13	...	Qe7
14	Nd2	Kh8!

Intending to play 15 ... Nxa4
which at this stage would be premature because of the very simple
reply 15 Qxa4 and if 15 ... Bxc5
then 16 Qc4+.

15 Ne4

The consequences of the acceptance
of the Black pawn would not be
satisfactory for White: 15 Bxd6
cxd6 16 Nxb6 axb6 17 Bxc6 bxc6
18 Rxc6 Rxa2 19 Rxb6 d5!,
threatening 20 ... fxg3, followed
by 21 ... Qc5 or vice versa.

15	...	Bxc5

After this exchange the threat to
the pawn at b7 will turn out to be
less effective than Black's pressure
in the centre.

16	Naxc5	Nd4

With the strong threat of 17 ... f3,
against which White finds the only
adequate reply.

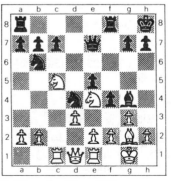

Position after 16 ... Nd4

17 Nb3!

After this there is no apparent
variation giving Black a definite
advantage. For example:

(a) 17 ... f3 18 Nxd4 fxg2 19 Nf3.
(b) 17 ... Nxe2+ 18 Rxe2 f3? 19
Re1.
(c) 17 ... Bxe2 18 Rxe2 f3? 19
Nxd4.
(d) 17 ... Nxb3 18 Qxb3 f3 19
Bxf3 Bxf3 20 exf3 Rxf3 21 Re3
with equal opportunities.

17	...	c6

Black proceeds along quiet positional lines, but as the move ... Rad8
(protecting d4) will be necessary
anyway, it should have been played
first. If now 18 Nxd4 exd4 19 Qd2
then 19 ... Nd5 20 Qa5 b6 21
Qxa7 Qb4, with ample compensation for the pawn. After the move
selected, White manages to balance
the position.

18	Nxd4	exd4
19	Qd2	Nd5
20	Rc4	Qe5
21	b4	

Threatening to gain a pawn with 22
Qb2. White has obtained something
of a counter-attack.

21	...	Rad8
22	Qb2	Nb6
23	Rc5	Rd5

Threatening 24 ... Na4!

24	Qa3	Nd7

Also protecting the rook at f8, a
point that will have great importance
in the future.

25 Rxd5?

The fact that White has played a few aggressive moves makes him too optimistic; from now on his position will be definitely inferior. Better was the modest 25 Rcc1 (25 Ra5 a6 26 Nc5 would be refuted as in the actual game by 26 . . . f3!) with the possible idea 26 Nc5.

25 . . .   cxd5

The obligatory displacement of the White knight will permit Black to execute now the very effective latent threat . . . f3.

26 Nc5

Black to move

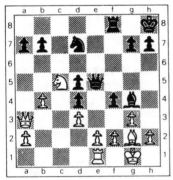

Position after 26 Nc5

26 . . .   f3

This would have been the beginning of an interesting attack if White had adopted the best defensive line which consisted of 27 Nxd7 Bxd7 28 Bf1! (and not 28 b5 Kg8!, after which White's b-pawn would be open to capture). The continuation would be 28 . . . h5 29 Qc1 (with the aim of stopping Black's 29 . . . h4, followed by 30 . . . hxg3 31 hxg3 Qxg3+!) Re8 30 e3 h4 with

the strong threat of . . . Re6-h6 etc. White's next move allows a quicker and more convincing solution.

27 h3   fxg2!

28 hxg4   Nf6!

If now 29 Nxb7 then 29 . . . Nxg4 winning straight away.

29 b5

Parrying the threat of 29 . . . Nxg4 (because of 30 Nd7 and wins).

29 . . .   Qe7!

The poor knight is impaled; 30 Qc1 does not help owing to the new threat 30 . . . Rc8, and 30 Qxa7 would be met by the threat of mate beginning with 30 . . . Nxg4.

30 Qb4

This saves the king (30 . . . Nxg4 31 Qxd4) but loses the knight.

30 . . .   Nd7

31 Qxd4

31 Na6 Qf6! would be hopeless.

31 . . .   Nxc5

Technically simpler than 31 . . . Qxc5 32 Qxc5 Nxc5 33 Rc1, followed by 34 Kxg2.

32 Qxd5

Or 32 Kxg2 b6 33 Qxd5 Rd8 34 Qf3 Nxd3.

32 . . .   Rd8

33 Qf3   Rxd3

And not 33 . . . Nxd3 34 Rd1 Ne5 35 Rxd8+, followed by 36 Qxb7 with a real counter-attack.

34 exd3   Qxe1+

35	Kxg2	Qe7
36	d4	Ne4
37	Qe3	Qe8
38	f3	Nf6
39	Qe5	

There are games in which it is truly difficult to determine the right moment to resign. Since White has not done so before, he now has to fight on till the end.

39	. . .	Kg8
40	g5	Qxe5
41	dxe5	Nd5
42	f4	Nc3

43	Kf3	Nxa2
44	f5	Nc3
45	b6	a5

The simplest.

46	Ke3	Nd5+
47	Kd4	Nxb6
48	e6	a4
49	f6	gxf6

Instead of this, 49 . . . a3? would have lost after 50 e7 Kf7 51 fxg7.

50	gxf6	a3
51	White resigns	

GAME 98

Munich 1941
English Opening

White: P. LEEPIN
Black: A. ALEKHINE

1	c4	e5
2	Nc3	Nf6
3	g3	d5
4	cxd5	Nxd5
5	Bg2	Nb6
6	a4	

This move is not recommendable at this stage of the game, since White obtains no advantage and at the same time gives up to Black the square b4.

6	. . .	a5
7	d3	Bb4

The first consequence of White's sixth move; otherwise the bishop would modestly have had to satisfy itself with the square e7.

8	Nf3	Nc6
9	0-0	0-0
10	Be3	Bg4
11	Rc1	f5!

A precisely calculated pawn sacrifice, the acceptance of which leads to rapid destruction foreseen by Black here on the eleventh move.

White to move

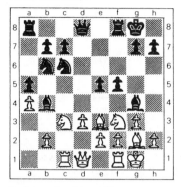

Position after 11 . . . f5

12 Ng5

Apparently effective in view of the threats 13 Ne6 and 13 Qb3+.

12 . . .	f4!
13 Bxb6	Qxg5
14 Bxc7	Qh5

More efficacious than 14 . . . Nd4, to which White would have been able to respond with 15 f3. But now this move is impossible in view of 15 . . . Bc5+ with an immediate win.

15 Bxc6

This eliminates one enemy but there still remain sufficient reserves. 15 Bf3 would also have lost quickly after 15 . . . Bxf3, followed by 16 . . . Rf6.

15 . . .	bxc6

16 Rc2

If 16 Re1 then 16 . . . fxg3 17 hxg3 Rxf2! 18 Kxf2 Bc5+.

16 . . .	Bxc3

The most exact. In the continuation from the plausible 16 . . . f3 White

would have been able to stop the direct mating threats with 17 h4! Bxc3 18 Rxc3 fxe2 19 Qb3+, followed by 20 Re1 etc.

17 Rxc3

If 17 bxc3 then 17 . . . f3 wins at once.

17 . . .	Bxe2
18 Qb3+	Kh8

19 Re1

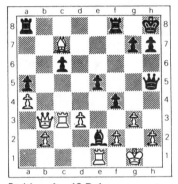

Position after 19 Re1

19 . . .	Qh3!

This reveals the idea behind the exchange on the sixteenth move. For the only plausible move, 20 f3, I had prepared mate in eight moves: 20 . . . fxg3! 21 Rxe2 Rxf3 22 Rc1 Raf8 23 Qd1 (or 23 Rg2 gxh2+ and mate in two) Rf2! 24 Rxf2 gxf2+ 25 Kh1 f1(Q)+ etc.

20 Bxe5

After this move Black has the agreeable choice between mate with 20 . . . f3 or with 20 . . . Bf3.

20 . . .	f3!

21 White resigns

GAME 99

Munich 1942
English Opening

White: P. KERES
Black: K. RICHTER

1 c4	e5
2 Nc3	Nf6
3 Nf3	Nc6
4 d4	exd4
5 Nxd4	Bb4
6 Bg5	h6
7 Bh4	g5

Unexpected, but a stroke that is characteristic of the German player.

8 Bg3	d6
9 Rc1	

Better would have been 9 e3 or 9 f3.

9 . . .	Nxd4
10 Qxd4	Bf5
11 h4?	

A considerable loss of time. 11 f3 would be better.

11 . . .	Kd7!

Intrepid and well inspired. If now 12 Be5 then 12 . . . Bc5 13 Bxf6 Bxd4 14 Bxd8 Raxd8 with advantage to Black.

12 Rd1	Ne4
13 Qe5	Bxc3+
14 bxc3	Nxg3
15 fxg3	

Also after 15 Qxg3 b6 Black would

have the better game.

15 . . .	Bg6
16 hxg5	Qxg5

At this moment White has some counter-attacking chances and Keres makes use of them with the ingenious spirit in which he specializes. This opportunity could be avoided by means of 16 . . . hxg5 17 Rxh8 Qxh8 and White's disorganized pawns would guarantee Black a good endgame.

17 Qf4	Rae8
18 Rd5!	

Forcing the undoubling of one of the pawns.

18 . . .	Qxf4
19 gxf4	b6
20 Kf2	h5
21 e3	h4
22 Be2	Be4
23 Rg5	Reg8
24 Bg4+	Kc6
25 Rxg8	Rxg8
26 Rxh4	Kc5
27 Bf3	Bxf3
28 Kxf3	Kxc4

In spite of all his efforts, the White king has not succeeded in counterbalancing all the advantages that his rival obtained in the opening. However, as we shall see later on, this advantage should not be decisive.

29	Rh7	Rf8
30	g4	Kxc3
31	Ke4!	c5
32	g5	c4
33	Kd5	Kb4
34	e4	c3
35	Rh2	Rc8
36	Rc2	b5
37	f5	a5

Position after 37 . . . a5

38 Kxd6?

The decisive mistake. Instead of this unfortunate move, necessary was 38 Kd4 with good chances of salvation. Let us look at two principal variations:

(a) 38 . . . Rg8 39 Rg2! c2 40 Rxc2 Rxg5 41 Kd5 Rg4 42 Re2 Kc3 43 Kxd6 Kd3 44 Rf2.

(b) 38 . . . a4 39 Kd3 Ka3 40 Rxc3+ Rxc3+ 41 Kxc3 b4+ 42 Kd4 b3 43 g6.

38	. . .	Kc4
39	e5	b4
40	Kd7	Ra8
41	e6	fxe6
42	f6	a4
43	g6	b3
44	axb3+	axb3
45	Rxc3+	Kxc3
46	f7	b2
47	g7	b1(Q)
48	f8(Q)	Qb7+?

Immediately decisive was 48 . . . Qb5+ because if 49 Kxe6 then 49 . . . Ra6+ winning in a few moves.

49	Kxe6	Ra6+
50	Ke5	Qb5+
51	Kf4	Ra4+
52	Kg3	Qd3+
53	Qf3	Ra8
54	g8(Q)	Rxg8+

Here or on the previous move exchanging queens would have sufficed.

55	Kh2	Rh8+
56	Kg1	

A king that does not want to resign!

56	. . .	Rg8+
57	Kh2	Kc2
58	Qc6+	Kd1
59	Qf3+	Qe2+
60	White resigns	

GAME 100

Prague 1943
English Opening

White: J. SAJTAR
Black: A. ALEKHINE

1 Nf3	Nf6
2 c4	e6
3 b3	c5
4 Bb2	Nc6
5 e3	d5
6 d4	

White now prefers the weakness of the diagonal e1-a5 in exchange for rapidly completing his development. But the prospect of permitting the advance . . . d4 would in any event not be attractive for the first player.

6 ...	cxd4
7 Nxd4	

If 7 exd4 there follows 7 . . . Bb4+ 8 Bc3 Bxc3+ 9 Nxc3 Ne4! and Black has the initiative.

7 ...	Bb4+
8 Bc3	

Relatively better than 8 Nc3 Ne4.

8 ...	Bxc3+
9 Nxc3	e5!
10 Nxc6	bxc6
11 cxd5	cxd5
12 Bb5+	Bd7
13 Bxd7+	Qxd7

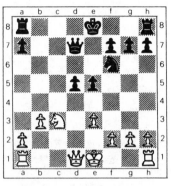

Position after 13 . . . Qxd7

Black has obtained the type of position that is produced for White after 1 d4 d5 2 c4 e6 3 Nf3 Nf6 4 Nc3 c5 5 cxd5 Nxd5 6 e4 Nxc3 7 bxc3 cxd4 8 cxd4 Bb4+ 9 Bd2 Bxd2+ 10 Qxd2 etc. White's chances rest in his queen-side pawn majority which could be menacing in the endgame. Black's opportunities consist of the creation at the right moment of a passed pawn on the d-file, which will be able to exercise strong pressure on his opponent's position during the middle-game. Consequently, whereas White concentrates on simplifying the game, Black's tactics will involve preventing such a design, eluding exchanges.

14 0-0	0-0
15 Qd3	Rfd8
16 Rfd1	Rac8

17 Rac1   Rc6!

With the object of avoiding the exchange of rooks, conserving greater attacking chances.

18 h3   h6

Both contestants permit themselves a breathing space to eliminate any combination by the enemy arising out of the kings' positions on the back rank. It will shortly be seen how useful this precaution turns out to be for Black.

19 Ne2   Rd6!

Giving White the c-file in the (correct) belief that his threats on the king's side will not leave his opponent enough time to derive benefit from this advantage.

20 Rc2

Against 20 Ng3 the reply would also have been 20 . . . Ne4!

20 . . .   Ne4

21 f3

Black was threatening 21 . . . Rg6.

21 . . .   Ng5

With the clear threat 22 . . . Nxf3+ (or 22 . . . Nxh3+) 23 gxf3 Qxh3 24 Kf2 e4 winning. This threat is, to be sure, easily parried, but it gives Black the necessary time to organize his main action in the centre.

22 Kh2   Qe7

23 Ng1

My opponent, one of the young Czech hopes (in this tournament he won fourth prize equal with Foltys, ahead of Opocensky, Sämisch, and many

other players), defends himself in irreproachable fashion. Black was threatening 23 . . . e4, which would now be dealt with by 24 Qd4.

23 . . .   d4

24 Re1!

Again the only possible move. It is evident that after 24 e4 Ne6 Black, with his solidly protected passed pawn, would have achieved a strategically won game. How can he induce his opponent to liquidate the tension in the centre by exd4 or e4? The aggressive move 24 . . . e4 would not work after 25 fxe4 Qe5+ 26 Kh1 Nxe4 27 Nf3 Qf5 28 Kg1!

Black to move

Position after 24 Re1

24 . . .   Rg6!!

Less in order to deal a direct attacking blow than to provide the square d6 for the queen; amongst other considerations, this is based on the view that the plausible reply 25 Kh1 would hardly be satisfactory because of 25 . . . e4 26 fxe4 Nxe4 27 Nf3 Rc6! and now 28 Nxd4 is impossible owing to 28 . . . Rxc2 29 Qxc2 Rxd4 30 exd4 Ng3+ 31

Kh2 Qxe1.

25 exd4

Resigning himself to the inevitable, since in this position there exists no more profitable move.

25 ...   **Qd6!**

Clearly the complement of the previous move. He obtains a passed pawn and the aim of the following play will be to unblock it. As will be seen, it is far from easy to attain this objective.

26 Kh1   **exd4**

27 Ne2   **Ne6**

28 Rec1

The exchange of one pair of rooks that follows this move is practically unavoidable, and will allow White to obtain some chances on the queen's wing.

28 ...   **Qe5**

29 Rc8   **Rxc8**

30 Rxc8+   **Kh7**

31 Rc1

Against 31 Rc2 the answer would be 31 ... Qa5 and if then 32 Qd2 Qf5 etc.

31 ...   **Nc5!**

Permitting the passed pawn to be protected by the rook.

32 Qd2   **Rd6**

Premature would be 32 ... d3 33 Nf4 Rd6 34 b4.

33 b4   **Ne6**

34 Qd3+   **g6**

35 a4   **Kg7**

With the intention of playing 36 ... a5 37 b5 Nc5 which at this moment would be ineffective owing to 38 Qc4.

36 a5   **a6**

37 Rd1

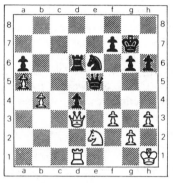

Position after 37 Rd1

37 ...   **Rd5!**

With the plan of regrouping his forces by means of 38 ... Qd6 etc. It should be observed that White cannot play 38 Nc3 because of 38 ... dxc3! 39 Qxd5 Qxd5 40 Rxd5 c2 and wins. Against 38 Qxa6 the continuation would be 38 ... d3 39 Ng1 Nf4 (threatening 40 ... Qb2) 40 Qc4 Rd4 41 Qb3 (or 41 Qc3 Nd5) Nh5 42 g4 Ng3+ 43 Kg2 Ne2 44 Nxe2 Qxe2+ 45 Kg3 h5 (threatening mate in three moves), with a triumphant attack.

38 Qe4

White tries to eliminate the danger by proposing an exchange of queens, but Black's course of action is not going to offer him any chances of resistance.

38 ...   **Qd6!**

Threatening 39 ... Re5 and 39 ...
d3.

39	f4	d3
40	Nc3	Rd4
41	Qe5+	Qxe5
42	fxe5	Nf4

This is not the simplest solution
(that would clearly be 42 ... Rxb4
43 Rxd3 Rb3, followed by 44 ...
Ra3 finally winning thanks to the
a-pawn), but it is certainly the most
elegant. I chose it because, by virtue
of the tactical possibilities, it seemed
to me easier to force victory with a
pawn on the b-file.

43 b5

The only chance of counter-play.

43 ... Ne2

Of course White cannot take the
knight. After 44 bxa6 Black would
have played 44 ... Nxc3! 45 a7
Nxd1! (and not 45 ... Rd8 46
Rxd3) 46 a8(Q) d2 winning. The
following move is therefore forced.

44	Nb1	axb5
45	a6	Ra4

And not 45 ... Nf4 46 Nc3!

| 46 | Rxd3 | Rxa6 |

The rest is a matter of technique.

47	Rd2	Ng3+!
48	Kg1	b4
49	Rd3	Ne2+
50	Kf2	Nf4
51	Rd4	Ra2+
52	Kf3	Nxg2
53	Rxb4	Ne1+!

The point of the preceding
manoeuvre. Now Black easily wins
the e-pawn. For example: 54 Kg4
Rg2+ 55 Kf4 Nd3+ 56 Kf3 Rf2+
57 Ke3 Nxb4 58 Kxf2 Nd3+.

54	Ke4	Re2+
55	Kd5	Rxe5+
56	White resigns	

Réti's Opening

GAME 101

Buenos Aires 1939
Réti's Opening

White: L. ENGELS (Germany)
Black: N. BERGQVIST (Sweden)

1	Nf3	e6		2	g3	d5

3	Bg2	Nf6
4	0-0	Be7
5	c4	0-0
6	b3	Ne4

A little-played and scarcely recommendable manoeuvre whereby he sacrifices two valuable tempi in the hope of enticing White to obstruct his a1-h8 diagonal by playing d4. But the first player finds an ingenious way of parrying this positional threat.

7 a3

With the unconcealed intention of dislodging the central knight with 8 d3.

7	...	f5?

Owing to his inferior development he cannot yet prepare a direct attack and this advance therefore means nothing except the weakening of his central position. 7 . . . Bf6 8 Ra2 c5 9 Rc2 dxc4 10 bxc4 Nc6 11 d3 Nd6, although not very promising, would at least be consistent.

8	d3	Bf6
9	Ra2	Nc5

9 . . . Nc3 10 Nxc3 Bxc3 11 d4 would also be hardly satisfactory but 9 . . . Nd6 could and should have been tried.

10	b4	Ncd7?

No opening can stand four inferior moves in the first ten. 10 . . . Nca6 would doubtless have been an emergency measure of the saddest kind but it would have at least avoided the following break-up of

the centre that will soon guarantee White complete domination of the board.

11	cxd5	exd5
12	Qb3	c6
13	e4	

From an elevated point of view this is a strategic decision.

13	...	Nb6

Black has clearly become demoralized. Otherwise he would have preferred 13 . . . fxe4 14 dxe4 Nb6 15 e5 Be7 16 Nd4 a5, after which he would retain at least some prospects for his queen's bishop.

14	e5	Be7
15	Re2	

Showing that his manoeuvre begun on the seventh move has contributed to the most effective mobilization of his queen's rook.

15	...	a5

The only counter-demonstration that Black will be able to attempt throughout the whole game. The opening of the a-file does not have much importance, since Black's minor pieces are hoarded together and cannot work jointly to utilize it.

16	Bd2	axb4
17	axb4	Na6
18	Na3	Nc7
19	Nc2	Be6

Nor would 19 . . . Ne6 be any use because White, after the exchange of one of his knights, would permanently occupy d4 with the other one.

20	Nfd4	Qd7
21	f4	Ra6
22	Ref2	

Expecting 22 . . . g6, after which he would have to prepare for the advance g4 by playing h3, Bf3, and Rg2. Meanwhile Black would be condemned to total passivity.

22	. . .	Kh8?

But Black delivers an immediate invitation to unfold the attack.

White to play

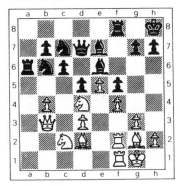

Position after 22 . . . Kh8

23   g4

This forces a simple and vulnerable weakness on the f-pawn after 23 . . . g6 24 gxf5 gxf5 25 Bh3 or else (as happens in the game) complete domination of the centre by the two adjoining pawns at e5 and f5. The tactical justification for the text move is shown by the following variation: 23 . . . Bh4 24 Re2 fxg4 25 f5 Bxf5 26 e6 and Black, as a consequence of his unfortunate move 22 . . . Kh8?, has no other reply but 26 . . . Bxe6.

23	. . .	Bh4

More prolonged resistance would be possible after 23 . . . g6. After the text move by the bishop this defence will not be possible since if 24 . . . g6 the bishop will fall into the snare of 25 g5, followed by 26 Nf3.

24	Re2	fxg4
25	f5	Bg8
26	Bf4	

White will not advance either of his central pawns unless it may be done with decisive effect. The text move has chiefly a positional value by preparing, according to circumstances, for action against Black's king's side, beginning with Ne3.

26	. . .	Nb5
27	Nxb5	cxb5
28	Nd4	Rfa8
29	Qb2!	

This prevents the more or less worrying possibility of 29 . . . Ra1 and at the same time proposes the exchange of the queen for the two Black rooks. White rightly believes that this transaction will facilitate the strengthening of the central pawns.

29	. . .	Ra2!

Black, on the other hand, has very little to lose and he is disposed to run the risk.

30	Qxa2	Rxa2
31	Rxa2	Qe7

This only precipitates the inevitable end. If 31 . . . Be7 (relatively better), White would play 32 Bd2, threatening 33 f6 and 33 Ra5.

32 f6!

Threatening to win a piece by 33 Nf5 etc.

32	...	Qd7
33	Re2	gxf6

Or 33 ... Be6 34 Nxe6 Qxe6 35 Bg3 Bxf6 36 exf6 Qxe2 37 f7 and wins.

34	e6	Qe8

35 Nf5   Bxe6

If 35 ... Bg5 then 36 Bxg5 fxg5 37 e7 Nc8 38 Rc1 winning.

36	Nxh4	Qd7
37	Rfe1	Bg8

38 Re7

With the unavoidable threat of Bh6-g7 mate.

38 ...   Black resigns

GAME 102

Buenos Aires 1939
Réti's Opening

White: G. STAHLBERG (Sweden)
Black: E. ROJAHN (Norway)

1	Nf3	Nf6
2	c4	b6
3	g3	Bb7
4	Bg2	g6

There is not much in this double fianchetto because of White's adoption of a particular pawn structure in the centre. More flexible is 4 ... c5 and 5 ... Qc8, preparing for an eventual ... d5 or ... Nc6 and leaving open both possibilities for the development of the king's bishop.

5	Nc3	Bg7
6	0-0	c5

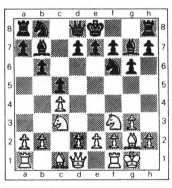

Position after 6 ... c5

7 d3!!

Taking advantage of the fact that, owing to the lack of protection of the queen's bishop, Black cannot play 7 ... d5 (because of 8 Ne5 0-0 9 Bg5), White adopts a modern stratagem used in other systems of

development such as the English
and the Sicilian. This consists of
'sacrificing' (that is, leaving without
adequate protection) a central
square (here d4) with the purpose
of obtaining control of all the
neighbouring squares. The present
short game shows in a convincing
way how effective this strategy can
be if the opponent does not
immediately take steps to oppose
it.

| 7 | . . . | 0-0 |
| 8 | e4 | d6?? |

After playing this 'plausible' move
Black will soon be led into a
desperate position. White's
strategic threat of Nh4, followed by
f4 and then f5 can only be prevented by 8 . . . e6 9 Nh4 Ne8
10 f4 f5, after which his position
although somewhat inferior, would
be defensible.

| 9 | Nh4 | Nc6 |
| 10 | f4 | Qd7 |

10 . . . Nd4 could not be played
because of 11 e5.

| 11 | h3 | Rad8 |
| 12 | Kh2 | e6 |

Weakening f6 without any necessity
or compensation. But White's plan
would have been Be3, Qd2, and f5
in any case.

| 13 | Be3 | Nd4 |
| 14 | Qd2 | Ne8 |

Very late, because evidently White
is not going to permit . . . f5. Without any piece or pawn exchanged
Black has no effective remedy. The

game is an instructive lesson in
modern opening strategy.

White to play

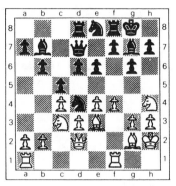

Position after 14 . . . Ne8

| 15 | f5! | exf5 |

This loses faster than 15 . . . e5
but there is no doubt possible that
the attempt to block the position
would not be successful. After 16
Bh6 Qe7 17 Rf2, followed by 18
Raf1, Black would be almost compelled to alter the pawn position,
to his disadvantage. After the text
move Ståhlberg rapidly obtains a
mating attack.

| 16 | exf5 | Bxg2 |
| 17 | Qxg2 | Bf6 |

There was practically nothing to be
done against Nd5, followed by f6.

| 18 | Nd5 | Bxh4 |
| 19 | gxh4 | Kh8 |

19 . . . Nxf5 is of no use because of
20 Rxf5.

20	Bxd4+	cxd4
21	fxg6	hxg6
22	Rae1	Ng7

23	Qg5	Nf5
24	Rxf5!	Black resigns

The rook cannot be taken because of mate in two.

GAME 103

Buenos Aires 1939
Réti's Opening

White: G. STAHLBERG (Sweden)
Black: M. CASTILLO (Chile)

1	d4	Nf6
2	c4	g6
3	g3	d5
4	cxd5	Nxd5
5	Nf3	Bg7
6	Bg2	0-0
7	0-0	c5
8	Nc3	Nxc3
9	bxc3	

The position thus reached can be obtained from different lines of play: firstly, Réti's Opening; secondly, the Catalan System; thirdly, the Grünfeld Defence. According to the present state of theory (the most recent well-known experience is the game Pirc-Bogoljubov, Bad Sliac, 1932; previous games are Bogoljubov-Euwe, match 1928 and Kashdan-Bogoljubov, Bled, 1931) the position is considered favourable to White, although Black is not without counter-chances in practice. These are based mainly on the combined activity of his free bishops.

9	...	Nc6

And not 9 . . . cxd4 10 Nxd4 with clear advantage to White.

10	e3	Qa5
11	Qb3	Rb8
12	Bd2?	

Since the above-mentioned game Bogoljubov-Euwe the text move has (rightly) been deemed inferior on account of the possibility of 12 . . . Bg4 with the threat 13 . . . Bxf3 14 Bxf3 cxd4 winning material. And if 12 Ba3? then the blockading manoeuvre 12 . . . c4! 13 Qb2 Bf5 is permitted. The precise developing move at this stage is 12 Bb2.

12	...	cxd4?

After 12 . . . Bg4 the artificial reply 13 Rfb1 would have been virtually forced. The manoeuvre in the text will be convincingly refuted by White's fourteenth move.

13	cxd4	Qh5
14	Rac1	

Parrying the threat 14 . . . Bg4 because of 15 Rc5.

14	...	Be6
15	Qa3	Rfd8

16	Rc5	f5
17	h4	

With the intention of exploiting to the maximum the bad position of the Black queen.

17	...	h6

White to play

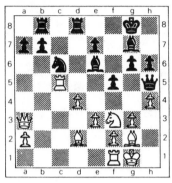

Position after 17 ... h6

18 Nh2

An original manoeuvre; White liberates the imprisoned queen with the aim of catching her again in the middle of the board. The preparatory move 18 Re1 would be inadequate because of the defence 18 ... g5 19 Nh2 Qf7.

18	...	Qe2

19 Nf3!

This move is like the opening and closing of the door in order to take the queen in a better situation.

19	...	Rd6

The only defence against the terrible threat of 20 Re1. But now White secures a decisive positional advantage in the endgame.

20	Re1	Qa6

21	Qxa6	bxa6
22	Rc1	Nb4

Hoping to find some compensation in the two bishops.

23	Bxb4	Rxb4
24	Rc7	Bxa2

Or 24 ... Bf6 25 Ne5 with clear advantage.

25	Rxe7	Rb1
26	Rxb1	Bxb1
27	Nd2	Ba2
28	Rxa7	Rb6!
29	Bf1	Rb2
30	Bc4+	Bxc4
31	Nxc4	Ra2
32	d5?	

Up until here Ståhlberg has simplified material in a totally logical way, despite Black's tenacious defence. But here, evidently, he commits an error of judgement. Instead of advancing the passed pawn, which increases the Black bishop's field of action, he could easily augment his positional advantage by the manoeuvre 32 h5! g5 (or 32 ... gxh5 33 Nd6 f4 34 Nf5 Bf8 35 gxf4) 33 Nd6 f4 34 Nf5 Bf8 35 gxf4 gxf4 36 exf4 and wins.

32	...	Rc2
33	Rc7	a5
34	Kg2?	

This weak move can also be explained only by shortage of time. What objection could be made to 34 d6 a4 35 d7 Bf6 36 Rc6 Be7 37 Rxg6+ Kf8 38 Rc6 etc.? 38 ...

a3 would not work because of 39 Rc8+.

34	...	a4
35	Rc8+	Bf8
36	d6	Kg7
37	d7	Be7
38	Nd6	Rd2
39	d8(Q)	Bxd8
40	Rxd8	Kh7

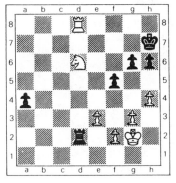

Position after 40 . . . Kh7

Incredible but true. Black is still alive and even threatens in passing to win a piece by advancing his a-pawn. It is rather peculiar that White cannot prevent this by playing 41 Rd7+ Kg8 42 Ne4 Rxd7 43 Nf6+ Kf7 44 Nxd7 a3 45 Nc5 a2 46 Nb3 Ke6 47 Kf3 Kd5 48 Ke2 Kc4 49 Na1 Kc3 50 Kd1 because of 50 . . . Kd3 with a draw in sight.

41	Rd7+	Kg8
42	h5!	gxh5
43	Kf3!	

But this method is quite safe and convincing.

43	...	a3
44	Kf4	a2
45	Ra7	Rxd6
46	Kxf5	Rd2
47	f4	Rg2
48	e4	Rxg3
49	Rxa2	h4
50	e5	**Black resigns**

Catalan System

GAME 104

Buenos Aires 1939
Catalan System

White: J. FOLTYS (Czechoslovakia)
Black: P. MICHEL (Germany)

1	Nf3	d5	2	g3	c5

3	Bg2	Nc6
4	d4	

White plays the Grünfeld Defence with an extra tempo, but his advantage will be sufficient to obtain only equality.

4	...	e6
5	0-0	Nf6
6	c4	

Attaining one of the positions typical of the evocative Catalan System, in which Black has a fairly good chance of finding a satisfactory continuation.

6	...	Be7

Also playable here is 6 ... dxc4 7 Qa4 Bd7 8 dxc5 Bxc5 9 Qxc4 Be7 10 Nc3 0-0 (Pelikan-Guimard, Buenos Aires, 1939).

7	dxc5?	

This inexact move is the cause of White's subsequent downfall. If he wished to obtain, by transposition of moves, a variation of the Tarrasch Defence, he should have begun with 7 cxd5 and if 7 ... exd5 then 8 Nc3 0-0 9 Bg5.

7	...	Bxc5
8	cxd5	exd5
9	Nbd2?	

The idea of blocking the isolated pawn instead of attacking it is bad. Comparatively better would be 9 Bg5 0-0 10 Nc3 d4 11 Bxf6 Qxf6 12 Ne4 Qe7 13 Nxc5 Qxc5 14 Rc1 Qb6, reaching a well known position.

9	...	0-0

10	Nb3	Bb6
11	Nbd4	Re8
12	e3?	

The third inexactitude, as a result of which Black's chances (on account of the weakness of the white squares in the enemy position) become clearly superior. 12 Be3 and if 12 ... Ng4 then 13 Bg5 would be natural.

12	...	Bg4
13	Nxc6	

Evidently fortifying Black's central position; after 13 b3 Nxd4 14 exd4 Ne4 White's game would remain manifestly inferior.

13	...	bxc6
14	h3	Bh5
15	b3	Ne4
16	Bb2	Qd6

White to move

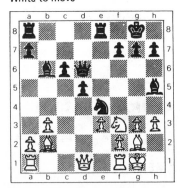

Position after 16 ... Qd6

17	g4	

It is easy to criticise this move, the weakness of which consists of compromising even more the king's position without increasing White's opportunities elsewhere on the board. But a desirable line of play would now be almost unimaginable; Black has the possibility of a sacrificial combination at f2 or g3, threatening to create a formidable passed pawn after . . . c5, . . . Rad8 and . . . d4. Clearly White has not understood the spirit of the variation chosen by his adversary.

17 . . .	Bg6
18 Rc1	Bc7

The first direct threat (19 . . . Ng5).

| 19 Re1 | f6! |

A timely protection of the squares e5 and g7.

| 20 Kf1 | |

With the aim of weakening the effect of . . . Ng5.

20 . . .	Rad8
21 Nd4	c5
22 Nb5	Qa6
23 Qe2	Bb6
24 a4	

24 Nc3 is not possible because of 24 . . . Ng3+ 25 fxg3 Bd3, winning.

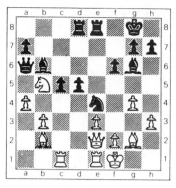

Position after 24 a4

| 24 . . . | d4 |

The triumph of Tarrasch's central pawn.

25 Red1	d3
26 Qf3	d2
27 Ra1	Ba5
28 Kg1	Qe6

Leading to the gain of material.

| 29 Rab1 | |

In a desperate position any move looks like a mistake.

29 . . .	Ng5
30 Qc6	Bxb1
31 White resigns	

In my opinion this game, on account of the purity of style, is one of the finest productions of the 1939 tournament.

GAME 105

Munich 1942
Catalan System

White: G. BARCZA
Black: E. BOGOLJUBOV

1	Nf3	c5
2	g3	d5
3	Bg2	Nf6
4	0-0	Nc6
5	d4	e6
6	c4	

The strength of White's treatment of the opening is more apparent than real. As this game also demonstrates, Black can reach a comfortable position without great effort.

6	...	dxc4
7	Qa4	Bd7
8	dxc5	Na5!
9	Qc2	Bxc5
10	Ne5	Rc8
11	Bd2	b5

The simple reply 11 ... 0-0 would also be fairly acceptable. But Black is more ambitious.

12	Nxd7	Nxd7
13	Qc3	Nc6
14	Bxc6	Rxc6
15	Qxg7	Qf6
16	Qg4	Qd4!
17	Qxd4	Bxd4
18	Bc3	e5?

With the simple move 18 ... Bxc3 19 Nxc3 a6 Black would have assured himself of a comfortable and favourable endgame.

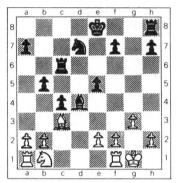

Position after 18 ... e5

19 a4!

A powerful move which changes the aspect of the battle.

19	...	b4
20	Bxb4	Bxb2
21	Ra2	c3

Also after 21 ... Bd4 22 Rc2 the c-pawn would finally succumb.

22	Bxc3!	Bxc3
23	Rc1	Ke7
24	Rxc3	Rhc8
25	Rxc6	Rxc6
26	Nd2	Rc3

Notwithstanding his pawn advantage, the final phase is not an expeditious triumph for White since Black has greater space available for his forces. Barcza treats the ending with exquisite finesse until obtaining victory.

27	f3	Nc5
28	Kf2	f5
29	Rb2!	Kd6
30	a5	Kc7
31	Rb5	e4?

Greater drawing chances were offered by 31 . . . a6 32 Rb6 Ra3 etc.

32	fxe4	fxe4
33	Nf1	Kc6
34	Rb8	Ra3
35	Rh8	Rxa5

36	Rxh7	Ra2
37	g4	

The advance of this pawn quickly forces victory.

37	. . .	a5
38	g5	Rb2
39	g6	Rb8
40	g7	Rg8
41	Ne3	Ne6
42	Nf5	Kc5
43	Rh8	Rxg7
44	Nxg7	Nxg7
45	h4	**Black resigns**

GAME 106

Munich 1942
Catalan System

White: A. ALEKHINE
Black: B. RABAR

1	d4	Nf6
2	c4	e6
3	g3	d5
4	Bg2	dxc4
5	Qa4+	Bd7
6	Qxc4	Bc6
7	Nf3	Bd5

Black loses too many tempi with these bishop moves. Better is 7 . . . Nbd7 and if 8 Nc3 then 8 . . . Nb6 9 Qd3 Bb4, as was played in the game Junge-Alekhine in the same tournament.

8	Qd3	c5

9	Nc3	Bc6

If 9 . . . cxd4 there would follow 10 Nxd5 Qxd5 11 0-0 with the strong threat of 12 Nxd4.

10	0-0	Nbd7
11	Rd1	cxd4

If 11 . . . Be7 then 12 e4 and White, with the threat of 13 d5, would practically force the exchange at d4, which would guarantee him the advantage of the bishop pair.

12	Nxd4	Bxg2
13	Kxg2	Be7
14	Qf3!	

The queen now exerts strong pressure on the enemy queen's side.

14 ...   Qb6

This move will be refuted by energetic combinative play. But 14 ... Qb8 15 Nb3 with the threat of 16 Bf4 would be equally unsatisfactory.

15 Be3!

The consequences of this move are not very difficult to calculate, but it is interesting to prove that from this moment onwards Black already lacks any satisfactory defence. Against 15 ... Qxb2 White replies 16 Ncb5 and if 15 ... Ne5 there would follow 16 Ndb5!

15 ...   0-0

16 Nf5   Bc5

This apparent salvation will be refuted by a well-concealed combination. Nor would the alternative 16 ... Qd8 17 Nxe7+ Qxe7 18 Qxb7 Rfb8 19 Qc7 Rxb2 20 Bd4 have saved the game.

17 Na4   Qa5

18 Nxc5   Nxc5

White to move

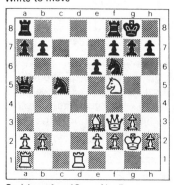

Position after 18 ... Nxc5

19 Nxg7!

This wins at least a pawn and leads to a simply won ending. The only reply — excluding the text — would be 19 ... Nce4, against which White would first have forced the Black queen to abandon the fifth rank and would then have occupied the long diagonal with the bishop, with decisive effect: 20 b4! Qe5 21 Bf4 Qb5 (or 21 ... Qc3 22 Nh5!!) 22 a4! Qxb4 23 Be5 etc.

19 ...   Kxg7

20 Bd4

The strength of this move lies mainly in the fact that after 20 ... Nd7 White simply plays 21 Bc3, with the unavoidable threat of 22 Rxd7.

20 ...   Ne4

21 Qxe4   Qf5

22 Qxf5

The endgame that follows is without any technical difficulties.

22 ...   exf5

23 Rac1   Rfe8

24 Rc7   Rxe2

25 Rxb7   Kg6

26 Bxf6   Kxf6

27 Rd6+   Black resigns

If 27 ... Kg7 there follows 28 Rdd7 Rf8 29 Kf3 Rc2 30 Rdc7 Rd2 31 Ke3.

GAME 107

Exhibition Game, Warsaw 1943
Catalan System

White: A. ALEKHINE
Black: E. BOGOLJUBOV

1	d4	d5
2	c4	e6
3	Nf3	Nf6
4	g3	dxc4
5	Qa4+	Qd7

The exchange of queens that Black will force with this manoeuvre gives him very few advantages, because it does not solve the chief problem, which is the development of the queen's bishop.

6	Qxc4	Qc6
7	Nbd2	Qxc4
8	Nxc4	Bb4+
9	Bd2	Bxd2+
10	Ncxd2	

Preferable to 10 Nfxd2 which, after 10 ... Nc6 11 Nf3 Nb4! would have offered Black some chances. Despite the simplification Black still faces a difficult problem: if he is compelled to play ... c6 what future will be left for the bishop? Bogoljubov takes a radical measure; with the aim of protecting the points he prepares to castle long. In the continuation we shall see the weak side of this strategy.

10	...	Nc6
11	Bg2	Bd7
12	0-0	0-0-0

13	Rac1	Rhe8
14	Nc4	

It goes without saying that White will not allow ... e5.

14	...	Re7
15	a3	Be8
16	Rfd1	Nd5
17	b4	Nb6

White to move

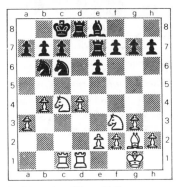

Position after 17 ... Nb6

18 b5!

An important move which forces the knight to withdraw and permits the blocking of the queen's side. For if 18 ... Nxc4 then 19 bxc6 Nxa3 20 cxb7+ Kxb7 21 Ne5+ Kc8 22 Nc6 Bxc6 23 Bxc6 Rd6 24 Rc3, followed by 25 Ra1 and wins.

18	...	Nb8
19	Nxb6+	axb6

20	a4	f6
21	Bh3	

Threatening to advance the d-pawn.

21	...	Bd7

Now it seems that Black is at last going to free himself by 22 . . . e5.

White to move

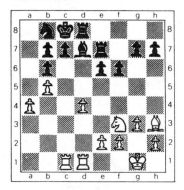

Position after 21 . . . Bd7

22 Nd2!!

Decisive, because if 22 . . . e5 there follows 23 Nc4 with the threat of 24 Nxb6 mate. What follows now is practically all forced.

22	...	Rf8

23	Bg2!	

23 Nc4 would allow Black to play 23 . . . Kd8, followed by 24 . . . Bc8.

23	...	c6
24	Nc4	Kc7
25	e4	cxb5

Desperation, since there is no defence against the advance of the d-pawn.

26	axb5	Bxb5
27	d5!	

More accurate than 27 Na3+ Bc6 28 d5, after which Black would not have been under any obligation to exchange pawns.

27	...	exd5
28	Na3+	Bc6
29	exd5	Rd7
30	Nb5+	Kd8
31	dxc6	bxc6
32	Nd4!	

This wins at least a pawn.

32	...	**Black resigns**

An instructive game from the strategic point of view.

Index of Players

All references are to game-numbers

Alekhine 5, 6, 7, 9, 10, 11, 12, 13, 19, 23, 26, 31, 33, 34, 39, 40, 43, 49, 50, 55, 57, 64, 83, 92, 94, 96, 97, 98, 100, 106, 107
Apscheneek 18, 34

Barcza 10, 105
Bartosek 31
Bergqvist 101
Bogoljubov 15, 26, 73, 85, 96, 105, 107
Bolbochán 65
Brinckmann 41

Capablanca 42, 67, 68, 82
Castillo 103
Charlier 57, 94
Cruz, O. 57, 94
Cruz, W. 18, 57
Czerniak 42, 52, 75, 91, 93, 97

Danielsson 51
De Ronde 45
Dulanto 27

Eliskases 39, 53
Endzelins 29
Enevoldsen 64, 68, 71
Engels 101

Flores 32, 74, 75
Foltys 8, 44, 47, 48, 104
Friedemann 1

Graf 56
Grau 53, 77, 90

Hasenfuss 46
Heinicke 41

Junge 9, 73

Kahn 59
Kashdan 2, 4, 16, 17, 60, 63, 70, 78, 79, 80, 81

Keres 3, 8, 24, 30, 32, 35, 47, 83, 84, 99
Kieninger 19, 37
Kunerth 55

Leepin 98
Lundin 20, 28, 58, 62

Medina 24, 89
Menchik 56
Michel 20, 104
Mikenas 35, 66, 67, 77, 91, 92
Milner-Barry 44

Naharro 43
Najdorf 74

Opocensky 62, 82, 84, 86

Pahl 21
Pérez 14
Petrov 66, 87, 90
Piazzini 22, 54
Pleci 1, 29
Podgorny 50
Pomar 12, 14, 25, 33, 36, 38, 69, 72
Poulsen 65

Rabar 3, 106
Raud 28
Reed 51
Rellstab 85
Reshevsky 2, 4, 16, 17, 60, 63, 70, 78, 79, 80, 81
Rey Ardid 6
Ribeiro 25, 72
Richter 37, 40, 99
Rico 36
Rohacek 13
Rojahn 52, 102
Rometti 45
Röpstorff 15
Russher 76

Sajtar 100

Index of Players

Sämisch 11, 89
Sanz 38
Schmidt 5, 59
Silva Rocha 57, 58, 94
Ståhlberg 30, 54, 61, 102, 103
Stoltz 48

Tartakower 22, 71, 87, 88, 93
Teteris 46
Ticoulat 69
Trompowsky 94, 95
Tsvetkov 49

Vaitonis 95
Van Scheltinga 61, 86, 88
Von Bardeleben 23

Walcicer 76
Werkmeister 21

Yanofsky 27

Zollner 7

A CATALOG OF SELECTED

DOVER BOOKS

IN ALL FIELDS OF INTEREST

A CATALOG OF SELECTED DOVER
BOOKS IN ALL FIELDS OF INTEREST

CONCERNING THE SPIRITUAL IN ART, Wassily Kandinsky. Pioneering work by father of abstract art. Thoughts on color theory, nature of art. Analysis of earlier masters. 12 illustrations. 80pp. of text. 5⅜ x 8½.   23411-8 Pa. $3.95

ANIMALS: 1,419 Copyright-Free Illustrations of Mammals, Birds, Fish, Insects, etc., Jim Harter (ed.). Clear wood engravings present, in extremely lifelike poses, over 1,000 species of animals. One of the most extensive pictorial sourcebooks of its kind. Captions. Index. 284pp. 9 x 12.   23766-4 Pa. $12.95

CELTIC ART: The Methods of Construction, George Bain. Simple geometric techniques for making Celtic interlacements, spirals, Kells-type initials, animals, humans, etc. Over 500 illustrations. 160pp. 9 x 12. (USO)   22923-8 Pa. $9.95

AN ATLAS OF ANATOMY FOR ARTISTS, Fritz Schider. Most thorough reference work on art anatomy in the world. Hundreds of illustrations, including selections from works by Vesalius, Leonardo, Goya, Ingres, Michelangelo, others. 593 illustrations. 192pp. 7⅛ x 10¼.   20241-0 Pa. $9.95

CELTIC HAND STROKE-BY-STROKE (Irish Half-Uncial from "The Book of Kells"): An Arthur Baker Calligraphy Manual, Arthur Baker. Complete guide to creating each letter of the alphabet in distinctive Celtic manner. Covers hand position, strokes, pens, inks, paper, more. Illustrated. 48pp. 8¼ x 11.   24336-2 Pa. $3.95

EASY ORIGAMI, John Montroll. Charming collection of 32 projects (hat, cup, pelican, piano, swan, many more) specially designed for the novice origami hobbyist. Clearly illustrated easy-to-follow instructions insure that even beginning papercrafters will achieve successful results. 48pp. 8¼ x 11.   27298-2 Pa. $3.50

THE COMPLETE BOOK OF BIRDHOUSE CONSTRUCTION FOR WOODWORKERS, Scott D. Campbell. Detailed instructions, illustrations, tables. Also data on bird habitat and instinct patterns. Bibliography. 3 tables. 63 illustrations in 15 figures. 48pp. 5¼ x 8½.   24407-5 Pa. $2.50

BLOOMINGDALE'S ILLUSTRATED 1886 CATALOG: Fashions, Dry Goods and Housewares, Bloomingdale Brothers. Famed merchants' extremely rare catalog depicting about 1,700 products: clothing, housewares, firearms, dry goods, jewelry, more. Invaluable for dating, identifying vintage items. Also, copyright-free graphics for artists, designers. Co-published with Henry Ford Museum & Greenfield Village. 160pp. 8¼ x 11.   25780-0 Pa. $10.95

HISTORIC COSTUME IN PICTURES, Braun & Schneider. Over 1,450 costumed figures in clearly detailed engravings—from dawn of civilization to end of 19th century. Captions. Many folk costumes. 256pp. 8⅜ x 11¾.   23150-X Pa. $12.95

THE BEST TALES OF HOFFMANN, E. T. A. Hoffmann. 10 of Hoffmann's most important stories: "Nutcracker and the King of Mice," "The Golden Flowerpot," etc. 458pp. 5⅜ x 8½. 21793-0 Pa. $9.95

FROM FETISH TO GOD IN ANCIENT EGYPT, E. A. Wallis Budge. Rich detailed survey of Egyptian conception of "God" and gods, magic, cult of animals, Osiris, more. Also, superb English translations of hymns and legends. 240 illustrations. 545pp. 5⅜ x 8½. 25803-3 Pa. $13.95

FRENCH STORIES/CONTES FRANÇAIS: A Dual-Language Book, Wallace Fowlie. Ten stories by French masters, Voltaire to Camus: "Micromegas" by Voltaire; "The Atheist's Mass" by Balzac; "Minuet" by de Maupassant; "The Guest" by Camus, six more. Excellent English translations on facing pages. Also French-English vocabulary list, exercises, more. 352pp. 5⅜ x 8½. 26443-2 Pa. $8.95

CHICAGO AT THE TURN OF THE CENTURY IN PHOTOGRAPHS: 122 Historic Views from the Collections of the Chicago Historical Society, Larry A. Viskochil. Rare large-format prints offer detailed views of City Hall, State Street, the Loop, Hull House, Union Station, many other landmarks, circa 1904-1913. Introduction. Captions. Maps. 144pp. 9⅜ x 12¼. 24656-6 Pa. $12.95

OLD BROOKLYN IN EARLY PHOTOGRAPHS, 1865-1929, William Lee Younger. Luna Park, Gravesend race track, construction of Grand Army Plaza, moving of Hotel Brighton, etc. 157 previously unpublished photographs. 165pp. 8⅞ x 11¾. 23587-4 Pa. $13.95

THE MYTHS OF THE NORTH AMERICAN INDIANS, Lewis Spence. Rich anthology of the myths and legends of the Algonquins, Iroquois, Pawnees and Sioux, prefaced by an extensive historical and ethnological commentary. 36 illustrations. 480pp. 5⅜ x 8½. 25967-6 Pa. $8.95

AN ENCYCLOPEDIA OF BATTLES: Accounts of Over 1,560 Battles from 1479 B.C. to the Present, David Eggenberger. Essential details of every major battle in recorded history from the first battle of Megiddo in 1479 B.C. to Grenada in 1984. List of Battle Maps. New Appendix covering the years 1967-1984. Index. 99 illustrations. 544pp. 6½ x 9¼. 24913-1 Pa. $14.95

SAILING ALONE AROUND THE WORLD, Captain Joshua Slocum. First man to sail around the world, alone, in small boat. One of great feats of seamanship told in delightful manner. 67 illustrations. 294pp. 5⅜ x 8½. 20326-3 Pa. $5.95

ANARCHISM AND OTHER ESSAYS, Emma Goldman. Powerful, penetrating, prophetic essays on direct action, role of minorities, prison reform, puritan hypocrisy, violence, etc. 271pp. 5⅜ x 8½. 22484-8 Pa. $6.95

MYTHS OF THE HINDUS AND BUDDHISTS, Ananda K. Coomaraswamy and Sister Nivedita. Great stories of the epics; deeds of Krishna, Shiva, taken from puranas, Vedas, folk tales; etc. 32 illustrations. 400pp. 5⅜ x 8½. 21759-0 Pa. $10.95

BEYOND PSYCHOLOGY, Otto Rank. Fear of death, desire of immortality, nature of sexuality, social organization, creativity, according to Rankian system. 291pp. 5⅜ x 8½. 20485-5 Pa. $8.95

A THEOLOGICO-POLITICAL TREATISE, Benedict Spinoza. Also contains unfinished Political Treatise. Great classic on religious liberty, theory of government on common consent. R. Elwes translation. Total of 421pp. 5⅜ x 8½. 20249-6 Pa. $9.95

STICKLEY CRAFTSMAN FURNITURE CATALOGS, Gustav Stickley and L. & J. G. Stickley. Beautiful, functional furniture in two authentic catalogs from 1910. 594 illustrations, including 277 photos, show settles, rockers, armchairs, reclining chairs, bookcases, desks, tables. 183pp. 6½ x 9¼. 23838-5 Pa. $9.95

AMERICAN LOCOMOTIVES IN HISTORIC PHOTOGRAPHS: 1858 to 1949, Ron Ziel (ed.). A rare collection of 126 meticulously detailed official photographs, called "builder portraits," of American locomotives that majestically chronicle the rise of steam locomotive power in America. Introduction. Detailed captions. xi + 129pp. 9 x 12. 27393-8 Pa. $12.95

AMERICA'S LIGHTHOUSES: An Illustrated History, Francis Ross Holland, Jr. Delightfully written, profusely illustrated fact-filled survey of over 200 American lighthouses since 1716. History, anecdotes, technological advances, more. 240pp. 8 x 10¾. 25576-X Pa. $12.95

TOWARDS A NEW ARCHITECTURE, Le Corbusier. Pioneering manifesto by founder of "International School." Technical and aesthetic theories, views of industry, economics, relation of form to function, "mass-production split" and much more. Profusely illustrated. 320pp. 6⅛ x 9¼. (USO) 25023-7 Pa. $9.95

HOW THE OTHER HALF LIVES, Jacob Riis. Famous journalistic record, exposing poverty and degradation of New York slums around 1900, by major social reformer. 100 striking and influential photographs. 233pp. 10 x 7⅞. 22012-5 Pa. $10.95

FRUIT KEY AND TWIG KEY TO TREES AND SHRUBS, William M. Harlow. One of the handiest and most widely used identification aids. Fruit key covers 120 deciduous and evergreen species; twig key 160 deciduous species. Easily used. Over 300 photographs. 126pp. 5⅜ x 8½. 20511-8 Pa. $3.95

COMMON BIRD SONGS, Dr. Donald J. Borror. Songs of 60 most common U.S. birds: robins, sparrows, cardinals, bluejays, finches, more–arranged in order of increasing complexity. Up to 9 variations of songs of each species. Cassette and manual 99911-4 $8.95

ORCHIDS AS HOUSE PLANTS, Rebecca Tyson Northen. Grow cattleyas and many other kinds of orchids–in a window, in a case, or under artificial light. 63 illustrations. 148pp. 5⅜ x 8½. 23261-1 Pa. $4.95

MONSTER MAZES, Dave Phillips. Masterful mazes at four levels of difficulty. Avoid deadly perils and evil creatures to find magical treasures. Solutions for all 32 exciting illustrated puzzles. 48pp. 8¼ x 11. 26005-4 Pa. $2.95

MOZART'S DON GIOVANNI (DOVER OPERA LIBRETTO SERIES), Wolfgang Amadeus Mozart. Introduced and translated by Ellen H. Bleiler. Standard Italian libretto, with complete English translation. Convenient and thoroughly portable–an ideal companion for reading along with a recording or the performance itself. Introduction. List of characters. Plot summary. 121pp. 5¼ x 8½. 24944-1 Pa. $2.95

TECHNICAL MANUAL AND DICTIONARY OF CLASSICAL BALLET, Gail Grant. Defines, explains, comments on steps, movements, poses and concepts. 15-page pictorial section. Basic book for student, viewer. 127pp. 5⅜ x 8½. 21843-0 Pa. $4.95

BRASS INSTRUMENTS: Their History and Development, Anthony Baines. Authoritative, updated survey of the evolution of trumpets, trombones, bugles, cornets, French horns, tubas and other brass wind instruments. Over 140 illustrations and 48 music examples. Corrected and updated by author. New preface. Bibliography. 320pp. 5⅜ x 8½. 27574-4 Pa. $9.95

HOLLYWOOD GLAMOR PORTRAITS, John Kobal (ed.). 145 photos from 1926-49. Harlow, Gable, Bogart, Bacall; 94 stars in all. Full background on photographers, technical aspects. 160pp. 8⅜ x 11¼. 23352-9 Pa. $12.95

MAX AND MORITZ, Wilhelm Busch. Great humor classic in both German and English. Also 10 other works: "Cat and Mouse," "Plisch and Plumm," etc. 216pp. 5⅜ x 8½. 20181-3 Pa. $6.95

THE RAVEN AND OTHER FAVORITE POEMS, Edgar Allan Poe. Over 40 of the author's most memorable poems: "The Bells," "Ulalume," "Israfel," "To Helen," "The Conqueror Worm," "Eldorado," "Annabel Lee," many more. Alphabetic lists of titles and first lines. 64pp. 5$\frac{3}{16}$ x 8¼. 26685-0 Pa. $1.00

PERSONAL MEMOIRS OF U. S. GRANT, Ulysses Simpson Grant. Intelligent, deeply moving firsthand account of Civil War campaigns, considered by many the finest military memoirs ever written. Includes letters, historic photographs, maps and more. 528pp. 6⅛ x 9¼. 28587-1 Pa. $11.95

AMULETS AND SUPERSTITIONS, E. A. Wallis Budge. Comprehensive discourse on origin, powers of amulets in many ancient cultures: Arab, Persian Babylonian, Assyrian, Egyptian, Gnostic, Hebrew, Phoenician, Syriac, etc. Covers cross, swastika, crucifix, seals, rings, stones, etc. 584pp. 5⅜ x 8½. 23573-4 Pa. $12.95

RUSSIAN STORIES/PYCCKNE PACCKA3bl: A Dual-Language Book, edited by Gleb Struve. Twelve tales by such masters as Chekhov, Tolstoy, Dostoevsky, Pushkin, others. Excellent word-for-word English translations on facing pages, plus teaching and study aids, Russian/English vocabulary, biographical/critical introductions, more. 416pp. 5⅜ x 8½. 26244-8 Pa. $8.95

PHILADELPHIA THEN AND NOW: 60 Sites Photographed in the Past and Present, Kenneth Finkel and Susan Oyama. Rare photographs of City Hall, Logan Square, Independence Hall, Betsy Ross House, other landmarks juxtaposed with contemporary views. Captures changing face of historic city. Introduction. Captions. 128pp. 8¼ x 11. 25790-8 Pa. $9.95

AIA ARCHITECTURAL GUIDE TO NASSAU AND SUFFOLK COUNTIES, LONG ISLAND, The American Institute of Architects, Long Island Chapter, and the Society for the Preservation of Long Island Antiquities. Comprehensive, well-researched and generously illustrated volume brings to life over three centuries of Long Island's great architectural heritage. More than 240 photographs with authoritative, extensively detailed captions. 176pp. 8¼ x 11. 26946-9 Pa. $14.95

NORTH AMERICAN INDIAN LIFE: Customs and Traditions of 23 Tribes, Elsie Clews Parsons (ed.). 27 fictionalized essays by noted anthropologists examine religion, customs, government, additional facets of life among the Winnebago, Crow, Zuni, Eskimo, other tribes. 480pp. 6⅛ x 9¼. 27377-6 Pa. $10.95

FRANK LLOYD WRIGHT'S HOLLYHOCK HOUSE, Donald Hoffmann. Lavishly illustrated, carefully documented study of one of Wright's most controversial residential designs. Over 120 photographs, floor plans, elevations, etc. Detailed perceptive text by noted Wright scholar. Index. 128pp. 9¼ x 10¾. 27133-1 Pa. $11.95

THE MALE AND FEMALE FIGURE IN MOTION: 60 Classic Photographic Sequences, Eadweard Muybridge. 60 true-action photographs of men and women walking, running, climbing, bending, turning, etc., reproduced from rare 19th-century masterpiece. vi + 121pp. 9 x 12. 24745-7 Pa. $10.95

1001 QUESTIONS ANSWERED ABOUT THE SEASHORE, N. J. Berrill and Jacquelyn Berrill. Queries answered about dolphins, sea snails, sponges, starfish, fishes, shore birds, many others. Covers appearance, breeding, growth, feeding, much more. 305pp. 5¼ x 8¼. 23366-9 Pa. $8.95

GUIDE TO OWL WATCHING IN NORTH AMERICA, Donald S. Heintzelman. Superb guide offers complete data and descriptions of 19 species: barn owl, screech owl, snowy owl, many more. Expert coverage of owl-watching equipment, conservation, migrations and invasions, etc. Guide to observing sites. 84 illustrations. xiii + 193pp. 5⅜ x 8½. 27344-X Pa. $8.95

MEDICINAL AND OTHER USES OF NORTH AMERICAN PLANTS: A Historical Survey with Special Reference to the Eastern Indian Tribes, Charlotte Erichsen-Brown. Chronological historical citations document 500 years of usage of plants, trees, shrubs native to eastern Canada, northeastern U.S. Also complete identifying information. 343 illustrations. 544pp. 6½ x 9¼. 25951-X Pa. $12.95

STORYBOOK MAZES, Dave Phillips. 23 stories and mazes on two-page spreads: Wizard of Oz, Treasure Island, Robin Hood, etc. Solutions. 64pp. 8¼ x 11. 23628-5 Pa. $2.95

NEGRO FOLK MUSIC, U.S.A., Harold Courlander. Noted folklorist's scholarly yet readable analysis of rich and varied musical tradition. Includes authentic versions of over 40 folk songs. Valuable bibliography and discography. xi + 324pp. 5⅜ x 8½. 27350-4 Pa. $9.95

MOVIE-STAR PORTRAITS OF THE FORTIES, John Kobal (ed.). 163 glamor, studio photos of 106 stars of the 1940s: Rita Hayworth, Ava Gardner, Marlon Brando, Clark Gable, many more. 176pp. 8⅜ x 11¼. 23546-7 Pa. $12.95

BENCHLEY LOST AND FOUND, Robert Benchley. Finest humor from early 30s, about pet peeves, child psychologists, post office and others. Mostly unavailable elsewhere. 73 illustrations by Peter Arno and others. 183pp. 5⅜ x 8½. 22410-4 Pa. $6.95

YEKL and THE IMPORTED BRIDEGROOM AND OTHER STORIES OF YIDDISH NEW YORK, Abraham Cahan. Film Hester Street based on Yekl (1896). Novel, other stories among first about Jewish immigrants on N.Y.'s East Side. 240pp. 5⅜ x 8½. 22427-9 Pa. $6.95

SELECTED POEMS, Walt Whitman. Generous sampling from *Leaves of Grass*. Twenty-four poems include "I Hear America Singing," "Song of the Open Road," "I Sing the Body Electric," "When Lilacs Last in the Dooryard Bloom'd," "O Captain! My Captain!"—all reprinted from an authoritative edition. Lists of titles and first lines. 128pp. 5⁵⁄₁₆ x 8¼. 26878-0 Pa. $1.00

AUTOBIOGRAPHY: The Story of My Experiments with Truth, Mohandas K. Gandhi. Boyhood, legal studies, purification, the growth of the Satyagraha (nonviolent protest) movement. Critical, inspiring work of the man responsible for the freedom of India. 480pp. 5⅜ x 8½. (USO) 24593-4 Pa. $8.95

CELTIC MYTHS AND LEGENDS, T. W. Rolleston. Masterful retelling of Irish and Welsh stories and tales. Cuchulain, King Arthur, Deirdre, the Grail, many more. First paperback edition. 58 full-page illustrations. 512pp. 5⅜ x 8½. 26507-2 Pa. $9.95

THE PRINCIPLES OF PSYCHOLOGY, William James. Famous long course complete, unabridged. Stream of thought, time perception, memory, experimental methods; great work decades ahead of its time. 94 figures. 1,391pp. 5⅜ x 8½. 2-vol. set.
Vol. I: 20381-6 Pa. $12.95
Vol. II: 20382-4 Pa. $12.95

THE WORLD AS WILL AND REPRESENTATION, Arthur Schopenhauer. Definitive English translation of Schopenhauer's life work, correcting more than 1,000 errors, omissions in earlier translations. Translated by E. F. J. Payne. Total of 1,269pp. 5⅜ x 8½. 2-vol. set. Vol. 1: 21761-2 Pa. $11.95
Vol. 2: 21762-0 Pa. $12.95

MAGIC AND MYSTERY IN TIBET, Madame Alexandra David-Neel. Experiences among lamas, magicians, sages, sorcerers, Bonpa wizards. A true psychic discovery. 32 illustrations. 321pp. 5⅜ x 8½. (USO) 22682-4 Pa. $8.95

THE EGYPTIAN BOOK OF THE DEAD, E. A. Wallis Budge. Complete reproduction of Ani's papyrus, finest ever found. Full hieroglyphic text, interlinear transliteration, word-for-word translation, smooth translation. 533pp. 6½ x 9¼.
21866-X Pa. $10.95

MATHEMATICS FOR THE NONMATHEMATICIAN, Morris Kline. Detailed, college-level treatment of mathematics in cultural and historical context, with numerous exercises. Recommended Reading Lists. Tables. Numerous figures. 641pp. 5⅜ x 8½.
24823-2 Pa. $11.95

THEORY OF WING SECTIONS: Including a Summary of Airfoil Data, Ira H. Abbott and A. E. von Doenhoff. Concise compilation of subsonic aerodynamic characteristics of NACA wing sections, plus description of theory. 350pp. of tables. 693pp. 5⅜ x 8½. 60586-8 Pa. $14.95

THE RIME OF THE ANCIENT MARINER, Gustave Doré, S. T. Coleridge. Doré's finest work; 34 plates capture moods, subtleties of poem. Flawless full-size reproductions printed on facing pages with authoritative text of poem. "Beautiful. Simply beautiful."–*Publisher's Weekly*. 77pp. 9¼ x 12. 22305-1 Pa. $6.95

NORTH AMERICAN INDIAN DESIGNS FOR ARTISTS AND CRAFTSPEOPLE, Eva Wilson. Over 360 authentic copyright-free designs adapted from Navajo blankets, Hopi pottery, Sioux buffalo hides, more. Geometrics, symbolic figures, plant and animal motifs, etc. 128pp. 8⅜ x 11. (EUK) 25341-4 Pa. $8.95

SCULPTURE: Principles and Practice, Louis Slobodkin. Step-by-step approach to clay, plaster, metals, stone; classical and modern. 253 drawings, photos. 255pp. 8⅛ x 11.
22960-2 Pa. $11.95

MY BONDAGE AND MY FREEDOM, Frederick Douglass. Born a slave, Douglass became outspoken force in antislavery movement. The best of Douglass' autobiographies. Graphic description of slave life. 464pp. 5⅜ x 8½. 22457-0 Pa. $8.95

FOLLOWING THE EQUATOR: A Journey Around the World, Mark Twain. Fascinating humorous account of 1897 voyage to Hawaii, Australia, India, New Zealand, etc. Ironic, bemused reports on peoples, customs, climate, flora and fauna, politics, much more. 197 illustrations. 720pp. 5⅜ x 8½. 26113-1 Pa. $15.95

THE PEOPLE CALLED SHAKERS, Edward D. Andrews. Definitive study of Shakers: origins, beliefs, practices, dances, social organization, furniture and crafts, etc. 33 illustrations. 351pp. 5⅜ x 8½. 21081-2 Pa. $8.95

THE MYTHS OF GREECE AND ROME, H. A. Guerber. A classic of mythology, generously illustrated, long prized for its simple, graphic, accurate retelling of the principal myths of Greece and Rome, and for its commentary on their origins and significance. With 64 illustrations by Michelangelo, Raphael, Titian, Rubens, Canova, Bernini and others. 480pp. 5⅜ x 8½. 27584-1 Pa. $9.95

PSYCHOLOGY OF MUSIC, Carl E. Seashore. Classic work discusses music as a medium from psychological viewpoint. Clear treatment of physical acoustics, auditory apparatus, sound perception, development of musical skills, nature of musical feeling, host of other topics. 88 figures. 408pp. 5⅜ x 8½. 21851-1 Pa. $10.95

THE PHILOSOPHY OF HISTORY, Georg W. Hegel. Great classic of Western thought develops concept that history is not chance but rational process, the evolution of freedom. 457pp. 5⅜ x 8½. 20112-0 Pa. $9.95

THE BOOK OF TEA, Kakuzo Okakura. Minor classic of the Orient: entertaining, charming explanation, interpretation of traditional Japanese culture in terms of tea ceremony. 94pp. 5⅜ x 8½. 20070-1 Pa. $3.95

LIFE IN ANCIENT EGYPT, Adolf Erman. Fullest, most thorough, detailed older account with much not in more recent books, domestic life, religion, magic, medicine, commerce, much more. Many illustrations reproduce tomb paintings, carvings, hieroglyphs, etc. 597pp. 5⅜ x 8½. 22632-8 Pa. $11.95

SUNDIALS, Their Theory and Construction, Albert Waugh. Far and away the best, most thorough coverage of ideas, mathematics concerned, types, construction, adjusting anywhere. Simple, nontechnical treatment allows even children to build several of these dials. Over 100 illustrations. 230pp. 5⅜ x 8½. 22947-5 Pa. $7.95

DYNAMICS OF FLUIDS IN POROUS MEDIA, Jacob Bear. For advanced students of ground water hydrology, soil mechanics and physics, drainage and irrigation engineering, and more. 335 illustrations. Exercises, with answers. 784pp. 6⅛ x 9¼. 65675-6 Pa. $19.95

SONGS OF EXPERIENCE: Facsimile Reproduction with 26 Plates in Full Color, William Blake. 26 full-color plates from a rare 1826 edition. Includes "The Tyger," "London," "Holy Thursday," and other poems. Printed text of poems. 48pp. 5¼ x 7. 24636-1 Pa. $4.95

OLD-TIME VIGNETTES IN FULL COLOR, Carol Belanger Grafton (ed.). Over 390 charming, often sentimental illustrations, selected from archives of Victorian graphics—pretty women posing, children playing, food, flowers, kittens and puppies, smiling cherubs, birds and butterflies, much more. All copyright-free. 48pp. 9¼ x 12¼. 27269-9 Pa. $7.95

PERSPECTIVE FOR ARTISTS, Rex Vicat Cole. Depth, perspective of sky and sea, shadows, much more, not usually covered. 391 diagrams, 81 reproductions of drawings and paintings. 279pp. 5⅜ x 8½. 22487-2 Pa. $7.95

DRAWING THE LIVING FIGURE, Joseph Sheppard. Innovative approach to artistic anatomy focuses on specifics of surface anatomy, rather than muscles and bones. Over 170 drawings of live models in front, back and side views, and in widely varying poses. Accompanying diagrams. 177 illustrations. Introduction. Index. 144pp. 8⅜ x11¼. 26723-7 Pa. $8.95

GOTHIC AND OLD ENGLISH ALPHABETS: 100 Complete Fonts, Dan X. Solo. Add power, elegance to posters, signs, other graphics with 100 stunning copyright-free alphabets: Blackstone, Dolbey, Germania, 97 more–including many lower-case, numerals, punctuation marks. 104pp. 8⅛ x 11. 24695-7 Pa. $8.95

HOW TO DO BEADWORK, Mary White. Fundamental book on craft from simple projects to five-bead chains and woven works. 106 illustrations. 142pp. 5⅜ x 8. 20697-1 Pa. $4.95

THE BOOK OF WOOD CARVING, Charles Marshall Sayers. Finest book for beginners discusses fundamentals and offers 34 designs. "Absolutely first rate . . . well thought out and well executed."–E. J. Tangerman. 118pp. 7¾ x 10⅝. 23654-4 Pa. $6.95

ILLUSTRATED CATALOG OF CIVIL WAR MILITARY GOODS: Union Army Weapons, Insignia, Uniform Accessories, and Other Equipment, Schuyler, Hartley, and Graham. Rare, profusely illustrated 1846 catalog includes Union Army uniform and dress regulations, arms and ammunition, coats, insignia, flags, swords, rifles, etc. 226 illustrations. 160pp. 9 x 12. 24939-5 Pa. $10.95

WOMEN'S FASHIONS OF THE EARLY 1900s: An Unabridged Republication of "New York Fashions, 1909," National Cloak & Suit Co. Rare catalog of mail-order fashions documents women's and children's clothing styles shortly after the turn of the century. Captions offer full descriptions, prices. Invaluable resource for fashion, costume historians. Approximately 725 illustrations. 128pp. 8⅜ x 11¼. 27276-1 Pa. $11.95

THE 1912 AND 1915 GUSTAV STICKLEY FURNITURE CATALOGS, Gustav Stickley. With over 200 detailed illustrations and descriptions, these two catalogs are essential reading and reference materials and identification guides for Stickley furniture. Captions cite materials, dimensions and prices. 112pp. 6½ x 9¼. 26676-1 Pa. $9.95

EARLY AMERICAN LOCOMOTIVES, John H. White, Jr. Finest locomotive engravings from early 19th century: historical (1804–74), main-line (after 1870), special, foreign, etc. 147 plates. 142pp. 11⅜ x 8¼. 22772-3 Pa. $10.95

THE TALL SHIPS OF TODAY IN PHOTOGRAPHS, Frank O. Braynard. Lavishly illustrated tribute to nearly 100 majestic contemporary sailing vessels: Amerigo Vespucci, Clearwater, Constitution, Eagle, Mayflower, Sea Cloud, Victory, many more. Authoritative captions provide statistics, background on each ship. 190 black-and-white photographs and illustrations. Introduction. 128pp. 8⅞ x 11¾. 27163-3 Pa. $13.95

EARLY NINETEENTH-CENTURY CRAFTS AND TRADES, Peter Stockham (ed.). Extremely rare 1807 volume describes to youngsters the crafts and trades of the day: brickmaker, weaver, dressmaker, bookbinder, ropemaker, saddler, many more. Quaint prose, charming illustrations for each craft. 20 black-and-white line illustrations. 192pp. 4⅝ x 6. 27293-1 Pa. $4.95

VICTORIAN FASHIONS AND COSTUMES FROM HARPER'S BAZAR, 1867–1898, Stella Blum (ed.). Day costumes, evening wear, sports clothes, shoes, hats, other accessories in over 1,000 detailed engravings. 320pp. 9⅜ x 12¼. 22990-4 Pa. $14.95

GUSTAV STICKLEY, THE CRAFTSMAN, Mary Ann Smith. Superb study surveys broad scope of Stickley's achievement, especially in architecture. Design philosophy, rise and fall of the Craftsman empire, descriptions and floor plans for many Craftsman houses, more. 86 black-and-white halftones. 31 line illustrations. Introduction 208pp. 6½ x 9¼. 27210-9 Pa. $9.95

THE LONG ISLAND RAIL ROAD IN EARLY PHOTOGRAPHS, Ron Ziel. Over 220 rare photos, informative text document origin (1844) and development of rail service on Long Island. Vintage views of early trains, locomotives, stations, passengers, crews, much more. Captions. 8⅞ x 11¾. 26301-0 Pa. $13.95

THE BOOK OF OLD SHIPS: From Egyptian Galleys to Clipper Ships, Henry B. Culver. Superb, authoritative history of sailing vessels, with 80 magnificent line illustrations. Galley, bark, caravel, longship, whaler, many more. Detailed, informative text on each vessel by noted naval historian. Introduction. 256pp. 5⅜ x 8½. 27332-6 Pa. $7.95

TEN BOOKS ON ARCHITECTURE, Vitruvius. The most important book ever written on architecture. Early Roman aesthetics, technology, classical orders, site selection, all other aspects. Morgan translation. 331pp. 5⅜ x 8½. 20645-9 Pa. $8.95

THE HUMAN FIGURE IN MOTION, Eadweard Muybridge. More than 4,500 stopped-action photos, in action series, showing undraped men, women, children jumping, lying down, throwing, sitting, wrestling, carrying, etc. 390pp. 7⅞ x 10⅝. 20204-6 Clothbd. $25.95

TREES OF THE EASTERN AND CENTRAL UNITED STATES AND CANADA, William M. Harlow. Best one-volume guide to 140 trees. Full descriptions, woodlore, range, etc. Over 600 illustrations. Handy size. 288pp. 4½ x 6⅜. 20395-6 Pa. $6.95

SONGS OF WESTERN BIRDS, Dr. Donald J. Borror. Complete song and call repertoire of 60 western species, including flycatchers, juncoes, cactus wrens, many more–includes fully illustrated booklet. Cassette and manual 99913-0 $8.95

GROWING AND USING HERBS AND SPICES, Milo Miloradovich. Versatile handbook provides all the information needed for cultivation and use of all the herbs and spices available in North America. 4 illustrations. Index. Glossary. 236pp. 5⅜ x 8½. 25058-X Pa. $6.95

BIG BOOK OF MAZES AND LABYRINTHS, Walter Shepherd. 50 mazes and labyrinths in all–classical, solid, ripple, and more–in one great volume. Perfect inexpensive puzzler for clever youngsters. Full solutions. 112pp. 8⅛ x 11. 22951-3 Pa. $4.95

PIANO TUNING, J. Cree Fischer. Clearest, best book for beginner, amateur. Simple repairs, raising dropped notes, tuning by easy method of flattened fifths. No previous skills needed. 4 illustrations. 201pp. 5⅜ x 8½.   23267-0 Pa. $6.95

A SOURCE BOOK IN THEATRICAL HISTORY, A. M. Nagler. Contemporary observers on acting, directing, make-up, costuming, stage props, machinery, scene design, from Ancient Greece to Chekhov. 611pp. 5⅜ x 8½.   20515-0 Pa. $12.95

THE COMPLETE NONSENSE OF EDWARD LEAR, Edward Lear. All nonsense limericks, zany alphabets, Owl and Pussycat, songs, nonsense botany, etc., illustrated by Lear. Total of 320pp. 5⅜ x 8½. (USO)   20167-8 Pa. $6.95

VICTORIAN PARLOUR POETRY: An Annotated Anthology, Michael R. Turner. 117 gems by Longfellow, Tennyson, Browning, many lesser-known poets. "The Village Blacksmith," "Curfew Must Not Ring Tonight," "Only a Baby Small," dozens more, often difficult to find elsewhere. Index of poets, titles, first lines. xxiii + 325pp. 5⅜ x 8¼.   27044-0 Pa. $8.95

DUBLINERS, James Joyce. Fifteen stories offer vivid, tightly focused observations of the lives of Dublin's poorer classes. At least one, "The Dead," is considered a masterpiece. Reprinted complete and unabridged from standard edition. 160pp. 5³⁄₁₆ x 8¼.
26870-5 Pa. $1.00

THE HAUNTED MONASTERY and THE CHINESE MAZE MURDERS, Robert van Gulik. Two full novels by van Gulik, set in 7th-century China, continue adventures of Judge Dee and his companions. An evil Taoist monastery, seemingly supernatural events; overgrown topiary maze hides strange crimes. 27 illustrations. 328pp. 5⅜ x 8½.   23502-5 Pa. $8.95

THE BOOK OF THE SACRED MAGIC OF ABRAMELIN THE MAGE, translated by S. MacGregor Mathers. Medieval manuscript of ceremonial magic. Basic document in Aleister Crowley, Golden Dawn groups. 268pp. 5⅜ x 8½.
23211-5 Pa. $8.95

NEW RUSSIAN-ENGLISH AND ENGLISH-RUSSIAN DICTIONARY, M. A. O'Brien. This is a remarkably handy Russian dictionary, containing a surprising amount of information, including over 70,000 entries. 366pp. 4½ x 6⅛.
20208-9 Pa. $9.95

HISTORIC HOMES OF THE AMERICAN PRESIDENTS, Second, Revised Edition, Irvin Haas. A traveler's guide to American Presidential homes, most open to the public, depicting and describing homes occupied by every American President from George Washington to George Bush. With visiting hours, admission charges, travel routes. 175 photographs. Index. 160pp. 8¼ x 11.   26751-2 Pa. $11.95

NEW YORK IN THE FORTIES, Andreas Feininger. 162 brilliant photographs by the well-known photographer, formerly with *Life* magazine. Commuters, shoppers, Times Square at night, much else from city at its peak. Captions by John von Hartz. 181pp. 9¼ x 10¾.   23585-8 Pa. $12.95

INDIAN SIGN LANGUAGE, William Tomkins. Over 525 signs developed by Sioux and other tribes. Written instructions and diagrams. Also 290 pictographs. 111pp. 6⅛ x 9¼.   22029-X Pa. $3.95

ANATOMY: A Complete Guide for Artists, Joseph Sheppard. A master of figure drawing shows artists how to render human anatomy convincingly. Over 460 illustrations. 224pp. 8⅜ x 11¼. 27279-6 Pa. $10.95

MEDIEVAL CALLIGRAPHY: Its History and Technique, Marc Drogin. Spirited history, comprehensive instruction manual covers 13 styles (ca. 4th century thru 15th). Excellent photographs; directions for duplicating medieval techniques with modern tools. 224pp. 8⅜ x 11¼. 26142-5 Pa. $12.95

DRIED FLOWERS: How to Prepare Them, Sarah Whitlock and Martha Rankin. Complete instructions on how to use silica gel, meal and borax, perlite aggregate, sand and borax, glycerine and water to create attractive permanent flower arrangements. 12 illustrations. 32pp. 5⅜ x 8½. 21802-3 Pa. $1.00

EASY-TO-MAKE BIRD FEEDERS FOR WOODWORKERS, Scott D. Campbell. Detailed, simple-to-use guide for designing, constructing, caring for and using feeders. Text, illustrations for 12 classic and contemporary designs. 96pp. 5⅜ x 8½. 25847-5 Pa. $2.95

SCOTTISH WONDER TALES FROM MYTH AND LEGEND, Donald A. Mackenzie. 16 lively tales tell of giants rumbling down mountainsides, of a magic wand that turns stone pillars into warriors, of gods and goddesses, evil hags, powerful forces and more. 240pp. 5⅜ x 8½. 29677-6 Pa. $6.95

THE HISTORY OF UNDERCLOTHES, C. Willett Cunnington and Phyllis Cunnington. Fascinating, well-documented survey covering six centuries of English undergarments, enhanced with over 100 illustrations: 12th-century laced-up bodice, footed long drawers (1795), 19th-century bustles, 19th-century corsets for men, Victorian "bust improvers," much more. 272pp. 5⅜ x 8¼. 27124-2 Pa. $9.95

ARTS AND CRAFTS FURNITURE: The Complete Brooks Catalog of 1912, Brooks Manufacturing Co. Photos and detailed descriptions of more than 150 now very collectible furniture designs from the Arts and Crafts movement depict davenports, settees, buffets, desks, tables, chairs, bedsteads, dressers and more, all built of solid, quarter-sawed oak. Invaluable for students and enthusiasts of antiques, Americana and the decorative arts. 80pp. 6½ x 9¼. 27471-3 Pa. $8.95

HOW WE INVENTED THE AIRPLANE: An Illustrated History, Orville Wright. Fascinating firsthand account covers early experiments, construction of planes and motors, first flights, much more. Introduction and commentary by Fred C. Kelly. 76 photographs. 96pp. 8¼ x 11. 25662-6 Pa. $8.95

THE ARTS OF THE SAILOR: Knotting, Splicing and Ropework, Hervey Garrett Smith. Indispensable shipboard reference covers tools, basic knots and useful hitches; handsewing and canvas work, more. Over 100 illustrations. Delightful reading for sea lovers. 256pp. 5⅜ x 8½. 26440-8 Pa. $7.95

FRANK LLOYD WRIGHT'S FALLINGWATER: The House and Its History, Second, Revised Edition, Donald Hoffmann. A total revision—both in text and illustrations—of the standard document on Fallingwater, the boldest, most personal architectural statement of Wright's mature years, updated with valuable new material from the recently opened Frank Lloyd Wright Archives. "Fascinating"–*The New York Times*. 116 illustrations. 128pp. 9¼ x 10¾. 27430-6 Pa. $11.95

PHOTOGRAPHIC SKETCHBOOK OF THE CIVIL WAR, Alexander Gardner. 100 photos taken on field during the Civil War. Famous shots of Manassas Harper's Ferry, Lincoln, Richmond, slave pens, etc. 244pp. 10⅝ x 8¼. 22731-6 Pa. $9.95

FIVE ACRES AND INDEPENDENCE, Maurice G. Kains. Great back-to-the-land classic explains basics of self-sufficient farming. The one book to get. 95 illustrations. 397pp. 5⅜ x 8½. 20974-1 Pa. $7.95

SONGS OF EASTERN BIRDS, Dr. Donald J. Borror. Songs and calls of 60 species most common to eastern U.S.: warblers, woodpeckers, flycatchers, thrushes, larks, many more in high-quality recording. Cassette and manual 99912-2 $9.95

A MODERN HERBAL, Margaret Grieve. Much the fullest, most exact, most useful compilation of herbal material. Gigantic alphabetical encyclopedia, from aconite to zedoary, gives botanical information, medical properties, folklore, economic uses, much else. Indispensable to serious reader. 161 illustrations. 888pp. 6½ x 9¼. 2-vol. set. (USO) Vol. I: 22798-7 Pa. $9.95
Vol. II: 22799-5 Pa. $9.95

HIDDEN TREASURE MAZE BOOK, Dave Phillips. Solve 34 challenging mazes accompanied by heroic tales of adventure. Evil dragons, people-eating plants, blood-thirsty giants, many more dangerous adversaries lurk at every twist and turn. 34 mazes, stories, solutions. 48pp. 8¼ x 11. 24566-7 Pa. $2.95

LETTERS OF W. A. MOZART, Wolfgang A. Mozart. Remarkable letters show bawdy wit, humor, imagination, musical insights, contemporary musical world; includes some letters from Leopold Mozart. 276pp. 5⅜ x 8½. 22859-2 Pa. $7.95

BASIC PRINCIPLES OF CLASSICAL BALLET, Agrippina Vaganova. Great Russian theoretician, teacher explains methods for teaching classical ballet. 118 illus-trations. 175pp. 5⅜ x 8½. 22036-2 Pa. $5.95

THE JUMPING FROG, Mark Twain. Revenge edition. The original story of The Celebrated Jumping Frog of Calaveras County, a hapless French translation, and Twain's hilarious "retranslation" from the French. 12 illustrations. 66pp. 5⅜ x 8½. 22686-7 Pa. $3.95

BEST REMEMBERED POEMS, Martin Gardner (ed.). The 126 poems in this superb collection of 19th- and 20th-century British and American verse range from Shelley's "To a Skylark" to the impassioned "Renascence" of Edna St. Vincent Millay and to Edward Lear's whimsical "The Owl and the Pussycat." 224pp. 5⅜ x 8½. 27165-X Pa. $4.95

COMPLETE SONNETS, William Shakespeare. Over 150 exquisite poems deal with love, friendship, the tyranny of time, beauty's evanescence, death and other themes in language of remarkable power, precision and beauty. Glossary of archaic terms. 80pp. 5³⁄₁₆ x 8¼. 26686-9 Pa. $1.00

BODIES IN A BOOKSHOP, R. T. Campbell. Challenging mystery of blackmail and murder with ingenious plot and superbly drawn characters. In the best tradition of British suspense fiction. 192pp. 5⅜ x 8½. 24720-1 Pa. $6.95

THE WIT AND HUMOR OF OSCAR WILDE, Alvin Redman (ed.). More than 1,000 ripostes, paradoxes, wisecracks: Work is the curse of the drinking classes; I can resist everything except temptation; etc. 258pp. 5⅜ x 8½. 20602-5 Pa. $5.95

SHAKESPEARE LEXICON AND QUOTATION DICTIONARY, Alexander Schmidt. Full definitions, locations, shades of meaning in every word in plays and poems. More than 50,000 exact quotations. 1,485pp. 6½ x 9¼. 2-vol. set.
Vol. 1: 22726-X Pa. $16.95
Vol. 2: 22727-8 Pa. $16.95

SELECTED POEMS, Emily Dickinson. Over 100 best-known, best-loved poems by one of America's foremost poets, reprinted from authoritative early editions. No comparable edition at this price. Index of first lines. 64pp. 5 3/16 x 8¼.
26466-1 Pa. $1.00

CELEBRATED CASES OF JUDGE DEE (DEE GOONG AN), translated by Robert van Gulik. Authentic 18th-century Chinese detective novel; Dee and associates solve three interlocked cases. Led to van Gulik's own stories with same characters. Extensive introduction. 9 illustrations. 237pp. 5⅜ x 8½. 23337-5 Pa. $6.95

THE MALLEUS MALEFICARUM OF KRAMER AND SPRENGER, translated by Montague Summers. Full text of most important witchhunter's "bible," used by both Catholics and Protestants. 278pp. 6⅝ x 10. 22802-9 Pa. $12.95

SPANISH STORIES/CUENTOS ESPAÑOLES: A Dual-Language Book, Angel Flores (ed.). Unique format offers 13 great stories in Spanish by Cervantes, Borges, others. Faithful English translations on facing pages. 352pp. 5⅜ x 8½.
25399-6 Pa. $8.95

THE CHICAGO WORLD'S FAIR OF 1893: A Photographic Record, Stanley Appelbaum (ed.). 128 rare photos show 200 buildings, Beaux-Arts architecture, Midway, original Ferris Wheel, Edison's kinetoscope, more. Architectural emphasis; full text. 116pp. 8¼ x 11. 23990-X Pa. $9.95

OLD QUEENS, N.Y., IN EARLY PHOTOGRAPHS, Vincent F. Seyfried and William Asadorian. Over 160 rare photographs of Maspeth, Jamaica, Jackson Heights, and other areas. Vintage views of DeWitt Clinton mansion, 1939 World's Fair and more. Captions. 192pp. 8⅞ x 11. 26358-4 Pa. $12.95

CAPTURED BY THE INDIANS: 15 Firsthand Accounts, 1750-1870, Frederick Drimmer. Astounding true historical accounts of grisly torture, bloody conflicts, relentless pursuits, miraculous escapes and more, by people who lived to tell the tale. 384pp. 5⅜ x 8½. 24901-8 Pa. $8.95

THE WORLD'S GREAT SPEECHES, Lewis Copeland and Lawrence W. Lamm (eds.). Vast collection of 278 speeches of Greeks to 1970. Powerful and effective models; unique look at history. 842pp. 5⅜ x 8½. 20468-5 Pa. $14.95

THE BOOK OF THE SWORD, Sir Richard F. Burton. Great Victorian scholar/adventurer's eloquent, erudite history of the "queen of weapons"–from prehistory to early Roman Empire. Evolution and development of early swords, variations (sabre, broadsword, cutlass, scimitar, etc.), much more. 336pp. 6⅛ x 9¼.
25434-8 Pa. $9.95

THE INFLUENCE OF SEA POWER UPON HISTORY, 1660–1783, A. T. Mahan. Influential classic of naval history and tactics still used as text in war colleges. First paperback edition. 4 maps. 24 battle plans. 640pp. 5⅜ x 8½.   25509-3 Pa. $12.95

THE STORY OF THE TITANIC AS TOLD BY ITS SURVIVORS, Jack Winocour (ed.). What it was really like. Panic, despair, shocking inefficiency, and a little heroism. More thrilling than any fictional account. 26 illustrations. 320pp. 5⅜ x 8½.
20610-6 Pa. $8.95

FAIRY AND FOLK TALES OF THE IRISH PEASANTRY, William Butler Yeats (ed.). Treasury of 64 tales from the twilight world of Celtic myth and legend: "The Soul Cages," "The Kildare Pooka," "King O'Toole and his Goose," many more. Introduction and Notes by W. B. Yeats. 352pp. 5⅜ x 8½.   26941-8 Pa. $8.95

BUDDHIST MAHAYANA TEXTS, E. B. Cowell and Others (eds.). Superb, accurate translations of basic documents in Mahayana Buddhism, highly important in history of religions. The Buddha-karita of Asvaghosha, Larger Sukhavativyuha, more. 448pp. 5⅜ x 8½.   25552-2 Pa. $12.95

ONE TWO THREE . . . INFINITY: Facts and Speculations of Science, George Gamow. Great physicist's fascinating, readable overview of contemporary science: number theory, relativity, fourth dimension, entropy, genes, atomic structure, much more. 128 illustrations. Index. 352pp. 5⅜ x 8½.   25664-2 Pa. $8.95

ENGINEERING IN HISTORY, Richard Shelton Kirby, et al. Broad, nontechnical survey of history's major technological advances: birth of Greek science, industrial revolution, electricity and applied science, 20th-century automation, much more. 181 illustrations. ". . . excellent . . ."–*Isis.* Bibliography. vii + 530pp. 5⅜ x 8¼.
26412-2 Pa. $14.95

DALÍ ON MODERN ART: The Cuckolds of Antiquated Modern Art, Salvador Dalí. Influential painter skewers modern art and its practitioners. Outrageous evaluations of Picasso, Cézanne, Turner, more. 15 renderings of paintings discussed. 44 calligraphic decorations by Dalí. 96pp. 5⅜ x 8½. (USO)   29220-7 Pa. $4.95

ANTIQUE PLAYING CARDS: A Pictorial History, Henry René D'Allemagne. Over 900 elaborate, decorative images from rare playing cards (14th–20th centuries): Bacchus, death, dancing dogs, hunting scenes, royal coats of arms, players cheating, much more. 96pp. 9¼ x 12¼.   29265-7 Pa. $11.95

MAKING FURNITURE MASTERPIECES: 30 Projects with Measured Drawings, Franklin H. Gottshall. Step-by-step instructions, illustrations for constructing handsome, useful pieces, among them a Sheraton desk, Chippendale chair, Spanish desk, Queen Anne table and a William and Mary dressing mirror. 224pp. 8⅛ x 11¼.
29338-6 Pa. $13.95

THE FOSSIL BOOK: A Record of Prehistoric Life, Patricia V. Rich et al. Profusely illustrated definitive guide covers everything from single-celled organisms and dinosaurs to birds and mammals and the interplay between climate and man. Over 1,500 illustrations. 760pp. 7½ x 10⅛.   29371-8 Pa. $29.95

Prices subject to change without notice.

Available at your book dealer or write for free catalog to Dept. GI, Dover Publications, Inc., 31 East 2nd St., Mineola, N.Y. 11501. Dover publishes more than 500 books each year on science, elementary and advanced mathematics, biology, music, art, literary history, social sciences and other areas.